Healthy Homestyle
Cooking

Healthy Homestyle
Cooking

200 of Your Favorite Family Recipes–
With a Fraction of the Fat

By Evelyn Tribole, M.S., R.D.

RODALE PRESS, EMMAUS, PENNSYLVANIA

Copyright © 1994 by Evelyn Tribole
Photographs copyright © 1994 by Rodale Press, Inc.

Printed in the United States of America on acid-free ∞, recycled paper containing a minimum of 10% post-consumer waste ♻

Front Cover:
Old-Fashioned Beef Stew, page 170

Design and Photography:
Tad Ware & Co., Inc.

Illustrations:
Tracy Turner

Library of Congress Cataloging-in-Publication Data

Tribole, Evelyn, 1959-
   Healthy homestyle cooking : 200 of your favorite family recipes, with a fraction of the fat / by Evelyn Tribole.
     p. cm.
   Includes index.
   ISBN 0-87596-212-2: hardcover
   1. Cookery. 2. Low-fat diet—Recipes. I. Title.
TX714.T76 1994
641.5'638—dc20   94-19580
                                    CIP

Distributed in the book trade by St. Martin's Press

2 4 6 8 10 9 7 5 3   hardcover

OUR MISSION

We publish books that empower people's lives.

RODALE ❦ BOOKS

To my family

CONTENTS

Acknowledgments

There are many people I would like to thank, without whose help, encouragement and inspiration this book would not have been possible. Creating and testing a cookbook can be a humbling process. So to the following people, I send my *sincere* thanks and appreciation.

Chef Patricia Hart, M.S., R.D., a friend who was immensely helpful in getting me through cooking crises with her personal culinary "911 Help Line." When I asked Patty which professional affiliation to use as an acknowledgment, she simply said, "Put me down as your friend." Done.

To those who established my roots in cooking: Terese Laurance, who first exposed me to the concept of "recipe modification" with contagious enthusiasm during my dietetic internship years. Jeanne Peters, R.D., who knew me in my days when "I didn't do food." Jeanne showed me how fun "lite" cooking could be as a vehicle for nutrition education without deprivation.

Barbara Harris, Editor in Chief of *Shape* magazine, who suggested turning my simple story idea "Recipe Makeovers" into a regular column in the magazine.

My "Recipe Makeover" column readers, workshop participants and clients, who taught me a lot from their feedback.

My taste testers, especially Nancy Dusenbury and Elaine Roberts, who were always ready at a moment's notice—I appreciated your candid feedback, even when I didn't want to hear it!

My literary agent, Jan Miller of the Dupree/Miller agency, who convinced me that the concept "Recipe Makeovers" should become a cookbook. And Cathy Harris, who brought us together. Also, Sunita Batra from the agency, who was consistent and persistent in following through.

My editor, Mary Jo Plutt, and the Rodale Food Center, who were patient and gave me helpful feedback. To Jean Rogers and Debora Tkac, also Rodale editors.

Finally, to my family: A special thanks to my husband, Jeff, for picking up the slack with unbridled support, especially during my kitchen fatigue spells. (Thank you for putting up with my crankies on the days the recipes weren't quite working out. I think the word "testy" originated from testing recipes.) And my wonderful daughter, Krystin, who after dining on a meal of appetizers wanted to know when we'd be eating "real" dinners again.

BALANCING PLEASURE AND NUTRITION

America is a land of fads and trends. Nowhere is this more evident than with regard to food. But healthy eating is not a fad; it's a way of life. Often, my first job in helping clients with a nutrition makeover is to convince them that the process is pretty painless.

Many people are afraid that eating healthier means sacrificing taste in pursuit of good nutrition. One of my new clients even said to me, "I ate two cheeseburgers, a large order of fries and anything else I could get my hands on before coming to see you." He thought I was going to take away all his favorite foods, so he indulged—with a capital I.

But I'm not the food police (nor do I want to be). Instead, I work to respect clients' taste buds and to assure them that discovering new eating habits will be enjoyable.

My clients are often pleased and surprised that nutrition and taste have equal priority when we're making over eating habits and recipes. They learn quickly that nutritious eating doesn't doom them to diet martyrdom—eating bland foods that taste like cardboard.

There seems to be a prevailing attitude that if a food tastes good, it must not be good for you and, conversely, that healthful foods taste bad. Unfortunately, this belief has been reinforced with inferior offerings that have recently besieged the grocery stores. We've chewed on rubbery fat-free cheeses, gummed our way through dry high-fiber muffins and nearly cut our tongues on gritty fat-free ice creams. At the homefront, some of us have surrendered the salt shaker at the stove and table, only to experience tasteless dinners. These kinds of experiences can squash our enthusiasm for nutritious eating. But it's important not to give up!

It is possible to balance pleasurable eating with good nutrition. In this chapter, we'll explore the basics of healthy eating and their relationship to good nutrition. Then in chapter 2, I'll give you a primer for recipe makeovers—cooking tips and techniques for making recipes healthier without compromising flavor and texture.

NUTRITION MATTERS

You can tell an awful lot about people from looking into their refrigerators or knowing their thoughts about food. Food is connected with so many aspects of our lives that it is very private. A client once told me, "Having you see and know what I eat is like seeing me naked." Because of the professional relationship I have with my clients, I don't disclose names or personal cases—whether I'm helping a waitress who's working her way through law school, a famous actor who's getting ready for a movie or a busy homemaker who wants to get her family's nutrition in check. Regardless of who I see, the issues are quite similar; after all, each of us has basic human needs, especially eating!

The people who come to me do so for a number of reasons, from wanting increased energy to breaking the chronic diet cycle to preventing disease. Many of my clients are hard-driven professionals. Some of them are into the salad-only mentality and don't realize that they need to eat other foods (especially carbohydrates) to fuel their bodies. It is very easy to cross the fine line between having a healthy interest in food and developing an eating disorder.

But we do have good reason to be concerned about what we eat, because according to several reports on nutrition and health:

- Over half of the top ten killer diseases in this country are related to what we eat, such as too much fat, sodium and cholesterol.

- One out of two Americans has a high blood cholesterol level.

- Americans consume an average of 34 percent of their total daily calories from fat. (That's higher than the recommended level of less than 30 percent.)

- One out of four Americans is overweight.

- Childhood obesity has doubled over the past decade.

- Most American diets exceed the recommended daily sodium level of 2,400 milligrams, putting susceptible people at risk of high blood pressure.

- Most Americans eat only half the recommended intake of fiber, increasing their risk of colon cancer and heart disease.

Ten Ways to Boost Your Fiber Intake

According to the National Cancer Institute, we should eat at least 20 to 35 grams of fiber each day. The average American, however, consumes only 11 grams. To make sure you don't come up shy, follow these tips.

1. Toss kidney beans, garbanzos or other varieties into your salads.

2. Sprinkle wheat germ or bran on your favorite hot cereal.

3. Use whole-wheat flour whenever possible in your cooking and baking.

4. Choose whole-grain breads, cereals and crackers.

5. Eat at least five servings of fruits and vegetables each day.

6. When possible, opt for whole fruits and vegetables rather than their juices.

7. Stir chopped dried fruits into your cookies, muffins and breads before baking.

8. Choose cereals with a minimum of five grams of fiber per serving.

9. Cook with brown rice rather than white rice.

10. Choose fiber-rich snacks such as popcorn, raw vegetables with a reduced-fat dip or whole-grain crackers with reduced-fat cheese.

RECIPE FOR A HEALTHY DIET

Clearly, what we eat has an impact on our health. However, all too often the focus on nutritious eating has been aimed at what to cut out or limit. That's part of the reason why it's rather common for my first-time patients to mini-binge the night before they come to see me. They expect that they'll have to say good-bye to the foods they love. (Don't worry, they don't have to—and neither do you.)

For many people, the idea of giving up or limiting their favorite foods is the main obstacle to changing their diets for the better. In one survey reported by the American Dietetic Association, a whopping 39 percent of American adults felt that way. That's why I prefer to take the emphasis off of totally avoiding certain foods and put it on maintaining a balance between pleasure and good nutrition. If a food tastes awful, you aren't likely to eat it for long, regardless of its nutritional benefits. And the deprivation approach to nutrition does not work.

If you think that healthy eating is synonymous with depriving yourself of tasty foods or denying yourself even one speck of fat, you could set yourself up for an eating backlash. Ice cream, for example, looks especially appealing when it's on your "list of forbidden foods." When you do finally eat some ice cream, you're more likely to indulge in *larger* quantities (no matter how frozen your tongue gets). This is especially true if you think you will never be able to eat ice cream again.

I see this vicious set-up in my clients over and over. I have to remind them that one snack, one meal, one day, even one week will not make or break health or waistlines. So let's get rid of food deprivation and guilt—and replace them with a healthy relationship with food. Otherwise you risk becoming food and fat phobic.

Healthy food choices can certainly help in disease prevention, and they can also help you feel more energized. If you feel better eating nutritiously—and the food you eat happens to taste great—you'll continue eating healthier (without feeling like a nutrition martyr).

One of the best ways to build a healthy diet that you'll enjoy eating is to include a lot of variety. The Food Guide Pyramid developed by the U. S. Department of Agriculture is an easy way to keep variety and nutrition in balance. The pyramid replaces the old basic four food groups that we all learned about in school. The emphasis is placed on a foundation of grains, lots of fruits and vegetables and modest amounts of dairy products and meats or other high-protein foods. (The illustration on page 5 shows how the

Learn the Secrets of the Pyramid

In many parts of the world, people eat a diet that's very different from ours. They concentrate on whole grains and fresh fruits and vegetables. They use meats and dairy products almost as condiments that give a flavor accent to meals without adding too much fat or too many calories. They also tend to consume oils and other fats sparingly.

The U.S. Department of Agriculture used just such an eating pattern as the model for their Food Guide Pyramid. As you can see by looking at this illustration, the base of the pyramid—and the foundation of a healthy diet—is the BREAD GROUP, which includes rice, other grains, pasta, cereals and baked goods (preferably whole grain and reduced fat).

One BREAD GROUP serving equals 1 slice of bread, 1 ounce of ready-to-eat cereal or ½ cup of cooked cereal, rice or pasta; one VEGETABLE GROUP serving equals 1 cup of raw leafy vegetables, ½ cup of other cooked or raw vegetables or ¾ cup of vegetable juice; one FRUIT GROUP serving equals 1 medium piece of fruit, ½ cup of chopped, cooked or canned fruit or ¾ cup of fruit juice; one MILK GROUP serving equals 1 cup of milk or yogurt, 1½ ounces of natural cheese or 2 ounces of processed cheese; one MEAT GROUP serving equals 2 to 3 ounces of cooked lean meat, poultry or fish or ½ cup of cooked dry beans (1 egg or 2 tablespoons of peanut butter count as 1 ounce of lean meat).

Fats, oils and sweets
Use sparingly

Meat, poultry, fish, dry beans, eggs and nuts group
2–3 servings

Milk, yogurt and cheese group
2–3 servings

Vegetable group
3–5 servings

Fruit group
2–4 servings

Bread, cereal, rice and pasta group
6–11 servings

different groups fit into the pyramid and what the recommended number of servings is for each group.)

The goal of eating a variety of foods is so sensible that we often take this bit of nutrition wisdom for granted. But a study reported in the *American Journal of Clinical Nutrition* looked at the impact of diet diversity on mortality. It showed that people who eliminated several whole food groups from their diets had an increased risk of premature death.

Clearly, what you eat does have an effect on your overall health. But what you *don't eat* can also have a major impact. As a nation we have several shortcomings. We "undereat" in key food categories. Let's focus first on what we need to eat more of.

GRAINS. This may be the country of amber waves of grain, but unfortunately the average American eats only half of the daily recommended amount! Many of my clients are afraid to eat grains. They think carbohydrates are fattening, so there is some initial resistance to adding carbohydrate foods to their diets. And they're apparently not alone in thinking that way. One recent Gallup poll found that nearly 75 percent of adults questioned said they averaged only 3 grain servings a day. That's half—or less—of the 6 to 11 servings recommended on the Food Guide Pyramid.

In fact, the whole premise of the pyramid is that the largest portion of your diet should come from grain foods, such as breads, cereals, rice and pasta. These foods provide complex carbohydrates, which are important sources of energy for our bodies. They also provide many essential vitamins and minerals. Yet all too often, my weight-conscious clients eat a light breakfast and a lunch of salad with iced tea, only to end up with brain drain and food cravings by midafternoon. The problem: not enough carbs. The solution: grains! Without enough carbohydrates, they're doing the equivalent of trying to run their cars on vapors instead of a good tank of fuel.

To get the most from your grains, choose whole-grain products—brown rice, whole-wheat flour, bulgur and so forth. Grains are commonly eaten in their refined form, which diminishes their nutrient profile. For example, white pasta is nutritionally equivalent to white bread. And although there's nothing wrong with a meal of white pasta, you could end up shortchanging yourself if all your other grain choices are refined products. So be sure to check labels for the term *whole wheat* to ensure you are getting a whole-grain product. The term *wheat* by itself is no guarantee that you are getting a whole-grain product.

FRUITS AND VEGETABLES. Many parents battle at mealtime to get their children to eat their fruits and vegetables. But often adults don't eat their fair share of veggies either. Currently, only 23 percent of Americans consume the recommended 5 or more servings of fruits and vegetables each day. The average intake is about 3½ servings. This difference may seem small, but by the end of a year, it adds up to a whopping deficit of 500 servings!

Research has shown that those who eat higher amounts of fruits and vegetables have lower rates of cancer and heart disease. To promote the benefits of fruits and vegetables, the National Cancer Institute is sponsoring a program called "5 a Day—for Better Health," which recommends eating a total of at least five servings of fruits and vegetables each day. The serving sizes follow those found on the pyramid. For example, one serving of vegetables is either 1 cup raw, ½ cup cooked or ¾ cup juice. A serving of fruit equals ¾ cup juice or ½ cup chopped, cooked or canned fruit.

Many of my clients believe they need to eat five servings of different fruits or vegetables. And while that would be a nice tribute to variety, it isn't necessary. You could meet your minimum produce quota with 1½ cups of cooked broccoli and 1½ cups of orange juice.

BEANS. I've always joked that if I were to give an Academy Award to one group of foods, it would be beans. It is no secret to my clients that I'm on the bean bandwagon (some people even call me the Bean Queen). I have a passion for beans because they are so rich in nutrients. They are high in dietary fiber, protein, iron, folic acid and complex carbohydrates, and they're low in fat and sodium—making them among the best foods around. In addition, beans contain high amounts of soluble fiber, the same type of fiber found in oat bran that can help lower cholesterol. If you're not particularly fond of oat bran, you might be happy to learn that one cup of cooked pinto beans, for instance, has three times the fiber of an equivalent amount of cooked oat bran (made from ⅓ cup of raw oat bran).

Unfortunately, even with all of these benefits, beans are still lonely heroes in the arena of nutritious eating. Often they are overlooked. In the Food Guide Pyramid, for instance, beans are lumped into the meat group. Other times, beans are outright snubbed. The California Department of Health, however, has taken the nutritional power of legumes seriously. In their latest dietary guidelines, they recommend eating at least three ½ cup servings each week.

Bean Power

Great things often come in small packages. That's certainly the case with dried beans. Each tiny bean is packed full of nutrition, yet it's low in calories and fat. Just 1 cup of cooked beans contains almost one-third of your Recommended Dietary Allowance of protein and iron. And beans can go a long way toward helping you eat the 20 to 35 grams of dietary fiber the National Cancer Institute advises you to get every day.

Eat them alone or use them to replace meat in casseroles, salads and soups. There's no end to the ways you can boost your diet with bean power. Here's how some of the most common varieties stack up in terms of calories, fat, sodium and fiber.

One note: These figures are for cooked dried beans. If you use canned beans (and they *are* convenient), the sodium level will go way up. You can wash away some of that sodium by pouring the beans into a strainer or sieve and rinsing them well with cold water.

BEAN (1 cup cooked)	CALORIES	FAT (g.)	SODIUM (mg.)	FIBER (g.)
Black	227	<1	1	12
Black-eyed peas	198	<1	6	9
Chick-peas (garbanzos)	269	4	11	8
Great Northern	210	<1	4	10
Kidney	225	<1	4	13
Lentils	231	<1	4	10
Lima	217	<1	4	8
Navy	259	1	2	13
Pinto	235	<1	3	11
Split peas	231	<1	4	5

LIGHTEN UP

If you stick with traditional fatty foods that are high in cholesterol and sodium, with little regard to nutrition, you may pay a hefty penalty with your health. Yet if you totally exile favorite foods, you could feel miserable and end up overeating. A better approach is to focus on where you can cut the fat (or cholesterol or sodium) and *not* miss it. For example, my clients are surprised to learn that I am fond of pancakes for breakfast—with syrup! The only thing I do differently than many people is leave out the butter. I don't miss the fatty little accoutrement, especially when I've got a rich maple syrup to keep my taste buds happy. And I don't feel deprived.

TOTAL FAT. There is a trend developing among restaurants of putting little bottles of olive oil on tables for patrons to drizzle on their bread instead of using butter. Ironically, people who are trying to cut down on fat think that olive oil is superior to butter. But it actually has more calories than butter, and it's still 100 percent fat. All fats need to be treated respectfully.

While health experts do not agree on the optimal total fat intake, nearly all believe that fat should not exceed 30 percent of your daily calories. By lowering your fat intake, you'll reduce your risk of developing chronic diseases such as heart disease, diabetes and certain types of cancer. The National Academy of Sciences has stated that "There is evidence that further reduction in fat intake [below 30 percent] may confer even greater health benefits." In addition, some studies suggest that lowering fat intake to as little as 10 percent may even widen partially clogged arteries.

A general rule of thumb I like to use for determining how much fat to eat is: Eat no more than three grams of fat for every 100 calories. This tip will help keep you below the 30 percent fat ceiling. Keep in mind, however, that the 30 percent recommendation is intended to be an average over time. It is not a mandate for each food or each meal; it should be an average over a day or week. The number of grams of fat can be easily found on food labels. To estimate your fat quota, see page 11.

As you cut down on your fat consumption, remember that fat is still an essential nutrient. So don't strive to entirely eliminate it from your diet. Every cell in your body requires fat. In particular, two fatty acids—linoleic and linolenic—found in fat are especially vital, like vitamins. If deprived of these two essential nutrients, you may experience dry and flaky skin, hair loss and impaired wound healing.

The bottom line with fat is to keep your total intake low (under 30 percent of calories). If you do that, the fat issue becomes one of taste. So whether you prefer olive oil, butter or margarine, keep the amounts small. If there's no difference in flavor, choose the lowest in saturated fat (canola oil, corn oil, safflower oil, sunflower oil and olive oil are the lowest). Better yet, vary the types of fat you eat. That's a great way to hedge your nutritional bets in the ever-changing world of nutrition research.

Sometimes we eat or prepare foods out of sheer habit, not necessarily because we prefer their taste. Perhaps you can do without the fat in a particular item that you are eating. Does having margarine or butter on toast with jam make a flavor difference to you? If you won't miss the fat, why bother with it? (In the next chapter, and throughout this book, you'll learn lots of ways you can cut the fat from recipes without missing it.)

My philosophy is that if I'm going to eat fat, I want to *taste* it. Adding mayonnaise to a sandwich does nothing for my taste buds, so I routinely hold the mayo. But on occasion I'll add a couple of avocado slices—they make a satisfying flavor difference to me.

SATURATED FAT. There are basically three types of fat: saturated, monounsaturated and polyunsaturated. Saturated fats— which are linked to heart disease and high blood cholesterol—are primarily found in animal foods such as meat, poultry and dairy products. Monounsaturated fats are found in olive oil and canola oil. Unsaturated fats are usually found in plants and fish.

Health experts agree that you should get only 10 percent of your total calories from saturated fat. Many recommend a lower intake—7 or 8 percent—on the theory that you'll reap even greater health benefits. One point most experts do agree on is that saturated fat can raise your levels of blood cholesterol. And high cholesterol puts you at risk for heart disease. To get a better handle on how much saturated fat you should eat in a day, see the table on the opposite page.

Here's something that often surprises my clients. Although saturated fat is primarily found in animal products, it is also present in plant foods, including oils. Even olive oil and canola oil, which are very low in saturated fat, contain some. And tropical oils like coconut oil and palm kernel oil are loaded with saturated fat— twice as much as lard!

CHOLESTEROL. We do not need cholesterol in our food. Our bodies make all the cholesterol they need for cellular health. Most health authorities recommend limiting your intake to 300 milligrams or less per day. That's because cholesterol in the diet is related to rising levels of blood cholesterol.

Dietary cholesterol comes only from meat, fish, poultry, eggs, dairy products and other animal foods. (Certain animal foods have

What's Your Daily Fat Quota?

Health experts tell us we should not consume more than 30 percent of our calories from fat. And we need to hold saturated fat to no more than 10 percent. But what do those limits really mean in practical terms? This table tells you how many grams of total fat and saturated fat you can have, based on your average calorie intake.

Calories	Total Fat (g.)	Saturated Fat (g.)
1,500	50	17
1,600	53	18
1,700	57	19
1,800	60	20
1,900	63	21
2,000	67	22
2,100	70	23
2,200	73	24
2,300	77	26
2,400	80	27
2,500	83	28
2,600	87	29
2,700	90	30
2,800	93	31
2,900	97	32
3,000	100	33

no cholesterol. Egg whites have none, and fat-free dairy products are virtually cholesterol free.)

Plant products—including fruits, vegetables, grains, nuts, beans and oils—do not contain any cholesterol. (Just remember that some of those foods can and often do contain fat.)

SODIUM. Your body needs dietary sodium to regulate the proper balance of vital fluids and chemicals in your system. But as is the case with fat and cholesterol, it's possible to get too much.

Diets high in sodium have been associated with high blood pressure, stroke and cancer of the stomach and esophagus. The recommended maximum intake is 2,400 milligrams a day—equivalent to about 1¼ teaspoons of salt. And 1,800 milligrams of sodium (or less) is an even healthier goal.

Although salt has been named as the main offender in the dietary sodium issue, only 15 percent of our consumption comes from table salt. Most of what we get in our diet comes from processed foods. Nonetheless, I've cut back on salt and high-sodium ingredients in this book. And in doing so, I've reduced the sodium in my recipes to about half of the original amounts.

One last point to remember—it's progress, not perfection that counts. Your body does not punch a time clock. One day or one week of less-than-optimum eating will not send you spiraling into a nutrient deficiency or turn you into a walking cholesterol bomb. It's what you do consistently over time that counts.

How I Did This Book

Recipe makeovers are my specialty. They're the subject of the column I do for *Shape* magazine, and they're a big hit among my clients. After all, people who want to eat better don't really want to forsake their old favorite foods—they just want versions of them that are lower in fat, calories and cholesterol.

I often hear comments like "My family loves that dish, but I just don't make it anymore because it's too high in fat." Such remarks inspire me to make sure popular foods remain a part of the family repertoire.

My usual procedure is to start with traditional recipes and work on them until they satisfy my standards for taste *and* nutrition. That's why many of the recipes in this book will probably have a familiar ring to them. I've collected favorites from all over. Friends, readers, workshop participants and family members contributed some. Others are modified forms of those in classic cookbooks—I chose the types of dishes that I know make frequent appearances at everyday meals as well as family reunions and other special celebrations. Often I was able to achieve big savings in fat and calories by making only a few simple changes.

I hope these new versions will become as popular at your house as they are at mine.

RECIPE MAKEOVER PRIMER

What one thing would make healthy eating easier and more enjoyable for most people? Being able to continue eating their favorite foods, with just a few adjustments. I began doing personal recipe makeovers for my clients with that philosophy in mind.

My clients are similar to the average American family—they tend to prepare the same 12 recipes 80 percent of the time. So making over their family favorites was the key to helping eat better. With a few nips and tucks, it's possible to create healthier versions of your favorite recipes. Of course, for this principle to work, the food must taste good.

During my recipe makeover workshops, we take recipes and make them more healthful. It is so much fun to watch people taste the difference. The process is part art, part science, and it is the best part of both.

There are an endless array of cooking tricks—ranging from changing a few simple cooking styles to substituting ingredients in beloved recipes—that can turn an unhealthy diet into a tasty, nutritious one that's the basis of a lifetime of eating enjoyment.

In this chapter, I'll reveal my tricks of the trade for slashing excess fat and calories from family favorites without sacrificing taste. In addition, throughout this cookbook, I'll clue you in to specific tips for converting traditional recipes into healthier versions. Each of the more than 200 recipes has been tested in my kitchen and tasted by my family and friends. And then the Rodale Food Center took their turn testing and tasting—to guarantee you success and good flavor in your new lighter style of cooking.

Go Slow

Basically, I use three methods to reduce the amount of fat and calories in a recipe:

- Replace a high-fat ingredient with a different one that's lower in fat and calories.

- Reduce the amount of a high-fat ingredient or eliminate it altogether.

- Use a reduced-fat cooking technique or method.

When modifying recipes, it is best to make only *one* change at a time. For instance, rather than changing *both* the ingredient and the method when preparing a recipe, change only the ingredient. If that works well, change the method when you make the recipe the second time. That way, if your dish doesn't turn out quite right, you know where the problem lies. I learned this the hard way. I once spent hours trying to create an ultra-nutritious soup—making changes *everywhere*—only to end up with inedible mush.

Try not to announce the health merits of your new creation until after your guests have taken a bite and evaluated it themselves. If you mention that it's a healthier version of a well-loved traditional dish, people are likely to think "If this is healthy, it won't taste good." Instead, be patient and let *them* make the first comment. You'll be surprised—often the comments run along the lines of "This is delicious. Can I have the recipe?"

Fat-Saving Substitutions

The easiest way to reduce the amount of fat in a recipe is to use a lower-fat version of an ingredient. Today, health-conscious consumers can choose from an array of reduced-fat and fat-free cheeses and other dairy products, salad dressings, canned cream soups, pasta sauces and much more.

It can be a little more complicated to use a lower-fat alternate ingredient instead of a fatty food. Beginning on page 17, you'll find a chart listing a variety of such substitutions, along with the fat and calorie savings you'll realize. Some of the highlights—and most surprising substitutions—include:

- **EVAPORATED SKIM MILK.** For a rich, creamy sauce or soup that's low in fat and calories, use evaporated skim milk instead of heavy cream. It has cream-like flavor and is richer in texture than regular skim milk. And best of all, you'll slim down your recipe by more than 80 grams of fat and 600 calories for every cup used.

- **FAT-FREE PLAIN YOGURT.** Use fat-free plain yogurt in place of sour cream. Hard to swallow, you say? I, too, was not particularly thrilled with this idea until I tried it in a stroganoff recipe and in an ambrosia fruit salad. I couldn't tell the difference, and neither could my family! While fat-free sour cream may seem like the logical substitution, it does not have the rich body or flavor of plain yogurt. And depending on the brands involved, fat-free yogurt is often much higher in calcium than sour cream.

- **APPLESAUCE.** Rather than using oil, margarine or butter in many baked products, I substitute applesauce. I save more than 900 calories and 100 grams of fat for each ½ cup used.

  This substitution works well for muffins, quick breads, cake mixes and cakes made from scratch. Applesauce is rich in a natural substance called pectin, which—like fat—prevents moisture loss during baking.

  In some recipes, when oil is the only liquid, I'll use a combination of half applesauce and half buttermilk. Substituting applesauce alone could result in an overly dry baked product. Buttermilk is a good choice because it's low in fat and has more body than other liquids, such as skim milk, fruit juice and water.

- **PRUNES.** Pureed prunes or baby food prunes are one of the best fat replacers in chocolate baked goodies, such as brownies and cakes. They add a naturally sweet flavor and chewy texture. And the dark color and rich flavor of chocolate help disguise the prunes, so you don't even notice they're there. Best yet, ½ cup of prune puree will save you nearly 800 calories and over 100 grams of fat in your recipe.

  For ease and convenience, I like using a jar of baby food prunes rather than prunes I've pureed myself. If you prefer to make your own puree, place ⅔ cup (4 ounces) of pitted prunes in a blender or small food processor. Add 3 tablespoons of hot water and blend or process until the prunes are smooth.

- **MARSHMALLOW CREME.** When you want a fluffy frosting, replace the margarine or butter in your recipe with marshmallow creme. It adds a creaminess to the frosting without contributing any fat.

- **REDUCED-CALORIE MARGARINE OR BUTTER.** If a recipe calls for a solid fat—such as shortening, butter or regular margarine—try replacing it with reduced-calorie margarine or butter. These products are made "light" by having water whipped into them. But remember, even though 1 tablespoon of a reduced-calorie product is lower in calories and fat than its regular counterpart, all of the calories still come from fat.

    Generally, it's best to use these products in foods that won't be cooked. In some recipes, such as cookies, the additional water from the margarine or butter will change the texture of the product.

- **FRUIT JUICE.** For a nonfat salad dressing or marinade, use a fruit juice. White grape, apple, orange and pineapple juices are all light-flavored alternatives to oil. Or combine the juice with defatted chicken broth for a less fruity liquid.

- **EGG WHITES.** For each whole egg, use two egg whites. Although you'll only save 5 grams of fat, the bigger savings will be in cholesterol. One egg yolk contains 213 milligrams of cholesterol!

- **COCOA POWDER.** For great chocolate flavor without the fat, use cocoa powder. For each ounce of unsweetened chocolate, use 3 tablespoons unsweetened cocoa powder.

    In my testing, I've also found that adding a small amount of instant coffee granules intensifies the chocolate flavor. I like using ½ to 1 teaspoon of granules in a recipe.

- **LOW-FAT CREAM SOUP.** Family-favorite casseroles almost always call for canned cream soups, which tend to be high in both fat and sodium. If your casserole or other recipe uses the soup in its condensed form, buy a condensed cream soup that's 99 percent fat free and that has ⅓ less sodium. Otherwise, make your own version of a cream soup. Here's how: In a small saucepan, use a wire whisk to stir together 1 cup evaporated skim milk, 1 tablespoon cornstarch and 1 teaspoon instant (preferably low-sodium) bouillon granules. Cook and stir until thickened and bubbly. Cook and stir for 1 minute more.

- **PHYLLO DOUGH.** When a dessert calls for a pastry pie crust, use the reduced-fat Graham Cracker Crust on page 317. Or opt for a flaky phyllo crust made with no-stick spray.

    To make a phyllo pastry shell: Cut three sheets of phyllo dough in half crosswise. Drape one half-sheet across a 9" pie plate. Press the phyllo into the plate and fold the overhanging edge toward the center, crumpling it slightly to fit. Lightly spray the dough with no-stick spray. Repeat layering and spraying with the remaining half-sheets. Bake at 375° for 4 to 6 minutes or until golden.

Easy Ways to Whittle Calories and Fat

It's amazing how many calories and how much fat you can trim from recipes just by making small changes. Here are a few of the ingredient substitutions that I use in my recipes.

INSTEAD OF	USE	CALORIES SAVED	FAT SAVED (g.)
DAIRY PRODUCTS			
4 ounces cheddar cheese	4 ounces reduced-fat cheddar cheese (less than 5 grams fat per ounce)	171	25
	OR		
	4 ounces fat-free cheddar cheese	293	38
4 ounces feta cheese	2 ounces feta cheese + 2 ounces fat-free cottage cheese	115	12
4 ounces chèvre (goat cheese)	2 ounces chèvre + 2 ounces fat-free ricotta cheese	160	16
8 ounces cream cheese	8 ounces light cream cheese	305	39
	OR		
	8 ounces fat-free cream cheese	588	79
	OR		
	8 ounces fat-free ricotta cheese	629	79
1 cup heavy cream	1 cup evaporated skim milk	621	87
1 cup sour cream	1 cup fat-free sour cream	347	48
	OR		
	1 cup fat-free plain yogurt	366	48
	OR		
	1 cup pureed fat-free cottage cheese + 1 tablespoon lemon juice	349	48
1 cup whole milk	1 cup skim milk	64	8

Instead of	Use	Calories Saved	Fat Saved (g.)
Fats and Oils			
½ cup oil (for baking)	½ cup applesauce	911	109
	OR		
	¼ cup applesauce + ¼ cup buttermilk	912	108
	OR		
	½ cup baby food prunes	799	109
½ cup oil (for marinades and salad dressings)	½ cup defatted chicken broth	945	109
	OR		
	½ cup unsweetened pineapple juice	894	109
½ cup margarine or butter (for baking)	½ cup reduced-calorie margarine (40% fat)	421	48
	OR		
	½ cup applesauce	760	92
	OR		
	¼ cup applesauce + ¼ cup buttermilk	761	91
	OR		
	½ cup baby food prunes	681	92
½ cup margarine or butter (for icings)	½ cup marshmallow creme	392	92
2 tablespoons oil (for sautéing)	2 tablespoons defatted broth	236	27
	OR		
	2 tablespoons unsweetened pineapple juice	223	27
	OR		
	2 tablespoons dry wine	221	27
Meats, Poultry, Fish and Eggs			
1 pound ground beef (80% lean)	1 pound lean ground beef (95% lean)	350	27
	OR		
	1 pound ground turkey breast	853	91
	OR		
	1 pound ground turkey	268	32
	OR		
	1 pound ground chicken	767	73
	OR		

INSTEAD OF	USE	CALORIES SAVED	FAT SAVED(g.)
	1 pound ground chicken breast OR	811	89
	1 pound ground pork tenderloin	761	80
3 slices pork bacon (¾ ounce total)	3 slices turkey bacon (¾ ounce total)	42	5
3 ounces roasted chicken thigh (with skin)	3 ounces roasted chicken breast (without skin)	70	10
6½ ounces canned oil-packed tuna	6½ ounces canned water-packed tuna	124	14
1 whole egg	2 egg whites	41	5

MISCELLANEOUS

INSTEAD OF	USE	CALORIES SAVED	FAT SAVED(g.)
1 cup chocolate chips	¾ cup chocolate chips OR	215	15
	⅔ cup chocolate chips OR	286	20
	½ cup chocolate chips	430	30
1 ounce unsweetened chocolate	3 tablespoons unsweetened cocoa powder	103	12
1 cup shredded coconut	½ cup shredded coconut OR	176	12
	1 teaspoon coconut flavoring	337	24
4 ounces sliced olives	2 ounces sliced olives	73	8
1 cup condensed canned cream soup	1 cup condensed canned 99% fat-free cream soup OR	112	13
	1 cup Low-Fat Cream Soup (page 16)	29	18
1 cup sugar	¾ cup sugar	192	0
1 cup walnuts	½ cup walnuts	385	37

HELPFUL, HEALTHFUL COOKING TIPS

Creating a reduced-fat recipe goes beyond using leaner ingredients. It also means using healthy cooking techniques. Below are a variety of ways you can reduce fat and calories in your recipes. (I relied on them when creating the recipes in this book.)

- Low- and no-fat cooking methods, such as steaming, poaching, stir-frying, broiling, grilling, microwaving, baking and roasting, are the best alternatives to frying.

- A good-quality set of no-stick saucepans, skillets and baking pans lets you "fry," sauté and bake without adding fat.

- No-stick spray or 1 to 2 tablespoons defatted broth, water, juice or wine can easily take the place of cooking oil when you're sautéing vegetables.

- Fat-free and reduced-fat cheeses have slightly different cooking characteristics than their fattier counterparts. Because they have less fat, they do not melt as smoothly. To overcome this, *finely* shred the cheese. When making sauces and soups, toss the cheese with a small amount of flour, cornstarch or arrowroot. When topping pizzas, casseroles or hot sandwiches, use reduced-fat rather than fat-free cheese.

- Trim all visible fat from steaks, chops, roasts and other meat cuts before preparing them.

- Replace one-quarter to one-half of the ground meat or poultry in a casserole or meat sauce with cooked brown rice, bulgur, couscous or cooked and chopped dried beans. You'll cut both fat and your food bill. (And you'll add fiber that meat lacks.)

- Remove the skin before cooking poultry, especially cuts like chicken breasts. (It is possible to keep the skin on until after cooking—skin helps prevent roasted or baked cuts from drying out. And studies have shown that the fat from the skin doesn't penetrate the meat during cooking. But if you do leave the skin on, make sure any seasonings you've applied go under the skin. Otherwise, you'll lose the flavor when you peel off the skin.)

- Skim and discard fat from hot soups or stews. Or chill the soup or stew and skim off the solid fat that forms at the top.

- Use pureed cooked vegetables—such as carrots, potatoes or cauliflower—to thicken soups and sauces instead of cream, egg yolks or a butter-and-flour roux.

- Select "healthier" fats when it is necessary to add fat to a recipe and it won't affect the flavor. That means replacing butter, lard or other highly saturated fats with oils such as canola, olive, safflower, sunflower, corn and others that are low in saturates. Keep in mind that sometimes it takes just a few drops of a very flavorful oil, such as extra-virgin olive, dark sesame, walnut or macadamia nut, to really perk up a dish. And just a *small* amount of butter can add a lot of flavor.

- Cut the fat where you won't miss it. But keep the characteristic flavor of fatty ingredients—such as nuts, coconut, chocolate chips and bacon—by reducing the quantity you use by 25 to 50 percent. For example, if a recipe calls for 1 cup of walnuts, use ½ cup. You'll save 385 calories and 37 grams of fat.

- Toast nuts to enhance their flavor and *finely* chop them so they are more distributed throughout a baked product.

- If sugar is the primary sweetener in a fruit sauce, beverage or other dish that isn't a baked good, scale the amount down by 25 percent. For instance, instead of using 1 cup of sugar, use ¾ cup. And if you like, add a pinch of cinnamon, nutmeg or allspice—you'll increase the perception of sweetness without adding calories.

  One word of caution: be careful when cutting back the amount of sugar in cakes, cookies and other baked products. Many times reducing the sugar will affect the texture or volume.

- Beat egg whites until soft peaks form before incorporating them into baked goods. This will increase volume and tenderness .

- Make a simple fat-free "frosting" for cakes or bar cookies by simply sprinkling the top with powdered sugar.

- Increase the fiber content and nutritional value of dishes by using whole-wheat flour for at least half of the all-purpose white flour. For cakes and other baked products that require a light texture, use whole-wheat pastry flour, which is available in health food stores and some well-stocked supermarkets.

As you make your favorite recipes into healthier versions, remember that it's progress, not perfection, that counts. Sometimes you won't be able to replace every fatty ingredient or to switch to a reduced-fat cooking method without compromising the taste or character of the recipe. If you were to entirely eliminate walnuts from a cookie recipe, for instance, you would probably notice the difference. The walnuts add both a unique flavor and a crunchy texture. In that case, just reducing the amount of nuts would be a nutritional improvement—and you'd still retain the cookies' flavor. Even making only one change to a recipe is a step in the right direction. And small steps add up!

Troubleshooting Your Recipe Makeovers

There's often a good scientific reason for including fat in a recipe. And simply removing it without making other adjustments can alter the finished product in undesirable ways. Here are some ways that I compensate for the change and still retain the taste and texture of the original recipe. Use these tips to help you make over your own family favorites.

PROBLEM	CAUSE	SOLUTION
MUFFINS AND BREADS		
Rubbery or tough texture	Ordinarily, fat is used to coat flour particles so the gluten will not develop during mixing. By eliminating the fat, you eliminate this protective coating.	Add a small amount of grated apple to the batter. This will add moistness and compensate for the tough texture. OR Add some fat *back* to the recipe. You may have taken out too much. OR Add chopped dried fruit and nuts to the batter to add another texture to the baked product.
Not enough body	Using a fat-free liquid substitute—such as skim milk, fruit juice or water—which is much less viscous than oil.	Use buttermilk as the liquid in the batter. OR Add a small amount of grated apple.
Wet texture	Different kinds of flours absorb different amounts of moisture from doughs and batters. All-purpose flour absorbs less water than whole-wheat flour.	Use whole-wheat flour when a recipe calls for it. OR Add a few tablespoons of wheat germ or oat bran.
	Underbaking muffins or bread.	Increase the baking time. OR Use an oven thermometer to check the temperature of your oven. Adjust the oven temperature, if necessary.

PROBLEM	CAUSE	SOLUTION
	Substituting two egg whites for each whole egg increases the moisture in baked products. (Egg whites are 88% water; yolks are 50% water.)	Decrease the baking temperature and increase the baking time. OR Use an oven thermometer to check the temperature of your oven. OR Stir an extra tablespoon of flour or cornstarch into the batter to absorb the excess moisture.

MEATS AND POULTRY

Dry and tough	Overcooking the meat or poultry.	Decrease the cooking time. Lean cuts of meat require less cooking time than their fattier counterparts. OR Add moisture to meats or poultry by: • covering or wrapping them in foil during roasting • searing the meat before roasting • marinating the meat or poultry in a no-oil marinade before cooking • coating small pieces of meat or poultry with fat-free bread or cracker crumbs.

SAUCES AND DIPS (YOGURT BASED)

Too thin	Overcooking the yogurt.	For cooked sauces and dips, stir in the yogurt at the very end. Cook *just* until heated through.
	Overstirring the yogurt.	For uncooked sauces and dips, gently stir in the yogurt.

PROBLEM	CAUSE	SOLUTION
SALAD DRESSINGS		
Too thin	Replacing the oil with a liquid that is thinner than oil.	Stir 1 to 2 teaspoons of arrowroot into the dressing using a wire whisk. Bring the mixture to a gentle boil, then cook and stir for 2 minutes more. OR Replace the oil with a fat-free or reduced-fat substance that has body, such as buttermilk, yogurt or sour cream.
CASSEROLES		
Too thin	Fat-free products, such as cream cheese and ricotta cheese, and reduced-calorie margarines contain more water than their regular counterparts. These products may contain gelatin, which breaks down and liquifies when heated.	Stir in a beaten egg white before baking to help thicken the mixture. OR Use light cream cheese or reduced-fat ricotta cheese.
	Many vegetables release water during baking.	Drain the vegetables well after cooking and before adding to the casserole.
Tough crust forms on top of the casserole	Fat-free cheeses tend to toughen and dry out quickly when melted in the oven or under the broiler.	*Finely* shred the cheese so it melts evenly. OR Use a reduced-fat cheese in place of fat-free cheese. OR Omit the cheese topping and serve the casserole with a reduced-fat cheese sauce, such as the one on page 262. OR Cover the casserole during baking.

OVEN-FRESH MUFFINS AND BREADS

Sweet sticky rolls filled with pecans . . . jumbo muffins spiked with chocolate chips . . . garlic bread crowned with a cheesy Parmesan topping—these goodies sound too good to be true on a reduced-fat diet. But my fondness for these specialties, served warm from the oven, sent me on my personal journey into the little-known realm of reduced-fat baking.

I soon realized that removing fat from muffins, quick breads and other such baked goods often left them with a rubbery texture. Fortunately, I learned that you can overcome this hurdle by replacing the fat with a combination of applesauce and buttermilk. Believe it or not, pectin in the applesauce acts like fat by preventing moisture loss during baking. And buttermilk contributes richness at a cost of only five grams of fat per cup.

I also found that reduced-fat muffins retain their moisture much better when baked in large muffin cups (the 3" size rather than the standard 2½" cups).

Those are just two of the many fat-busting techniques I use in this chapter. I hope they'll inspire you to reshape your own favorite baked recipes.

Berry Best Blueberry Muffins

Pictured on page 55

If you love blueberries, you'll enjoy these full-of-fruit muffins. Calories, fat and cholesterol were reduced by:

- Replacing butter with a combination of buttermilk and applesauce
- Using egg whites instead of a whole egg

Nutrition Scorecard (per large muffin)	Before	After
Calories	373	280
Fat (g.)	14	<1
% Calories from fat	32%	3%
Cholesterol (mg.)	69	0

> 1 cup all-purpose flour
> ¾ cup whole-wheat pastry flour
> ¾ cup sugar
> 1 tablespoon baking powder
> 1 teaspoon finely shredded lemon peel
> 2 egg whites
> ⅔ cup buttermilk
> ⅓ cup unsweetened applesauce
> 1 teaspoon vanilla
> 1 cup fresh or frozen blueberries (do not thaw frozen berries)

Preheat the oven to 400°. Spray six large, 3" muffin cups with no-stick spray and set aside.

In a large bowl, stir together the all-purpose flour, whole-wheat flour, sugar, baking powder and lemon peel. Make a well in the center of the mixture.

In a small bowl, beat the egg whites until foamy. Stir in the buttermilk, applesauce and vanilla. Add the buttermilk mixture to the flour mixture and stir just until moistened. Fold in the blueberries.

Spoon the batter into the prepared cups, filling each ¾ full. Bake for 22 to 25 minutes or until a toothpick inserted in the center comes out clean. Cool the muffins in the muffin cups for 5 minutes. Then remove the muffins and cool on a wire rack.

Makes 6 large muffins; 6 servings.

Note: To make standard-sized muffins, spray twelve 2½" muffin cups with no-stick spray. Spoon the batter into the cups, filling each ¾ full. Bake for 18 to 20 minutes or until done. Cool as directed above. (Per standard-sized blueberry muffin: 140 calories, <1 g. fat, 3% calories from fat, 0 mg. cholesterol.)

Apricot Oat Bran Muffins

Pictured on page 56

Here's a muffin recipe that I developed during the oat bran craze. Each time my clients tried these muffins and gave me their comments, I was able to make them better. I cut calories, fat and cholesterol by:

• Using egg whites instead of a whole egg

• Replacing oil with grated apples

Nutrition Scorecard (per large muffin)		
	Before	After
Calories	219	195
Fat (g.)	8	3
% Calories from fat	33%	14%
Cholesterol (mg.)	36	2

  2 *cups oat bran*
  ¼ *cup packed brown sugar*
  1 *tablespoon baking powder*
  2 *egg whites*
  1 *cup buttermilk*
  ⅓ *cup molasses*
  1 *large apple, peeled, cored and grated*
  ¾ *cup finely chopped dried apricots*

Preheat the oven to 400°. Spray six large, 3" muffin cups with no-stick spray and set aside.

In a large bowl, stir together the oat bran, brown sugar and baking powder. Make a well in the center of the mixture.

In a small bowl, beat the egg whites until foamy. Stir in the buttermilk and molasses. Add the buttermilk mixture to the oat-bran mixture and stir just until moistened. Fold in the apples and apricots.

Spoon the batter into the prepared cups, filling each ¾ full. Bake for 18 to 20 minutes or until a toothpick inserted in the center comes out clean. Cool the muffins in the muffin cups for 5 minutes. Then remove the muffins and cool on a wire rack.

Makes 6 large muffins; 6 servings.

Note: To make standard-sized muffins, spray twelve 2½" muffin cups with no-stick spray. Spoon the batter into the cups, filling each ¾ full. Bake for 15 to 17 minutes or until done. Cool as directed above. (Per standard-sized muffin: 98 calories, 2 g. fat, 14% calories from fat, 1 mg. cholesterol.)

Chocolate Chip Orange Muffins

Here's a delightfully delectable combination of flavors—the fresh orange zest really complements the chocolate in these muffins. You can use either regular or mini chips. I like to bite into larger chunks of chocolate, but some of my clients prefer to have the rich flavor of chocolate lavishly distributed throughout the muffins. Calories, fat and cholesterol were reduced by:

- Replacing oil with a combination of buttermilk and applesauce

- Using egg whites instead of a whole egg

- Reducing the amount of chocolate chips

Nutrition Scorecard
(per large muffin)

	Before	After
Calories	492	331
Fat (g.)	24	6
% Calories from fat	43%	15%
Cholesterol (mg.)	39	1

1 cup all-purpose flour
¾ cup whole-wheat pastry flour
¾ cup sugar
1 tablespoon baking powder
2 teaspoons finely shredded orange peel
2 egg whites
⅔ cup buttermilk
⅓ cup unsweetened applesauce
½ cup chocolate chips

Preheat the oven to 400°. Spray six large, 3" muffin cups with no-stick spray and set aside.

In a large bowl, stir together the all-purpose flour, whole-wheat flour, sugar, baking powder and orange peel. Make a well in the center of the mixture.

In a small bowl, beat the egg whites until foamy. Stir in the buttermilk and applesauce. Add the buttermilk mixture to the flour mixture and stir just until moistened. Fold in the chocolate chips.

Spoon the batter into the prepared cups, filling each ¾ full. Bake for 20 to 22 minutes or until a toothpick inserted in the center comes out clean. Cool the muffins in the muffin cups for 5 minutes. Then remove the muffins and cool on a wire rack.

Makes 6 large muffins; 6 servings.

Note: To make standard-sized muffins, spray twelve 2½" muffin cups with no-stick spray. Spoon the batter into the cups, filling each ¾ full. Bake for 15 to 17 minutes or until done. Cool as directed above. (Per standard-sized muffin: 166 calories, 3 g. fat, 15% calories from fat, 0 mg. cholesterol.)

Honey Bran Muffins

In the mornings, I love to treat my family to piping-hot muffins. And it's easy with these delicious, moist bran muffins. I prepare the batter the night before, then pop the muffins into the oven and let them bake while I get ready for work. Calories, fat and cholesterol were reduced by:

- Replacing butter with baby food prunes

- Using egg whites instead of a whole egg

Nutrition Scorecard
(per large muffin)

	Before	After
Calories	353	281
Fat (g.)	9	<1
% Calories from fat	22%	3%
Cholesterol (mg.)	58	2

1 cup 100% bran cereal (such as Kellogg's Bran Buds or
  Nabisco 100% Bran)
¾ cup all-purpose flour
¼ cup sugar
1 teaspoon baking soda
2 egg whites, lightly beaten
⅓ cup honey
1 (2½-ounce) jar baby food prunes
3 tablespoons molasses
1 cup buttermilk
½ cup raisins

In a large bowl, stir together the cereal, flour, sugar and baking soda. Make a well in the center of the mixture.

In a small bowl, stir together the egg whites, honey, prunes, molasses and buttermilk. Add the prune mixture to the flour mixture and stir just until moistened. Fold in the raisins. Transfer the batter to an airtight container. Seal and refrigerate overnight.

To bake the muffins, preheat the oven to 375°. Spray six large, 3" muffin cups with no-stick spray. Spoon the batter into the prepared cups, filling each ¾ full. Bake for 20 to 23 minutes or until a toothpick inserted in the center comes out clean. Cool the muffins in the muffin cups for 5 minutes. Then remove the muffins and cool on a wire rack.

Makes 6 large muffins; 6 servings.

Note: To make standard-sized muffins, spray twelve 2½" muffin cups with no-stick spray. Spoon the batter into the cups, filling each ¾ full. Bake for 16 to 19 minutes or until done. Cool as directed above. (Per standard-sized muffin: 141 calories, <1 g. fat, 3% calories from fat, 1 mg. cholesterol.)

Butterscotch Chip Muffins with Pecans

Hands down—these rich, cake-like muffins were voted "the best" among my taste testers. Serve the muffins with a glass of skim milk for a reduced-fat dessert or afternoon snack. I reduced calories, fat and cholesterol by:

- Replacing butter with a combination of buttermilk and applesauce

- Reducing the amount of butterscotch chips

- Reducing the amount of pecans

- Using egg whites instead of a whole egg

Nutrition Scorecard
(per muffin)

	Before	After
Calories	651	412
Fat (g.)	38	12
% Calories from fat	53%	27%
Cholesterol (mg.)	77	0

½ cup pecan halves
1 cup all-purpose flour
¾ cup whole-wheat pastry flour
½ cup packed brown sugar
¼ cup sugar
1 tablespoon baking powder
1 teaspoon ground cinnamon
2 egg whites
⅔ cup buttermilk
⅓ cup unsweetened applesauce
½ cup butterscotch chips

Preheat the oven to 400°. Spray six large, 3" muffin cups with no-stick spray and set aside. Set six of the pecan halves aside, then chop the remaining pecans.

In a large bowl, stir together the all-purpose flour, whole-wheat flour, brown sugar, sugar, baking powder and cinnamon. Make a well in the center of the mixture.

In a small bowl, beat the egg whites until foamy. Stir in the buttermilk and applesauce. Add the buttermilk mixture to the flour mixture and stir just until moistened. Fold in the chopped pecans and butterscotch chips.

Spoon the batter into the prepared cups, filling each ¾ full. Top each muffin with one of the reserved pecan halves. Bake for 22 to 25 minutes or until a toothpick inserted in the center comes out clean. Cool the muffins in the muffin cups for 5 minutes. Then remove the muffins and cool on a wire rack.

Makes 6 muffins; 6 servings.

Cinnamon Date and Walnut Muffins

Here's a great muffin for a nutritious, on-the-go breakfast. Eat one with a glass of milk and a piece of fruit and you'll have ample energy to get through the morning. Calories, fat and cholesterol were reduced by:

- Replacing butter with a combination of buttermilk and applesauce

- Using egg whites instead of a whole egg

- Reducing the amount of walnuts

Nutrition Scorecard (per large muffin)		
	Before	After
Calories	539	369
Fat (g.)	24	5
% Calories from fat	38%	12%
Cholesterol (mg.)	29	0

1 cup all-purpose flour
¾ cup whole-wheat pastry flour
¾ cup packed brown sugar
1 tablespoon baking powder
1 teaspoon finely shredded orange peel
½ teaspoon ground cinnamon
2 egg whites
⅔ cup buttermilk
⅓ cup unsweetened applesauce
⅔ cup pitted and snipped dates
⅓ cup chopped walnuts

Preheat the oven to 400°. Spray six large, 3" muffin cups with no-stick spray and set aside.

In a large bowl, stir together the all-purpose flour, whole-wheat flour, brown sugar, baking powder, orange peel and cinnamon. Make a well in the center of the mixture.

In a small bowl, beat the egg whites until foamy. Stir in the buttermilk and applesauce. Add the buttermilk mixture to the flour mixture and stir until moistened. Fold in the dates and walnuts.

Spoon the batter into the prepared cups, filling each ¾ full. Bake for 22 to 25 minutes or until a toothpick inserted in the center comes out clean. Cool the muffins in the muffin cups for 5 minutes. Then remove the muffins and cool on a wire rack.

Makes 6 large muffins; 6 servings.

Note: To make standard-sized muffins, spray twelve 2½" muffin cups with no-stick spray. Spoon the batter into the cups, filling each ¾ full. Bake for 15 to 17 minutes or until done. Cool as directed above. (Per standard-sized muffin: 185 calories, 3 g. fat, 12% calories from fat, 0 mg. cholesterol.)

Southwest Corn Muffins

Served with a big bowl of spicy chili or hearty soup, these giant cheddar-and-corn muffins are all you need to round out a simple meal. I slashed calories, fat and cholesterol by:

- Using egg whites instead of a whole egg

- Replacing oil with applesauce

- Using buttermilk instead of whole milk

- Reducing the amount of cheddar cheese and using its reduced-fat alternate (less than 5 grams of fat per ounce of cheese)

Nutrition Scorecard *(per large muffin)*		
	Before	After
Calories	425	263
Fat (g.)	21	3
% Calories from fat	45%	12%
Cholesterol (mg.)	61	12

1 cup yellow cornmeal
1 cup all-purpose flour
3 tablespoons sugar
1 tablespoon baking powder
2 egg whites, lightly beaten
1 cup buttermilk
¼ cup unsweetened applesauce
1 (4-ounce) can diced green chili peppers, drained
¾ cup (3 ounces) finely shredded reduced-fat sharp cheddar cheese

Preheat the oven to 400°. Spray six large, 3" muffin cups with no-stick spray and set aside.

In a large bowl, stir together the cornmeal, flour, sugar and baking powder. Make a well in the center of the mixture.

In a small bowl, stir together the egg whites, buttermilk and applesauce. Add the buttermilk mixture to the cornmeal mixture and stir just until moistened. Fold in the chili peppers and ½ cup of the cheese.

Spoon the batter into the prepared cups, filling each ¾ full. Top with the remaining ¼ cup of cheese. Bake for 20 to 22 minutes or until golden brown, and a toothpick inserted in the center comes out clean. Cool the muffins in the muffin cups for 5 minutes. Then remove the muffins and cool on a wire rack.

Makes 6 large muffins; 6 servings.

Note: To make standard-sized muffins, spray twelve 2½" muffin cups with no-stick spray. Spoon the batter into the cups, filling each ¾ full. Bake for 14 to 16 minutes or until done. Cool as directed above. (Per standard-sized muffin: 132 calories, 2 g. fat, 12% calories from fat, 6 mg. cholesterol.)

Buttermilk Cornbread

This quick bread is virtually fat free—less than 1 gram per serving! I like to serve it warm from the oven. That way, it's moist and tasty, and I don't need to spread on butter. Calories, fat and cholesterol were reduced by:

- Replacing oil with applesauce

- Using egg whites instead of a whole egg

- Using buttermilk instead of whole milk

Nutrition Scorecard
(per serving)

	Before	After
Calories	254	166
Fat (g.)	11	<1
% Calories from fat	40%	4%
Cholesterol (mg.)	31	1

1   cup all-purpose flour
1   cup yellow cornmeal
¼   cup sugar
1   tablespoon baking powder
½   teaspoon salt
2   egg whites, lightly beaten
1   cup buttermilk
⅓   cup unsweetened applesauce

Preheat the oven to 400°. Lightly spray an 8" × 8" × 2" baking pan and set aside.

In a large bowl, stir together the flour, cornmeal, sugar, baking powder and salt. Make a well in the center of the mixture.

In a small bowl, stir together the egg whites, buttermilk and applesauce. Add the buttermilk mixture to the flour mixture and stir just until moistened.

Pour the batter into the prepared pan. Bake about 25 minutes or until a toothpick inserted in the center comes out clean. Serve warm.

Makes 9 servings.

Lock in the Freshness

If you can't use it right away—freeze it! I found that reduced-fat breads, muffins, rolls and other baked items will stay tender and moist if you store them in the freezer rather than at room temperature. And for the best results, serve them warm.

For piping hot muffins and rolls, place the frozen bread items on a paper towel in a microwave oven. Two muffins or rolls will heat in about 30 to 60 seconds on high power (100%); four will heat in about 1 to 2 minutes.

Cinnamon Spiced Banana Nut Bread

Overripe bananas never need to go to waste in your house. Whenever you have them on hand, quickly whip up this wholesome nut bread. And if you can't use the bread right away, just wrap it and freeze it for later. Calories, fat and cholesterol were reduced by:

- Using egg whites instead of whole eggs

- Replacing whole milk with buttermilk

- Replacing shortening with applesauce

- Reducing the amount of walnuts

Nutrition Scorecard
(per serving)

	Before	After
Calories	275	215
Fat (g.)	11	4
% Calories from fat	36%	15%
Cholesterol (mg.)	37	0

1 cup all-purpose flour
1 cup whole-wheat pastry flour
1 cup packed brown sugar
1 tablespoon baking powder
1 teaspoon ground cinnamon
¼ teaspoon baking soda
4 egg whites
½ cup buttermilk
⅓ cup unsweetened applesauce
1 teaspoon vanilla
1 cup mashed ripe bananas (about 2 medium)
½ cup chopped walnuts

Preheat the oven to 350°. Spray a 9" × 5" × 3" loaf pan with no-stick spray and set aside.

In a large bowl, stir together the all-purpose flour, whole-wheat flour, brown sugar, baking powder, cinnamon and baking soda. Make a well in the center of the mixture.

In another large bowl, beat the egg whites until foamy. Stir in the buttermilk, applesauce and vanilla. Then stir in the bananas until well combined.

Add the banana mixture to the flour mixture and stir just until moistened. Fold in the walnuts.

Pour the batter into the prepared pan. Bake for 45 to 55 minutes or until a toothpick inserted in the center comes out clean. Cool the bread in the pan for 10 minutes. Then remove the bread and cool completely on a wire rack before slicing.

Makes 1 loaf; 12 servings.

Note: Store any leftover bread in the freezer. To thaw and reheat it, slice the frozen bread with a sharp knife and wrap each slice in a paper towel. Heat each slice in a microwave oven on high power (100%) about 30 seconds.

Spiced Pumpkin Bread

Pictured on page 57

Just one slice of this delicious quick bread provides you with 45 percent of your Recommended Dietary Allowance of cancer-preventing vitamin A, thanks to the pumpkin. I cut calories, fat and cholesterol by:

- Replacing shortening with a combination of applesauce and molasses

- Using egg whites instead of whole eggs

- Replacing whole milk with buttermilk

- Reducing the amount of walnuts

Nutrition Scorecard (per serving)	Before	After
Calories	254	199
Fat (g.)	10	3
% Calories from fat	36%	11%
Cholesterol (mg.)	37	0

¼ cup all-purpose flour
¾ cup whole-wheat pastry flour
1 cup packed brown sugar
1 tablespoon baking powder
1 teaspoon ground cinnamon
¼ teaspoon baking soda
¼ teaspoon ground nutmeg
⅛ teaspoon ground ginger
⅛ teaspoon ground cloves
4 egg whites
1 cup canned pumpkin
½ cup buttermilk
3 tablespoons unsweetened applesauce
2 tablespoons molasses
⅓ cup chopped walnuts

Preheat the oven to 350°. Spray an 8" × 4" × 2" loaf pan with no-stick spray and set aside.

In a large bowl, stir together the all-purpose flour, whole-wheat flour, brown sugar, baking powder, cinnamon, baking soda, nutmeg, ginger and cloves. Add the egg whites, pumpkin, buttermilk, applesauce, and molasses.

Use an electric mixer to beat on low speed just until blended, then beat on high speed for 2 minutes. Stir in the walnuts.

Pour the batter into the prepared pan. Bake for 55 to 65 minutes or until a toothpick inserted in the center comes out clean. Cool the bread in the pan for 10 minutes. Then remove the bread and cool completely on a wire rack before slicing.

Makes 1 loaf; 12 servings.

Whole-Wheat Zucchini Bread

This zucchini bread is one of my tastiest makeovers and much lower in fat than the original. It's also a lot higher in fiber and has a nutty flavor—thanks to the whole-wheat flour. Calories, fat and cholesterol were reduced by:

- Replacing oil with applesauce

- Using buttermilk instead of sour cream

- Using egg whites instead of whole eggs

- Reducing the amount of walnuts

Nutrition Scorecard
(per serving)

	Before	After
Calories	293	191
Fat (g.)	16	3
% Calories from fat	47%	15%
Cholesterol (mg.)	58	0

1	cup all-purpose flour
1	cup whole-wheat flour (not pastry flour)
1	cup sugar
2	teaspoons baking powder
1½	teaspoons ground cinnamon
1	teaspoon baking soda
¼	teaspoon salt
¼	teaspoon ground nutmeg
¼	teaspoon ground cloves
6	egg whites
½	cup unsweetened applesauce
½	cup buttermilk
1	teaspoon vanilla
1½	cups shredded unpeeled zucchini
½	cup chopped walnuts

Preheat the oven to 350°. Spray a 9" × 5" × 3" loaf pan with no-stick spray and set aside.

In a large bowl, stir together the all-purpose flour, whole-wheat flour, sugar, baking powder, cinnamon, baking soda, salt, nutmeg and cloves. Make a well in the center of the mixture.

In another large bowl, beat the egg whites until foamy. Stir in the applesauce, buttermilk and vanilla. Then stir in the zucchini until well combined.

Add the zucchini mixture to the flour mixture and stir just until moistened. Fold in the walnuts.

Pour the batter into the prepared pan. Bake for 40 to 50 minutes or until a toothpick inserted in the center comes out clean. Cool the bread in the pan for 10 minutes. Then remove the bread and cool completely on a wire rack before slicing.

Makes 1 loaf; 12 servings.

Harvest Apple Coffee Cake

Pictured on page 58

The applesauce plays a dual role in the production of this coffee cake—it replaces the oil and increases the apple flavor. I further reduced calories, fat and cholesterol by:

- Using egg whites instead of whole eggs

- Reducing the amount of sugar (and enhancing the sweetness by increasing the amount of cinnamon)

- Reducing the amount of walnuts

Nutrition Scorecard
(per serving)

	Before	After
Calories	617	320
Fat (g.)	35	4
% Calories from fat	51%	10%
Cholesterol (mg.)	53	0

    3 medium apples (about 1 pound)
 1½ cups sugar
    1 cup whole-wheat pastry flour
 1½ teaspoons ground cinnamon
    2 cups all-purpose flour
    1 teaspoon baking powder
    6 egg whites
    1 cup unsweetened applesauce
    1 teaspoon vanilla
  ½ cup chopped walnuts
    1 cup raisins
      Powdered sugar (optional)

Preheat the oven to 350°. Spray a 10" no-stick tube pan with no-stick spray and set aside. Peel, core, and finely chop the apples. Set the apples aside.

In a large bowl, stir together the all-purpose flour, whole-wheat flour, 1 cup of the sugar, the cinnamon and baking powder.

In another large bowl, beat the egg whites with clean, dry beaters until soft peaks form. Slowly beat in the remaining ½ cup of sugar. Slowly beat in the applesauce and vanilla. Then slowly beat in about one-quarter of the flour mixture.

Fold the egg white mixture into the remaining flour mixture. Then fold in the apples, walnuts and raisins.

Pour the batter into the prepared tube pan. Bake about 1 hour or until a toothpick inserted in the center comes out clean. Cool the cake in the pan for 10 minutes. Then invert the cake onto a serving platter and remove the pan. Cool slightly. If desired, lightly sift powdered sugar over top. Serve warm.

Makes 12 servings.

Cinnamon Streusel Coffee Cake

This coffee cake contains only a *third* of the fat of the original. But it retains the *full* amount of richness! Serve it warm for a midmorning break or an afternoon snack. Calories, fat and cholesterol were reduced by:

- Reducing the amount of butter in the topping

- Reducing the amount of walnuts in the topping

- Replacing the butter in the coffee cake with a combination of buttermilk and applesauce

- Replacing sour cream with fat-free yogurt

Nutrition Scorecard
(per serving)

	Before	After
Calories	462	328
Fat (g.)	23	7
% Calories from fat	45%	18%
Cholesterol (mg.)	96	6

STREUSEL TOPPING
- ¾ cup packed brown sugar
- 2 teaspoons ground cinnamon
- 2 tablespoons chilled butter
- ⅔ cup chopped walnuts

COFFEE CAKE
- 1½ cups all-purpose flour
- 1½ cups whole-wheat flour
- 1 cup sugar
- 1½ teaspoons baking powder
- 1½ teaspoons baking soda
- 6 egg whites
- ½ cup buttermilk
- ½ cup unsweetened applesauce
- ½ cup fat-free plain yogurt

TO MAKE THE STREUSEL TOPPING: In a small bowl, stir together the brown sugar and cinnamon. Use a pastry blender to cut in the butter until the mixture resembles coarse crumbs. Stir in the walnuts and set aside.

TO MAKE THE COFFEE CAKE: Preheat the oven to 350°. Spray a 10" fluted, no-stick tube pan with no-stick spray and set aside.

In a large bowl, stir together the all-purpose flour, whole-wheat flour, sugar, baking powder and baking soda.

In another large bowl, beat the egg whites with clean, dry beaters until soft peaks form. Slowly beat in the buttermilk, applesauce and yogurt. Then stir in the flour mixture just until well combined.

Place half of the topping mixture in the bottom of the prepared pan. Then add half of the batter to the pan and sprinkle with the remaining topping mixture. Carefully top with the remaining batter.

Bake for 40 to 50 minutes or until a toothpick inserted in the center comes out clean. Cool the cake in the pan for 10 minutes. Then invert the cake onto a serving platter and remove the pan. Cool slightly before slicing. Serve warm.

Makes 12 servings.

An Easy Way to Get Vitamin E

Vitamin E is a powerful antioxidant that helps to maintain healthy cells and bolster your immune system. Promising research has shown that this vitamin may also help in reducing the risk of heart disease.

When people go on a super-reduced-fat diet, their vitamin E intake often suffers. One of my favorite ways to add this nutrient to my diet is by sprinkling a little wheat germ on top of my cereal or by adding it to the baked goods. Just 2 tablespoons of wheat germ each day will provide you with about one-third of your vitamin E needs.

Glazed Cinnamon Rolls

Pictured on page 59

The biggest fat savings that I made in these tender sweet rolls came from using corn syrup instead of butter in the cinnamon filling. Calories, fat and cholesterol were also reduced by:

• Eliminating the butter in the dough

• Using egg whites instead of whole eggs

• Using skim milk in the dough and glaze instead of whole milk

Nutrition Scorecard
(per roll)

	Before	After
Calories	174	132
Fat (g.)	5	<1
% Calories from fat	26%	2%
Cholesterol (mg.)	30	0

SWEET DOUGH
2–2½ cups all-purpose flour
   2 cups whole-wheat flour (not pastry flour)
   1 package active dry yeast
   2 teaspoons ground cinnamon
   ½ teaspoon salt
   1 cup skim milk
   ⅓ cup sugar
   4 egg whites, lightly beaten

CINNAMON FILLING
   3 tablespoons light corn syrup
   ½ cup sugar
   3 teaspoons ground cinnamon

GLAZE
   ½ cup powdered sugar
   ¼ teaspoon vanilla
2–3 teaspoons skim milk

TO MAKE THE SWEET DOUGH: In a large bowl, stir together 1 cup of the all-purpose flour, 1 cup of the whole-wheat flour, the undissolved yeast, cinnamon and salt.

In a small saucepan, heat and stir the milk and sugar until very warm (120° to 130°). Stir the milk mixture into the flour mixture. Then add the egg whites. Using an electric mixer, beat on low speed just until blended. Then beat on high speed for 3 minutes. Gradually stir in the remaining 1 cup of whole-wheat flour. Then stir in enough of the remaining all-purpose flour to make a soft dough.

Sprinkle 1 tablespoon of the all-purpose flour evenly on a work surface. Then knead the dough for 6 to 8 minutes, incorporating as much of the remaining all-purpose flour as needed to produce a dough that's smooth and elastic. Shape the dough into a ball.

Spray a clean, dry large bowl with no-stick spray. Place the dough in the bowl and lightly coat the top with more spray. Cover and let rise, free from drafts, about 1 hour or until double in size.

Punch the dough down. Divide it in half. Cover and let rest for 10 minutes. Meanwhile, spray two 9" round baking pans with no-stick spray and set aside.

Sprinkle 1 tablespoon of the all-purpose flour evenly on a work surface. Roll half of the dough to a 12" × 10" rectangle. Repeat with more flour and the remaining dough.

TO MAKE THE CINNAMON FILLING: Brush each piece of dough with 1½ tablespoons of the corn syrup. In a small bowl, mix the sugar and cinnamon. Sprinkle it evenly over the dough pieces.

Roll up each piece of dough, starting at a long side, to form a cylinder. Pinch the seams together to seal. Cut each roll into 12 equal pieces. Divide the pieces between the prepared pans, positioning the rolls with their cut sides down.

Cover and let the rolls rise, free from drafts, about 30 minutes or until nearly double in size. Meanwhile, preheat the oven to 375°.

Uncover the rolls and bake them for 20 to 25 minutes. Cool the rolls in their pans for 5 minutes. Then invert them onto wire racks and remove the pans. Cool slightly.

TO MAKE THE GLAZE: In a small bowl, stir together the powdered sugar, vanilla and enough milk to make a glaze of the desired consistency. Drizzle the glaze over the warm rolls and serve.

Makes 24 cinnamon rolls; serves 24.

Note: If you want to freeze the baked rolls, do not top them with the glaze. Cool the rolls completely. Then tightly wrap them in heavy foil and freeze. To thaw, place the rolls, wrapped in foil, in a 300° oven and heat about 20 minutes. Drizzle the glaze over the rolls before serving.

Maple Pecan Sticky Rolls

Pictured on page 60

Who says gooey sweet rolls have no place in a healthy diet? Not me! My love for sticky rolls inspired me to find ways to cut their calories and fat without sacrificing their goodness. These rolls are best if served warm from the oven. I reduced calories, fat and cholesterol by:

- Eliminating the butter in the dough

- Using egg whites instead of whole eggs

- Reducing the amount of butter in the topping

- Reducing the amount of pecans in the topping and filling

- Replacing most of the butter in the topping and all of the butter in the filling with reduced-calorie maple syrup

Nutrition Scorecard
(per roll)

	Before	After
Calories	308	205
Fat (g.)	16	7
% Calories from fat	44%	29%
Cholesterol (mg.)	40	3

SWEET DOUGH
2–2½ cups all-purpose flour
    2 cups whole-wheat flour (not pastry flour)
    1 package active dry yeast
    1 teaspoon ground cinnamon
    ½ teaspoon salt
    1 cup skim milk
    ⅓ cup sugar
    4 egg whites

PECAN FILLING
    3 tablespoons reduced-calorie maple syrup
    ½ cup sugar
    1 teaspoon ground cinnamon
    ⅓ cup chopped pecans

PECAN TOPPING
    2 tablespoons butter
    ½ cup packed brown sugar
    ⅓ cup reduced-calorie maple syrup
   1⅓ cup chopped pecans

TO MAKE THE SWEET DOUGH: In a large bowl, stir together 1 cup of the all-purpose flour, 1 cup of the whole-wheat flour, the undissolved yeast, cinnamon and salt.

In a small saucepan, heat and stir the milk and sugar until very warm (120° to 130°). Stir the milk mixture into the flour mixture. Then add the egg whites. Using an electric mixer, beat on low speed just until blended. Then beat on high speed for 3 minutes. Gradually stir in the remaining 1 cup of whole-wheat flour. Then stir in enough of the remaining all-purpose flour to make a soft dough.

Sprinkle 1 tablespoon of the all-purpose flour evenly on a work surface. Then knead the dough for 6 to 8 minutes, incorporating as much of the remaining all-purpose flour as needed to produce a dough that's smooth and elastic. Shape the dough into a ball.

Spray a clean, dry large bowl with no-stick spray. Place the dough in the bowl and lightly coat the top with more spray. Cover and let rise, free from drafts, about 1 hour or until double in size.

Punch the dough down. Divide it in half. Cover and let rest for 10 minutes. Meanwhile, spray two 9" × 1½" round baking pans with no-stick spray and set aside.

Sprinkle 1 tablespoon of the all-purpose flour evenly on a work surface. Roll half of the dough to a 12" × 10" rectangle. Repeat with more flour and the remaining dough.

TO MAKE THE PECAN FILLING: Brush each piece of dough with 1½ tablespoons of the syrup. In a small bowl, mix the sugar and cinnamon. Sprinkle it evenly over the dough pieces. Sprinkle the pecans evenly over the dough.

Roll up each piece of dough, starting at a long side, to form a cylinder. Pinch the seams together to seal. Cut each roll into 12 equal pieces.

TO MAKE THE PECAN TOPPING: In a small saucepan, melt the butter. Stir in the brown sugar and syrup until combined. Evenly spread the mixture in the baking pans. Evenly sprinkle the pecans on top.

Divide the dough pieces between the prepared pans, positioning the rolls with their cut sides down.

Cover and let the rolls rise, free from drafts, about 30 minutes or until nearly double in size. Meanwhile, preheat the oven to 375°.

Uncover the rolls and bake them for 20 to 25 minutes. Cool the rolls in their pans for 10 minutes. Then invert them onto large plates or serving platters. Keep the pans on top of the rolls for 1 minute, then remove the pans. Serve warm.

Makes 24 rolls; serves 24.

Note: To freeze the baked rolls, cool them completely. Then tightly wrap the rolls in heavy foil and freeze. To thaw, place the rolls, wrapped in foil, in a 300° oven and heat about 20 minutes.

Better-for-You Popovers

Popovers are now healthier than ever! I increased their nutrient profile by replacing some of the all-purpose flour with whole-wheat flour. I reduced calories, fat and cholesterol by:

• Using egg whites instead of whole eggs

• Replacing the whole milk with skim milk

• Reducing the amount of oil

Nutrition Scorecard
(per popover)

	Before	After
Calories	146	111
Fat (g.)	6	2
% Calories from fat	34%	15%
Cholesterol (mg.)	77	0

4 egg whites
1 cup skim milk
2 teaspoons canola or corn oil
½ cup all-purpose flour
½ cup whole-wheat flour (not pastry flour)
¼ teaspoon salt

Preheat the oven to 400°. Spray six 6-ounce custard cups, 3" muffin cups or the cups in a popover pan with no-stick spray. Set the cups aside.

In a medium bowl, combine the egg whites, milk and oil. Add the all-purpose flour, whole-wheat flour and salt. Use a wire whisk to beat until smooth.

Pour the batter into the prepared cups, filling each halfway. If using custard cups, place them on a cookie sheet.

Bake about 40 minutes or until the tops are dry and firm. Immediately remove the popovers from the cups and serve hot.

Makes 6 popovers; 6 servings.

Note: Be sure the oven is preheated to 400° before baking these popovers. If the oven is not hot enough, the popovers will not rise properly.

Whole-Wheat Soda Bread

For a simple, hearty bread in a flash, I like to make this reduced-fat version of Irish soda bread. Soda bread is similar in texture and flavor to heavy whole-grain yeast bread but takes only a fraction of the time to make. Calories, fat and cholesterol were reduced by:

• Eliminating the butter in the dough

• Using egg whites instead of whole eggs

Nutrition Scorecard
(per serving)

	Before	After
Calories	181	141
Fat (g.)	6	<1
% Calories from fat	31%	5%
Cholesterol (mg.)	66	0

> 1 cup all-purpose flour
> 1 cup whole-wheat pastry flour
> 1 teaspoon baking powder
> ½ teaspoon baking soda
> ½ teaspoon salt
> 3 egg whites
> ¾ cup buttermilk

Preheat the oven to 375°. Spray a cookie sheet with no-stick spray and set aside.

In a large bowl, stir together the all-purpose flour, whole-wheat flour, baking powder, baking soda and salt. Make a well in the center of the mixture.

In a small bowl, lightly beat 2 of the egg whites. Stir in the buttermilk. Add the buttermilk mixture to the flour mixture and stir just until moistened.

Sprinkle 1 tablespoon of flour evenly on a work surface. Then knead the dough about 30 seconds or until almost smooth. Transfer the dough to the prepared cookie sheet and shape it into a round loaf, about 6" in diameter. Using a sharp knife, slash a cross on the top of the loaf.

Lightly beat the remaining 1 egg white, then brush it over the loaf. Bake about 35 minutes or until golden. Carefully transfer the loaf to a wire rack and cool slightly before slicing.

Makes 1 loaf; 8 servings.

Buttermilk Whole-Wheat Pancakes

Pictured on page 61

Although "light" commercial pancake mixes are available, I still prefer pancakes made from scratch. These fluffy, reduced-fat pancakes are my daughter's favorite. They were adapted from a recipe given to me by my friend's great-grandmother. Top them with reduced-calorie maple syrup or a low-sugar peach or pear sauce. Calories, fat and cholesterol were reduced by:

- Replacing the butter with additional buttermilk
- Using egg whites instead of whole eggs
- Using no-stick spray instead of oil to grease the griddle

Nutrition Scorecard
(per 2 pancakes)

	Before	After
Calories	290	186
Fat (g.)	15	1
% Calories from fat	46%	6%
Cholesterol (mg.)	140	3

½ cup all-purpose flour
½ cup whole-wheat pastry flour
1 tablespoon sugar
1¼ cups buttermilk
1 teaspoon baking soda
4 egg whites
1 teaspoon vanilla

In a medium bowl, stir together the all-purpose flour, whole-wheat flour and sugar. Make a well in the center of the mixture.

In small bowl, stir together the buttermilk and baking soda until dissolved. Stir in the egg whites and vanilla until well combined. Add the buttermilk mixture to the flour mixture and stir just until moistened.

Spray an unheated griddle or large skillet with no-stick spray. Heat the griddle or skillet over medium heat. For each pancake, pour a scant ¼ cup batter onto the hot griddle or in the skillet, spreading the batter to about a 4" circle. Cook until the pancakes are bubbly and slightly dry around the edges. Then turn over and cook until golden brown.

Makes 8 pancakes; 4 servings.

Hawaiian French Toast

This recipe starts with Hawaiian bread, which is a commercial sweet bread with a fine cake-like texture. It makes a wonderful base for French toast. If Hawaiian bread is unavailable in your area, use thick slices of French bread. I reduced calories, fat and cholesterol by:

- Using egg whites instead of whole eggs

- Replacing whole milk with evaporated skim milk

- Using no-stick spray instead of butter to grease the griddle

Nutrition Scorecard (per serving)		
	Before	After
Calories	362	267
Fat (g.)	16	4
% Calories from fat	40%	15%
Cholesterol (mg.)	136	22

8 ounces Hawaiian bread
4 egg whites
½ cup evaporated skim milk
1 teaspoon vanilla
⅛ teaspoon ground cinnamon

The night before, cut the bread into slices about ¾" to 1" thick. Spread the slices in a single layer to slightly dry them at room temperature overnight. (This will prevent the toast from becoming soggy.)

In the morning, in a shallow bowl, use a wire whisk to beat together the egg whites, milk, vanilla and cinnamon.

Spray an unheated griddle or large skillet with no-stick spray. Heat the griddle or skillet over medium heat. Meanwhile, dip the bread slices in the egg mixture, coating both sides. (Do not soak the bread slices in the egg mixture.)

Place the bread slices on the griddle or in the skillet and cook for 2 to 3 minute on each side or until golden.

Makes 4 servings.

Parmesan Garlic Bread

Pictured on page 62

Garlic bread has always been a favorite of mine, especially with pasta. But usually it's really high in fat because of the amount of butter spread on it. So instead, I chose olive oil—olive oil has more flavor than butter and a little goes a long way when brushed on the bread. I further slashed calories, fat and cholesterol by:

• Reducing the amount of oil used

Nutrition Scorecard
(per 2 slices)

	Before	After
Calories	272	215
Fat (g.)	13	6
% Calories from fat	42%	27%
Cholesterol (mg.)	33	2

> 3   tablespoons olive oil
> 4   cloves garlic, minced
> 1   (1-pound) loaf French or sourdough bread, cut lengthwise in half
> 4   tablespoons finely shredded Parmesan cheese
>   Paprika

Preheat the broiler. In a blender or small food processor, blend or process the oil and garlic until well combined. Brush the cut surfaces of the bread with the garlic mixture.

Sprinkle each bread half with 2 tablespoons of the cheese. Using a sharp knife, score each half diagonally into eight slices. Lightly sprinkle with the paprika. Broil for 3 to 4 minutes or just until golden. Serve warm.

Makes 16 slices; 8 servings.

APPETIZING TIDBITS

It's hard to eat just *one* appetizer. If you're like most people, one appetizer quickly leads to two, then three, then four. . . . Before you know it, you've filled up on little foods loaded with fat and calories.

It doesn't have to be that way. I've packed this chapter with all-time favorite appetizers and snacks. But these versions have less fat and fewer calories than the originals—and still taste great. Each recipe comes with easy fat- and calorie-cutting secrets, so you can use these tips to transform your own recipes into more healthful versions.

Some of my secrets may surprise you: pureed split peas replace part of the avocado in guacamole, for instance. I use no-stick spray between sheets of phyllo dough rather than melted butter to create flaky pastries. And fat-free yogurt cheese is a great skinny substitute for cream cheese.

So next time you feel like having a second, third or maybe even fourth appetizer, go ahead. With these lean appetizers and snacks, you won't be filling up on fat- and calorie-laden foods.

Savory Three-Cheese Ball

No one will guess that this rich-tasting cheese ball has about one-third of the calories and only a fraction of the fat of a standard cheese spread. I like to serve it with whole wheat crackers. I reduced calories, fat and cholesterol by:

- Using reduced-fat sharp cheddar cheese (less than 5 grams of fat per ounce of cheese)

- Replacing regular cream cheese with a combination of fat-free ricotta cheese and light cream cheese

- Using a small amount of poppy seeds instead of high-fat walnuts for coating the cheese ball

Nutrition Scorecard
(per 2 tablespoons)

	Before	After
Calories	113	42
Fat (g.)	11	2
% Calories from fat	88%	43%
Cholesterol (mg.)	23	5

1 cup (4 ounces) finely shredded reduced-fat sharp cheddar cheese
¼ cup soft-style light cream cheese
2 tablespoons fat-free ricotta cheese
1 tablespoon finely snipped fresh chives
1 tablespoon chopped bottled roasted red peppers
1 teaspoon Worcestershire sauce
1½ tablespoons poppy seeds

In a medium bowl, stir together the cheddar cheese, cream cheese and ricotta cheese until well combined. Stir in the chives, peppers and Worcestershire sauce. Cover and chill in the refrigerator for 4 to 24 hours.

Just before serving, shape the cheese mixture into a ball. Roll the ball in the poppy seeds. Let stand at room temperature for 15 minutes.

Makes about 1½ cups; 12 servings.

Hot Beer Cheese Dip

The beer imparts an enticing, characteristic flavor to this dip. If I'm serving guests who prefer not to consume alcohol, I make the dip with nonalcoholic beer. Serve the dip with your favorite raw vegetables or with bread cubes. Calories, fat and cholesterol were reduced by:

- Using no-stick spray instead of margarine or butter for sautéing the onions and garlic

- Using a combination of fat-free and reduced-fat (less than 5 grams of fat per ounce of cheese) cheddar cheeses

- Using fat-free yogurt instead of cream cheese

Nutrition Scorecard
(per 2 tablespoons)

	Before	After
Calories	86	38
Fat (g.)	7	1
% Calories from fat	73%	24%
Cholesterol (mg.)	21	5

¼ cup finely chopped green onions
1 clove garlic, minced
¼ teaspoon dried tarragon
1 cup (4 ounces) finely shredded fat-free cheddar cheese
1 cup (4 ounces) finely shredded reduced-fat sharp cheddar cheese
1 teaspoon cornstarch
¾ cup beer or nonalcoholic beer
¼ cup fat-free plain yogurt

Spray an unheated medium saucepan with no-stick spray. Add the onions, garlic and tarragon. Cook and stir over medium heat about 3 minutes or until the onions are tender.

Meanwhile, in a medium bowl combine the fat-free and reduced-fat cheeses. Sprinkle with the cornstarch and toss until coated.

Stir the beer into the onion mixture. Bring to a gentle simmer. Then slowly stir in the cheese mixture. Cook and stir just until melted. Remove from the heat and stir in the yogurt.

Makes 2 cups; 16 servings.

Hot Artichoke Parmesan Spread

The original version of this classic hot vegetable spread just drips with fat. But just by switching to lower-fat forms of sour cream and mayonnaise, I drastically cut the grams of fat. In addition, I reduced calories, fat and cholesterol by the steps below. I like to serve the dip with pita wedges.

- Using artichokes packed in water instead of those in oil

- Using reduced-fat Parmesan cheese (3 grams of fat per ounce of cheese)

Nutrition Scorecard *(per 2 tablespoons)*

	Before	After
Calories	156	51
Fat (g.)	15	3
% Calories from fat	87%	53%
Cholesterol (mg.)	14	2

1 cup grated reduced-fat Parmesan cheese
⅔ cup fat-free plain yogurt
½ cup fat-free sour cream
⅓ cup reduced-fat mayonnaise
1 clove garlic, minced
1 (14-ounce) can water-packed artichoke hearts, drained and chopped
2 tablespoons sliced green onions

In a medium microwave-safe bowl, stir together the Parmesan cheese, yogurt, sour cream, mayonnaise and garlic. Gently stir in the artichokes.

Cook in a microwave oven on high power (100%) about 2 minutes or until heated through, stirring every 60 seconds.

Stir before serving and sprinkle with the onions to garnish.

Makes 2 cups; 16 servings.

Vegetable Dill Dip

This dip is so creamy and full of body that my family and friends find it hard to believe it's so low in calories and fat. The dip is great served with any raw vegetables. I reduced calories, fat and cholesterol by:

- Using fat-free yogurt cheese instead of cream cheese

- Using a combination of fat-free ricotta cheese and fat-free sour cream

Nutrition Scorecard
(per 2 tablespoons)

	Before	After
Calories	80	29
Fat (g.)	8	1
% Calories from fat	90%	1%
Cholesterol (mg.)	22	2

1 cup Yogurt Cheese (page 83)
½ cup fat-free ricotta cheese
½ cup fat-free sour cream
1 tablespoon snipped fresh dill
1 teaspoon salt-free herb seasoning

In a medium bowl, stir together the yogurt cheese, ricotta, sour cream, dill and herb seasoning until well combined.

Makes 2 cups; 16 servings.

Note: To vary the dip, omit the dill and herb seasoning. Replace them with 1 tablespoon of your favorite dry dip or soup mix (such as ranch-style dip or onion soup).

Spinach and Chestnut Dip

Pictured on page 63

With only a few minor changes, I shaved calories and fat from a dip that's traditionally super high in calories and fat. But that's not all—I increased the spinach to pack the dip with more vitamins and minerals than ever before. Calories, fat and cholesterol were reduced by:

Nutrition Scorecard *(per 2 tablespoons)*		
	Before	After
Calories	82	31
Fat (g.)	8	2
% Calories from Fat	88%	58%
Cholesterol (mg.)	9	2

- Reducing the amount of mayonnaise and using its reduced-fat alternate

- Replacing the sour cream with fat-free yogurt and reducing the total amount

- Increasing the spinach to replace the volume lost by using less mayonnaise and sour cream

> 2 (10-ounce) packages frozen chopped spinach, thawed
> 1¾ cups fat-free plain yogurt
> ¾ cup reduced-fat mayonnaise
> 1 envelope vegetable soup mix
> 1 (8-ounce) can water chestnuts, drained and chopped
> 2 tablespoons chopped green onions

Squeeze excess liquid from the spinach. In a large bowl, stir together the yogurt, mayonnaise and soup mix. Then stir in the spinach, water chestnuts and green onions. Cover and chill in the refrigerator about 2 hours. Stir before serving.

Makes 5 cups; 40 servings.

Note: For an attractive presentation, cut a thin slice from the top of a medium head of red cabbage or a round loaf of bread. Then hollow out the cabbage or remove the soft center of the loaf to form a bowl. Spoon in the dip and serve with your favorite cut-up fresh vegetables or bread cubes.

Berry Best Blueberry Muffins (page 26)

55

Apricot Oat Bran Muffins (page 27)

Spiced Pumpkin Bread (page 35)

Harvest Apple Coffee Cake (page 37)

Glazed Cinnamon Rolls (page 40)

Maple Pecan Sticky Rolls (page 42)

Buttermilk Whole-Wheat Pancakes (page 46) with peach sauce

Parmesan Garlic Bread (page 48)

Spinach and Chestnut Dip (page 54)

Seven-Layer Tex-Mex Dip (page 74), Homemade Tortilla Chips (page 75)

Red Potatoes Stuffed with Cheese (page 84)

Marinated Tricolored Sweet Peppers (page 86)

Cocktail Party Meatballs (page 90)

Hawaiian Chicken (page 96)

Chicken à la Marengo (page 97)

69

Crispy Oven-Fried Chicken (page 99)

Hummus

Pictured on page 227

The unique flavor of traditional hummus comes from tahini, a peanut butter-like paste made from sesame seeds that's high in fat. By cutting back on the amount used, I removed a lot of fat. (Look for tahini in large supermarkets, health food stores and Middle Eastern markets.) I further reduced calories and fat by:

- Eliminating the traditional olive oil

- Replacing the oil and some of the tahini with liquid from the canned chick-peas

Nutrition Scorecard
(per 2 tablespoons)

	Before	After
Calories	109	74
Fat (g.)	6	2
% Calories from fat	46%	27%
Cholesterol (mg.)	0	0

1 (15-ounce) can chick-peas (garbanzo beans)
2 tablespoons fresh lemon juice
2 tablespoons tahini
1 clove garlic, minced
¼ teaspoon salt (optional)

Drain the chick-peas, reserving ¼ cup of the liquid. Rinse and drain the chick-peas.

In a blender or food processor, blend or process the reserved liquid, chick-peas, lemon juice, tahini and garlic until smooth and creamy. If desired, salt to taste.

Makes 1½ cups; 12 servings.

Note: Serve hummus with pita bread wedges, reduced-fat crackers or baguette slices.

Split Pea Guacamole

This version of the popular spicy dip looks and tastes just like the original but with a lot less fat. The Homemade Tortilla Chips on page 75 go especially well with this dip. Calories and fat were reduced by:

- Replacing some of the avocados with pureed split peas

Nutrition Scorecard
(per 2 tablespoons)

	Before	After
Calories	47	38
Fat (g.)	4	2
% Calories from fat	76%	47%
Cholesterol (mg.)	0	0

1 serrano chili pepper
2 teaspoons white vinegar
1 cup water
½ cup dried split peas
2 teaspoons fresh lemon juice
1 cup sliced green onions or chives
¾ cup loosely packed chopped fresh cilantro (see note)
½ teaspoon salt
½ teaspoon ground black pepper
2 very ripe avocados, halved, seeded and peeled
2 (4-ounce) cans diced green chili peppers (see note)

Wear disposable gloves or plastic bags over your hands to remove the seeds and finely mince the serrano chili pepper. Soak the minced chili peppers in the vinegar.

Meanwhile, in a medium saucepan, bring the water and split peas to a boil. Reduce the heat. Cover and simmer for 45 minutes. Add the chili-vinegar mixture. Cover and simmer about 10 minutes more or until the liquid is absorbed.

Transfer the split pea mixture to a food processor or blender. Add the lemon juice and puree until creamy. Transfer the pea mixture to a large bowl and stir in the green onions or chives, cilantro, salt and black pepper. Set aside.

In a large bowl, use a fork to mash the avocados to form a thick paste. Stir in the green chili peppers. Fold in the split pea mixture.

Makes 3¾ cups; 30 servings.

Note: If you prefer less spicy foods, use ¼ cup loosely packed cilantro and 1 (4-ounce) can diced green chili peppers.

Easy Green Chili Bean Dip

When friends drop in at the last minute, I quickly mix up this dip for a healthy impromptu snack. I serve the dip with Homemade Tortilla Chips (page 75). Calories, fat and cholesterol were reduced by:

- Using fat-free refried beans

- Eliminating the sour cream typically found in bean dip

- Using reduced-fat cheeses (less than 5 grams of fat per ounce of cheese)

Nutrition Scorecard *(per 2 tablespoons)*		
	Before	After
Calories	83	34
Fat (g.)	5	1
% Calories from fat	54%	26%
Cholesterol (mg.)	14	3

2 (16-ounce) cans fat-free refried beans
1 (7-ounce) can diced green chili peppers, drained
¼ cup + 1 tablespoon finely shredded reduced-fat Monterey Jack cheese
¼ cup + 1 tablespoon finely shredded reduced-fat cheddar cheese

In a large microwave-safe bowl, stir together the beans, chili peppers and ¼ cup each of the Monterey Jack cheese and cheddar cheese.

Cook in a microwave oven on high power (100%) for 90 seconds. Stir and cook on high about 30 seconds more or until the bean mixture is heated through and the cheeses are melted.

Transfer the dip to a serving bowl and sprinkle the remaining 2 tablespoons of cheeses on top.

Makes 4 cups; 32 servings.

Seven-Layer Tex-Mex Dip

Pictured on page 64

Guests will always come back for more after taking just one bite of this ever-so-popular, party-pleasing dip. Calories, fat and cholesterol were reduced by:

• Using fat-free refried beans

• Using fat-free yogurt cheese or fat-free sour cream instead of regular sour cream

• Reducing the amount of avocado

Nutrition Scorecard
(per serving of dip)

	Before	After
Calories	137	76
Fat (g.)	10	4
% Calories from fat	66%	47%
Cholesterol (mg.)	13	5

1 (16-ounce) can fat-free refried beans
½ cup salsa
1 cup Yogurt Cheese (page 83) or
   fat-free sour cream
1 cup (4 ounces) shredded reduced-fat Monterey Jack cheese
   or reduced-fat cheddar cheese
2 medium tomatoes, chopped
1 avocado, seeded, peeled and diced
¼ cup sliced green onions
2 tablespoons chopped ripe olives
   Homemade Tortilla Chips (opposite page)

In a medium bowl, stir together the refried beans and salsa. Spread the bean mixture on a 9" platter or in a pie plate.

Spread the yogurt cheese or sour cream on top of the bean layer. Then layer the shredded cheese, tomatoes, avocados, green onions and olives on top. If desired, cover and refrigerate for up to 4 hours. Serve with the tortilla chips.

Makes 16 servings.

Homemade Tortilla Chips

Pictured on page 64

After tasting one chip, my family became hooked! Now they won't go back to fatty store-bought chips. I slashed calories and fat by:

- Baking the chips instead of frying them
- Using no-stick spray instead of vegetable oil for oven frying

Nutrition Scorecard (per 6 chips)	Before	After
Calories	139	65
Fat (g.)	7	1
% Calories from fat	45%	14%
Cholesterol (mg.)	0	0

12 corn tortillas
Salt (optional)

Preheat the oven to 400°. Spray 2 cookie sheets with no-stick spray.

Stack the tortillas and cut the stack into six wedges. Place the tortillas on the prepared cookie sheets in a single layer. Lightly spray with no-stick spray. If desired, lightly sprinkle with the salt. Bake for 10 to 12 minutes or until lightly browned and crisp.

Makes 72 chips; 12 servings.

Fat-Free Foods

Fat-free foods can be an asset to reduced-fat cooking. Unfortunately, they are not all created equal in the taste department. There are winners and there are losers.

Keep an open mind when you're trying new fat-free foods. Soon you'll discover your favorites. Also, don't assume that if a food is fat-free, it's calorie-free too. Some fat-free foods are high in calories. Read the food labels to be sure of what you're getting.

Parmesan Wonton Crisps

	Nutrition Scorecard (per 4 chips)	
	Before	After
Calories	83	51
Fat (g.)	4	1
% Calories from fat	43%	18%
Cholesterol (mg.)	1	1

Finally, here's a thin, crispy chip for snacking that's low in calories and fat. I accomplished that by:

- Using olive oil no-stick spray instead of olive oil
- Baking the chips instead of frying them

30 wonton wrappers
¼ cup grated Parmesan cheese

Preheat the oven to 350°. Stack the wonton wrappers, then cut them in half diagonally to make 60 triangles.

Spray a cookie sheet with olive oil no-stick spray. Arrange the wonton wrappers in a single layer so the edges are not touching. Spray with the no-stick spray and sprinkle with the Parmesan cheese. Bake for 6 to 8 minutes or until light golden brown and crisp.

Makes 60 chips; 15 servings.

Cheddar Cheese Straws

Here's a cheesy snack that doubles as a great accompaniment to soup or salad. Calories, fat and cholesterol were reduced by:

- Using wonton wrappers instead of pastry dough

- Using reduced-fat sharp cheddar cheese (less than 5 grams of fat per ounce of cheese)

Nutrition Scorecard
(per 4 straws)

	Before	After
Calories	139	38
Fat (g.)	10	1
% Calories from fat	64%	23%
Cholesterol (mg.)	30	3

12 *wonton wrappers*
2 *teaspoons Worcestershire sauce*
½ *cup (2 ounces) finely shredded reduced-fat sharp cheddar cheese*
⅛ *teaspoon poppy seeds*

Preheat the oven to 350°. Stack the wonton wrappers. Cut the stack lengthwise into fourths, making 48 strips.

Line a cookie sheet with parchment paper or foil. Then spray the paper or foil with no-stick spray. Add the wonton strips in a single layer so the edges are not touching. Brush the wonton strips with the Worcestershire sauce. Sprinkle each strip with ½ teaspoon of the cheese. Then sprinkle with the poppy seeds. Bake for 8 to 10 minutes or until golden brown and crisp.

Makes 48 straws; 12 servings.

Peanut Butter Fruit Dip

Here's the perfect after-school snack—kids will love this dip for fruit and raw vegetables (apples, bananas, carrots and celery are particularly good). and it's good for them too. Calories and fat were reduced by:

- Using fat-free ricotta cheese
- Adding pureed cooked carrots (this tip came from Patricia Hart of the California Culinary Academy)

Nutrition Scorecard
(per 1 tablespoon)

	Before	After
Calories	95	52
Fat (g.)	8	3
% Calories from fat	76%	52%
Cholesterol (mg.)	0	0

¾ *cup fat-free ricotta cheese*
½ *cup natural-style peanut butter with oil drained off*
½ *cup marshmallow creme ice-cream topping*
1 *cup sliced carrots, cooked (see note)*
1 *tablespoon skim milk*

In a medium bowl, use an electric mixer to blend together the ricotta cheese and peanut butter until well combined. Mix in the marshmallow creme.

In a food processor or blender, puree the carrots with the milk. Stir the carrot mixture into the peanut butter mixture.

Makes 1½ cups; 24 servings.

Note: To save time, you can use ½ cup of strained baby-food carrots instead of the sliced carrots and milk.

Cream Cheese Fondue Dip for Fresh Fruit

Sometimes a failure is actually a success in the kitchen, as in the case of this recipe. This was my first attempt at making over a classic cream-cheese frosting. Unfortunately, it turned out too thin to spread on cakes but was just the right consistency for dipping fresh fruit. Calories, fat and cholesterol were also reduced by:

- Replacing regular cream cheese with a combination of vanilla yogurt cheese and light cream cheese

- Replacing butter in the original frosting recipe with additional vanilla yogurt cheese

Nutrition Scorecard
(per 2 tablespoons)

	Before	After
Calories	132	66
Fat (g.)	7	1
% Calories from fat	42%	10%
Cholesterol (mg.)	18	2

VANILLA YOGURT CHEESE
  3 (8-ounce) containers fat-free vanilla yogurt (made without gelatin)

FRUIT DIP
  1 cup vanilla yogurt cheese
  ½ cup soft-style light cream cheese
  1 teaspoon fresh lemon juice
  2½ cups powdered sugar
  Skim milk (optional)

TO MAKE THE VANILLA YOGURT CHEESE: Line a strainer with a double layer of cheesecloth or a coffee filter. Place the strainer over a deep bowl to allow the whey from the yogurt to drip into it.

Spoon the yogurt into the strainer. Place the strainer with the bowl in the refrigerator and let the yogurt drain for 14 to 24 hours or until thickened. Discard the whey. (You should have about 1 cup of yogurt cheese.)

TO MAKE THE FRUIT DIP: Transfer the yogurt cheese to a medium bowl. Beat in the cream cheese and lemon juice. Then slowly beat in the powdered sugar. If necessary, stir in enough of the milk to make a desired consistency.

Makes 2 cups; 16 servings.

Note: For a hint of flavoring, thin the dip with 1 tablespoon of amaretto, white crème de cacao or Grand Marnier instead of the milk.

Tortilla Pinwheels with Smoked Turkey

I always get compliments when I serve this impressive-looking, easy-to-make appetizer. For best results, don't make the pinwheels more than an hour before you're ready to serve them. Otherwise the tortillas may get soggy from the tomatoes. Calories, fat and cholesterol were reduced by:

• Using a mixture of fat-free yogurt cheese and fat-free ricotta instead of cream cheese

• Using lean smoked turkey breast instead of roast beef

Nutrition Scorecard
(per pinwheel)

	Before	After
Calories	97	59
Fat (g.)	6	1
% Calories from fat	56%	15%
Cholesterol (mg.)	26	9

½ *cup Yogurt Cheese (page 83)*
½ *cup fat-free ricotta cheese*
4 *large whole-wheat flour tortillas*
8 *romaine lettuce leaves*
16 *(1-ounce) slices cooked smoked turkey breast*
1 *cup chopped tomatoes*
¼ *cup sliced green onions*

In a small bowl, stir together the yogurt cheese and ricotta.

Spread one-fourth of the cheese mixture on each of the tortillas. On each tortilla, layer 2 lettuce leaves, 4 turkey slices, ¼ cup of the tomatoes and 1 tablespoon of the green onions.

Roll up each of the tortillas, jelly-roll fashion. Insert 6 toothpicks, about 1" apart, into each tortilla roll. Cut between the toothpicks and serve.

Makes 24 pinwheels; 24 servings.

Goat Cheese Rolled in Grape Leaves

If you don't have grape leaves, pipe the reduced-fat filling onto Belgian endive leaves or into pea pods. Calories, fat and cholesterol were reduced by:

- Reducing the quantity of goat cheese and replacing it with fat-free ricotta cheese

Nutrition Scorecard
(per appetizer)

	Before	After
Calories	17	11
Fat (g.)	1	1
% Calories from fat	63%	47%
Cholesterol (mg.)	4	2

1 (8-ounce) jar grape leaves, drained
½ cup fat-free ricotta cheese
3 ounces goat cheese, softened

At least 1 hour before assembling the rolls, rinse the grape leaves. If necessary, cut stems from the leaves. Then soak the leaves in a bowl of cold water to remove some of the brine.

Meanwhile, in a small bowl, stir together the ricotta cheese and goat cheese.

To assemble, drain the grape leaves and pat dry with paper towels. Spoon ½ teaspoon of the cheese mixture onto each grape leaf just below its center near the stem end. Fold in the sides of the grape leaves. Then roll up to enclose the filling, forming a cylindrical roll.

Makes 50 appetizers; 50 servings.

Mushrooms Stuffed with Turkey

This mushroom appetizer has a tasty turkey-and-bread stuffing instead of the normal, fat-laden sausage stuffing. I cut calories, fat and cholesterol by:

- Replacing the seasoned pork sausage with a combination of ground turkey breast and poultry seasoning

- Using fat-free Swiss cheese

- Using no-stick spray instead of margarine or butter for sautéing the mushroom-onion mixture

Nutrition Scorecard
(per appetizer)

	Before	After
Calories	49	32
Fat (g.)	3	1
% Calories from fat	55%	9%
Cholesterol (mg.)	8	5

24 medium to large fresh mushrooms
½ cup fine dry plain bread crumbs
½ cup cooked and crumbled ground turkey breast
3 tablespoons snipped fresh parsley
½ cup (2 ounces) finely shredded fat-free Swiss cheese
¼ cup sliced green onions
1 teaspoon poultry seasoning
1 clove garlic, minced

Preheat the oven to 425°. Gently wash the mushrooms and trim the tough ends from the stems. Then remove the mushroom stems from the caps and finely chop the stems. Set the chopped mushrooms and caps aside.

In a large bowl, stir together the bread crumbs, turkey and parsley until well combined. Then stir in the Swiss cheese and set the mixture aside.

Spray an unheated small skillet with no-stick spray. Add the chopped mushrooms, green onions, poultry seasoning and garlic. Cook and stir until tender.

Stir the mushroom-onion mixture into the bread crumb mixture. Spoon some of the mixture into each mushroom cap. Place the stuffed mushrooms on a cookie sheet. Bake for 8 to 10 minutes or until lightly browned.

Makes 24 appetizers; 24 servings.

Celery Stuffed with Blue Cheese

Here's an old-time favorite snack I updated with a new reduced-fat filling. Calories, fat and cholesterol were reduced by :

• Using fat-free yogurt cheese instead of cream cheese

• Eliminating margarine or butter from the filling

Nutrition Scorecard *(per 3 appetizers)*	Before	After
Calories	64	33
Fat (g.)	6	1
% Calories from fat	84%	27%
Cholesterol (mg.)	17	2

    ½ cup Yogurt Cheese (see below)
    1 tablespoon crumbled blue cheese
    1 teaspoon caraway seeds
    8 celery stalks, cut into thirds
       Paprika

In a small bowl, stir together the yogurt cheese, blue cheese and caraway seeds. Fill each of the celery pieces with about 1 teaspoon of the cheese mixture. Lightly sprinkle each with the paprika and serve.

Makes 24 appetizers; 8 servings.

Yogurt Cheese

Here's a great low-calorie substitute for cream cheese. Fat-free yogurt cheese is not only easy to make but also rich tasting. As you can tell from the figures listed, it beats regular cream cheese in every category. (By the way, I think yogurt cheese has a creamy texture that's superior to that of fat-free cream cheese.)

Nutrition Scorecard *(per 2 tablespoons)*	Before	After
Calories	104	31
Fat (g.)	10	0
% Calories from fat	87%	0%
Cholesterol (mg.)	33	1

   2 (16-ounce) containers fat-free plain yogurt (made without gelatin)

Line a strainer with a double layer of cheesecloth or a coffee filter. Place the strainer over a deep bowl to allow the whey from the yogurt to drip into it.

Spoon the yogurt into the strainer. Place the strainer with the bowl in the refrigerator and let the yogurt drain for 14 to 24 hours or until thickened. Discard the whey and transfer the yogurt cheese to a container. Cover and store in the refrigerator.

Makes 1½ cups; 12 servings.

Red Potatoes Stuffed with Cheese

Pictured on page 65

Here's a twice-baked potato in a mini-appetizer size. Calories, fat and cholesterol were reduced by:

- Using fat-free ricotta cheese instead of margarine or butter in the mashed potato stuffing

- Replacing sour cream with fat-free yogurt

- Using reduced-fat cheddar cheese (less than 5 grams of fat per ounce of cheese)

Nutrition Scorecard (per 2 wedges)		
	Before	After
Calories	72	36
Fat (g.)	5	1
% Calories from fat	56%	6%
Cholesterol (mg.)	12	1

> 10 *(2 pounds) red potatoes*
> ½ *cup fat-free ricotta cheese*
> ¼ *cup (1 ounce) finely shredded reduced-fat sharp cheddar cheese*
> ¼ *cup fat-free plain yogurt*
> *Crushed pink peppercorns (optional)*
> *Fresh chives (optional)*

Preheat the oven to 350°. Scrub the potatoes and pat dry. Using a fork, prick the potatoes. Bake about 45 minutes or until tender.

Cut the potatoes lengthwise into quarters (you will have a total of 40 wedges). Scoop out the pulp with a small spoon, leaving a sturdy, firm shell.

Transfer the potato pulp to a food processor or blender. Add the ricotta cheese, cheddar cheese and yogurt. Blend or process until smooth. If desired, spoon the potato mixture into a pastry bag fitted with a large star- or round-shaped pastry tip. Pipe or spoon a dollop of the mixture into each potato shell.

Place the filled shells on a cookie sheet and bake about 15 minutes or until heated through. If desired, sprinkle with the crushed pink peppercorns and top with the chives to garnish.

Makes 40 wedges; 20 servings.

Oven-Fried Potato Skins

By using reduced-fat ingredients and changing to a lean cooking method, I created a much more healthful appetizer than the traditional potato skins. Calories, fat and cholesterol were reduced by:

- Using a blend of reduced-fat cheddar cheese and reduced-fat Monterey Jack (less than 5 grams of fat per ounce of cheese)

- Using no-stick spray instead of margarine or butter for oven frying

Nutrition Scorecard
(per potato skin)

	Before	After
Calories	63	42
Fat (g.)	3	1
% Calories from fat	43%	21%
Cholesterol (mg.)	9	3

12 medium baking potatoes
1 cup (4 ounces) finely shredded reduced-fat Monterey Jack cheese
1 cup (4 ounces) finely shredded reduced-fat cheddar cheese
⅓ cup chopped green onions or snipped fresh chives

Preheat the oven to 425°. Using a fork, prick the potatoes. Bake for 40 to 50 minutes or until tender.

Cut the potatoes lengthwise into quarters. Scoop out the pulp with a small spoon, leaving ¼"-thick shells. (Set the pulp aside for another use.)

Spray a cookie sheet with no-stick spray. Place the potato shells on the sheet with the skin sides down. Spray the potatoes with the no-stick spray. Bake at 425° for 10 to 15 minutes or until crisp. Sprinkle the Monterey Jack cheese and cheddar cheese on the potatoes, then bake about 2 minutes more or until the cheeses are melted. Sprinkle with the green onions or chives and serve.

Makes 48 potato skins; 48 servings.

Marinated Tricolored Sweet Peppers

Pictured on page 66

I made only one simple change to this delicious, colorful combo that drastically lowered calories and fat:

• Using no-stick spray instead of oil for sautéing the peppers

Nutrition Scorecard (per 6 pepper strips)		
	Before	After
Calories	59	19
Fat (g.)	5	1
% Calories from fat	76%	1%
Cholesterol (mg.)	0	0

1 large sweet red pepper, cut into ½"-wide strips
1 large yellow pepper, cut into ½"-wide strips
1 large green pepper, cut into ½"-wide strips
¼ cup seasoned rice vinegar
2 tablespoons snipped fresh basil
 Lemon leaves (optional)
 Black olives (optional)
 Fresh pineapple sage (optional)

Spray a large skillet with no-stick spray. Add the red, yellow and green pepper strips. Cover and cook over medium heat about 5 minutes or until slightly tender.

Transfer the peppers to a glass or plastic bowl. Add the vinegar and basil, then toss until coated. Cover and chill in the refrigerator for at least 1 hour before serving. Garnish with lemon leaves, black olives and fresh pineapple sage, if desired.

Makes about 36 pepper strips; 6 servings.

A Little-Known Fact about Vitamin C

My clients are often amazed when I tell them that bell peppers are an even better source of vitamin C than oranges. One sweet red, green, yellow or other color pepper has more than twice the C of a medium orange. One pepper provides 141 milligrams of the vitamin; one orange has 70 milligrams. (The Recommended Dietary Allowance is 60 milligrams.)

Fresh Tomato-Topped Mini-Pizzas

These little pizzas make a great snack. They're also good as an easy, light meal—just add a salad. I reduced calories, fat and cholesterol by:

- Using reduced-fat whole-grain refrigerator biscuit dough instead of a regular biscuit dough for the crust

- Using plain tomato sauce instead of a commercial spaghetti sauce

- Using reduced-fat mozzarella cheese (less than 5 grams of fat per ounce of cheese)

- Using fresh tomatoes instead of pepperoni as the topper

Nutrition Scorecard (per pizza)		
	Before	After
Calories	202	131
Fat (g.)	13	4
% Calories from fat	58%	28%
Cholesterol (mg.)	18	5

1   (9-ounce) can whole-grain refrigerated biscuit dough (see note)
¼   cup tomato sauce
1   teaspoon dried Italian seasoning
⅔   cup (about 2½ ounces) finely shredded reduced-fat mozzarella cheese
1   cup chopped tomatoes
4   teaspoons grated Parmesan cheese

Preheat the oven to 375°. Spray a cookie sheet with no-stick spray. Separate the biscuit dough into eight biscuits. Flatten each biscuit into a 3½" circle and place on the prepared cookie sheet.

Spread the tomato sauce on top of the biscuits. Sprinkle with the Italian seasoning, then with the mozzarella cheese and tomatoes. Top the pizzas with the Parmesan cheese. Bake for 12 to 15 minutes or until the mozzarella cheese is melted and the pizzas are lightly browned around the edges.

Makes 8 pizzas; 8 servings.

Note: If the whole-grain refrigerated biscuit dough is unavailable, use 1 (10-ounce) can refrigerated pizza dough. Unroll the pizza dough onto a piece of wax paper. Press and form the dough into a 7½" square. Using a sharp 2½" biscuit cutter, cut the dough into eight rounds. Flatten each round into a 3½" circle.

Greek Spinach Triangles

Delicate, elegant and delicious! Best of all, these triangles have only half the calories and a fraction of the fat of the original version. The secret I found to making flaky reduced-fat phyllo pastries is to use no-stick spray between the layers of dough instead of melted butter. Calories, fat and cholesterol also were reduced by:

• Replacing some of the feta cheese with fat-free cottage cheese

Nutrition Scorecard
(per appetizer)

	Before	After
Calories	88	47
Fat (g.)	5	1
% Calories from fat	51%	19%
Cholesterol (mg.)	17	3

1 (10-ounce) package frozen chopped spinach, thawed
½ cup chopped onions
1 clove garlic, minced
3 ounces feta cheese, finely crumbled
½ cup fat-free cottage cheese
½ teaspoon dried oregano
12 sheets phyllo dough

Squeeze excess liquid from the spinach. Set the spinach aside.

Spray an unheated large skillet with olive oil no-stick spray. Add the onions and garlic. Cook and stir over medium heat about 3 minutes or until the onions are tender. Remove from the heat and stir in the spinach.

In a large bowl, combine the feta cheese, cottage cheese and oregano. Stir in the spinach mixture and set aside.

Preheat the oven to 375°. Spray a cookie sheet with the no-stick spray and set aside. Place one sheet of the phyllo dough on a large piece of wax paper. Spray the dough with the no-stick spray. Repeat layering and spraying the phyllo two more times (you will use a total of three sheets). Cover the remaining sheets of phyllo dough with a damp cloth to prevent drying out.

Cut the stack of prepared phyllo dough lengthwise into six strips. For each filled triangle, spoon about 1 tablespoon of the spinach mixture about 1" from one end of each strip. Fold the end over the spinach mixture at a 45° angle. Continue folding to form a triangle that encloses the spinach mixture (this procedure is like folding a flag).

After you've made the filled triangles from the first set of strips, repeat stacking the remaining phyllo sheets three more times and cutting each stack into strips as directed above. Then repeat the procedure for forming filled triangles.

Transfer the filled triangles to the prepared cookie sheet. Lightly spray them with the no-stick spray. Bake for 18 to 20 minutes or until golden brown. Serve warm.

Makes 24 appetizers; 24 servings.

Chinese Vegetable Egg Rolls

Chock-full of a mixture of vegetables, these crispy egg rolls are a welcome start to any meal. Calories and fat were reduced by:

- Using no-stick spray instead of oil to stir-fry the vegetables

- Using no-stick spray to pan-fry the egg rolls instead of deep-fat frying them

Nutrition Scorecard *(per egg roll)*		
	Before	After
Calories	163	93
Fat (g.)	9	1
% Calories from fat	50%	9%
Cholesterol (mg.)	0	0

2 tablespoons reduced-sodium soy sauce
1 teaspoon cornstarch
½ teaspoon dry mustard
¼ teaspoon ground black pepper
1 teaspoon oriental sesame oil
1 cup finely chopped celery
¼ cup finely chopped onions
1 teaspoon grated ginger root
1 clove garlic, minced
1 cup finely shredded Chinese cabbage
1 cup coarsely shredded carrots
1 cup fresh spinach, chopped
½ cup chopped fresh mushrooms
12 egg roll wrappers

In a small bowl, stir together the soy sauce, cornstarch, mustard and pepper until the cornstarch is dissolved. Set aside.

Spray a large skillet with no-stick spray, then add the oil. Heat the skillet over medium-high heat. Add the celery, onions, ginger and garlic. Stir-fry for 2 minutes. Then add the cabbage, carrots, spinach and mushrooms. Stir-fry for 1 minute more.

Stir in the soy sauce mixture and cook for 1 to 2 minutes or until the sauce mixture thickens and adheres to the vegetables. Remove from the heat.

To assemble the egg rolls, spoon ¼ cup of the vegetable mixture onto the center of each egg roll wrapper. Fold one corner of the wrapper over the vegetables, slightly tucking the corner under the filling. Then fold the side corners over the top. Lightly moisten the remaining corner with water. Then roll the egg roll toward the remaining corner and press firmly to seal.

Spray a griddle with the no-stick spray. (Or, wash and dry the large skillet, then spray it.) Heat the pan over medium-high heat. Add the egg rolls and cook on all sides until lightly browned. Serve warm.

Makes 12 egg rolls; 12 servings.

Cocktail Party Meatballs

Pictured on page 67

Meatballs are an all-time favorite at any party. Also, they can be prepared ahead, giving you more time with your guests. Just shape the meat mixture into balls and refrigerate them until the party. Then roll the balls in the coating mixture and broil. I reduced calories, fat and cholesterol by:

- Replacing the ground beef with a combination of ground turkey breast, ground turkey sausage and fat-free cottage cheese

- Using egg whites instead of a whole egg

Nutrition Scorecard (per meatball)

	Before	After
Calories	49	28
Fat (g.)	3	1
% Calories from fat	55%	32%
Cholesterol (mg.)	19	4

¼ cup fat-free cottage cheese
2 egg whites
2 teaspoons Worcestershire sauce
½ cup + 2 tablespoons dry plain bread crumbs
8 ounces ground turkey breast (see note)
6 ounces turkey sausage, removed from casings if necessary
2 tablespoons minced onions
2 tablespoons minced green peppers
½ cup snipped fresh parsley
¼ cup minced celery leaves

Spray a cookie sheet with no-stick spray and set aside. In a large bowl, stir together the cottage cheese, egg whites, Worcestershire sauce and ½ cup of the bread crumbs. Stir in the turkey breast, turkey sausage, onions and green peppers.

Shape the poultry mixture into 32 meatballs. On a sheet of wax paper, combine the parsley, celery leaves and remaining 2 tablespoons bread crumbs. Roll the meatballs in the parsley mixture until coated evenly.

Preheat the broiler. Transfer the meatballs to the prepared cookie sheet. Broil 3" to 4" from the heat for 10 to 12 minutes or until browned on all sides and no longer pink in the center, turning occasionally. Serve with cocktail toothpicks.

Makes 32 meatballs; 32 servings.

Note: To make sure you're buying the leanest ground turkey available, check the label. Look for products made with only turkey breast meat. Many ground turkey products contain the dark meat and the fatty skin.

Spicy Chicken Wings

You'll receive rave reviews when you serve this zesty finger-licking appetizer. Calories, fat and cholesterol were reduced by:

- Removing the skin from the chicken
- Baking the wings instead of frying them
- Reducing the amount of sugar in the sauce

Nutrition Scorecard
(per serving)

	Before	After
Calories	141	91
Fat (g.)	7	1
% Calories from fat	45%	10%
Cholesterol (mg.)	40	17

CHICKEN WINGS
14 chicken wing drummettes (see note)
¼ cup all-purpose flour
¼ teaspoon garlic powder
¼ teaspoon ground black pepper
2 egg whites, lightly beaten
¾ cup dry plain bread crumbs

SAUCE
½ cup reduced-sodium soy sauce
⅓ cup sugar
⅛ teaspoon crushed red pepper
Dash of hot-pepper sauce

TO MAKE THE CHICKEN WINGS: Preheat the oven to 400°. Spray a cookie sheet with no-stick spray. Using kitchen shears, remove the skin from the chicken drummettes.

On a piece of wax paper, combine the flour, garlic powder and pepper. Roll the chicken in the flour mixture, then dip into the egg whites. Finally, roll the pieces in the bread crumbs.

Place the coated chicken on the prepared cookie sheet and bake for 10 minutes. Turn the wings over and bake about 15 minutes more or until no longer pink. Transfer to a platter.

TO MAKE THE SAUCE: In a small bowl, stir together the soy sauce, sugar, red pepper and hot-pepper sauce. (If you prefer a hotter sauce, stir in additional hot-pepper sauce.) Pour the sauce over the chicken and serve.

Makes 14 drummettes; 14 servings.

Note: If chicken drummettes are unavailable at your supermarket, make your own using 14 chicken wings. Remove and discard the skin. Bend the two sections of each wing back and forth at their joints to break the cartilage. Then use a sharp knife to cut through the joints. Reserve the wing tips for another use (such as making chicken stock). For the remaining wing sections, start at the joint ends and use a small sharp knife to cut the cartilage around the bones. Then for each drummette, use your fingers to push the meat from the joint end of the bone to the other end to form a compact ball of meat.

HEARTY MAIN COURSES

Years ago, most of us learned to plan our meals around a hefty portion of meat or poultry. Vegetables, salads and other side dishes were treated as afterthoughts. They just weren't considered important.

Today, the previously neglected "extras" are now inching their way into the spotlight. We've come to realize that a pot-roast dinner, for instance, doesn't have to be heavy on the meat and light on the vegetables. The version I offer on page 110 has far less meat than usual and lots more carrots and potatoes. By the same token, my Healthy Homestyle Country Sausage on page 105 replaces the standard fatty pork with ground turkey, shredded apple and brown rice. It's as satisfying as the original but much leaner.

I updated other classic entrées by using healthier, lower-fat cooking methods. Instead of deep-frying breaded chicken, for example, I baked it. The coating is just as crisp as the standard version, but it's got only a speck of fat. And instead of pan-frying crab cakes in oil, I cooked them in a skillet using no-stick spray. These small changes make a world of difference!

Chicken Cordon Bleu

Here is one of my favorite makeovers. I was able to use a fat-free cheese and still get it to melt so that it oozes out when you cut into the rolled chicken. The secret to melting a fat-free cheese is to *finely* shred it. I cut calories, fat and cholesterol by:

- Replacing the ham with turkey ham

- Using fat-free Swiss cheese

- Using egg whites instead of a whole egg

Nutrition Scorecard
(per serving)

	Before	After
Calories	483	301
Fat (g.)	24	4
% Calories from fat	45%	11%
Cholesterol (mg.)	208	90

---

    4 (4-ounce) skinless, boneless chicken breast halves
    4 thin slices turkey ham
    1 cup (4 ounces) finely shredded fat-free Swiss cheese
    ⅓ cup all-purpose flour
    ¼ teaspoon salt
    ¼ teaspoon ground black pepper
    2 egg whites, lightly beaten
    ½ cup fine dry plain bread crumbs

Preheat the oven to 400°. Lightly spray a small cookie sheet or shallow baking pan with no-stick spray and set aside.

Place each chicken breast half between two pieces of plastic wrap. Working from the center to the edges, lightly pound with the flat side of a meat mallet to ¼" thickness. Remove the plastic wrap.

To assemble, place one slice of turkey ham on top of each breast half. Then place ¼ cup of the cheese, in a mound, on the center of each. Fold in the short sides, then roll the chicken and turkey ham around the cheese mound. Secure with wooden toothpicks.

In a shallow dish, stir together the flour, salt and pepper. To coat the chicken, first roll the bundles in the flour mixture to evenly cover all sides. Then dip the bundles in the egg whites and roll in the bread crumbs.

Spray an unheated, large no-stick skillet with no-stick spray. Heat the skillet over medium-low heat. Add the chicken bundles, seam side down. Cook and turn occasionally for 25 to 30 minutes or until the chicken is tender and no longer pink. Remove the toothpicks before serving.

Makes 4 servings.

Lemon Dijon Breasts of Chicken

Even though the original recipe I worked from had a head start on the road to healthier eating by calling for skinless chicken breasts, it still was high in fat. Most of the excess fat came from the oil in the marinade. So I switched to a no-oil marinade and slashed the percent of calories from fat. I reduced calories, fat and cholesterol by:

- Using wine instead of olive oil in the marinade

- Using no-stick spray instead of melted butter to cook the chicken

- Removing the fat from the chicken broth

Nutrition Scorecard
(per serving)

	Before	After
Calories	265	158
Fat (g.)	15	2
% Calories from fat	51%	11%
Cholesterol (mg.)	79	68

⅓ cup fresh lemon juice
¼ cup dry white wine or nonalcoholic white wine
3 tablespoons Dijon mustard
3 cloves garlic
¼ teaspoon dried rosemary
6 (4-ounce) skinless, boneless chicken breast halves
1 cup chicken broth, defatted
1 tablespoon cornstarch
1 teaspoon grated lemon peel
3 tablespoons chopped parsley

In a blender or small food processor, blend or process the lemon juice, wine, mustard, garlic and rosemary until well combined.

Place the chicken breast halves in a 13" × 9" × 2" baking dish in a single layer. Pour the lemon mixture over the chicken. Cover and marinate in the refrigerator for at least 1 hour.

Meanwhile, in a small bowl or cup, stir together 2 tablespoons of the chicken broth and the cornstarch until dissolved. Set the cornstarch mixture aside. Lightly spray an unheated large skillet with olive oil no-stick spray.

Remove the chicken from the marinade, reserving the marinade. Add the chicken to the skillet. Cook over medium heat for 4 minutes. Turn the chicken over and cook about 4 minutes more or until tender and no longer pink. Remove the chicken from the skillet and cover to keep warm.

Add the reserved marinade to the skillet. Using a wire whisk, stir in the cornstarch mixture and the remaining broth. Bring to a boil, stirring constantly. Then cook and stir for 2 minutes more. Stir in the lemon peel. Return the chicken to the skillet and heat through. Sprinkle with the parsley to garnish.

Makes 6 servings.

Chicken Marsala

Marsala is an Italian wine with a rich smoky flavor. When it's cooked with fresh mushrooms and chives, as in this recipe, it creates a wonderfully delicious, fat-free sauce. (If you'd rather not use Marsala, increase the amount of broth. The flavor of the dish will be altered, but you'll still get good results.) Calories, fat and cholesterol were reduced by:

- Using no-stick spray instead of butter to sauté the vegetables and chicken

- Removing the fat from the chicken broth

Nutrition Scorecard
(per serving)

	Before	After
Calories	268	192
Fat (g.)	10	2
% Calories from fat	35%	8%
Cholesterol (mg.)	91	68

4 (4-ounce) skinless, boneless chicken breast halves
¼ cup all-purpose flour
¼ teaspoon dried marjoram
⅛ teaspoon salt
⅛ teaspoon ground black pepper
1½ cups sliced fresh mushrooms
3 tablespoons snipped fresh chives
⅓ cup chicken broth, defatted
⅓ cup dry Marsala

Place each chicken breast half between two pieces of plastic wrap. Working from the center to the edges, lightly pound with the flat side of a meat mallet to ⅛" thickness. Remove the plastic wrap.

In a flat dish, combine the flour, marjoram, salt and pepper. Lightly press the chicken pieces into the flour mixture, coating both sides and shaking off any excess flour mixture.

Lightly spray an unheated large skillet with no-stick spray. Add the mushrooms and chives. Cook and stir until tender. Remove the mushroom mixture from the skillet. Add the chicken to the skillet and cook over medium-high heat for 4 minutes, turning to brown evenly.

Return the mushroom mixture to the skillet. Carefully add the broth and Marsala. Cook, uncovered, for 2 to 3 minutes or until the mushroom mixture slightly thickens, stirring occasionally. Transfer the chicken to a serving platter. Spoon the mushroom mixture over the chicken.

Makes 4 servings.

Hawaiian Chicken

Pictured on page 68

Here's a recipe for classic sweet-and-sour chicken that's healthier (and less messy!) than usual. Instead of dipping the chicken into a thin batter and deep-frying it, I dust the chicken with flour, pan-fry it until golden and then finish it off in the oven. I also reduced calories, fat and cholesterol by:

• Using chicken breasts without the skin

• Using no-stick spray instead of oil to cook the chicken

• Reducing the amount of sugar

• Using pineapple canned in its own juice

Nutrition Scorecard
(per serving)

	Before	After
Calories	785	400
Fat (g.)	32	2
% Calories from fat	36%	4%
Cholesterol (mg.)	92	68

CHICKEN
> 4 (4-ounce) skinless, boneless chicken breast halves
> ¼ cup all-purpose flour

SAUCE
> 1 (20-ounce) can pineapple slices (packed in juice)
> ¾ cup sugar
> ½ cup cider vinegar
> 2 tablespoons cornstarch
> 1 tablespoon reduced-sodium soy sauce
> 1 teaspoon grated ginger root
> 1 teaspoon chicken bouillon granules
> 1 large green pepper, cut into ¼" thick rings
>   Hot cooked brown rice (optional)

TO MAKE THE CHICKEN: Spray a large skillet with no-stick spray; heat. Meanwhile, coat both sides of the chicken with the flour. Shake off any excess flour. Add the chicken to the hot skillet and brown on both sides. Transfer the chicken to an 8" × 8" × 2" baking dish; set aside.

TO MAKE THE SAUCE: Drain the pineapple, reserving the juice. Transfer the juice to a 2-cup measuring cup. Add enough water to make 1¼ cups.

In a medium saucepan, use a wire whisk to stir together the juice mixture, sugar, vinegar, cornstarch, soy sauce, ginger and bouillon granules. Bring to a boil over medium heat. Slightly reduce the heat and gently boil for 4 minutes, stirring often.

Pour half of the sauce mixture over the chicken. Arrange the pineapple slices and pepper rings on top. Then pour on the remaining sauce mixture. Bake for 30 to 40 minutes or until the chicken is tender and no longer pink. If desired, serve with the rice.

Makes 4 servings.

Chicken à la Marengo

Pictured on page 69

This legendary dish was developed by Napoleon's Swiss chef in celebration of the victory over Austrian troops at Marengo. By making just two small changes, I was able to cut the calories and fat by more than half and still uphold the classic flavor. Serve the chicken over rice and with a romaine salad for a satisfying dinner. Calories, fat and cholesterol were reduced by:

• Removing the skin from the chicken

• Using no-stick spray instead of oil to brown the chicken and sauté the vegetables

Nutrition Scorecard
(per serving)

	Before	After
Calories	566	224
Fat (g.)	37	4
% Calories from fat	61%	19%
Cholesterol (mg.)	157	92

> 2½ pounds chicken pieces, skin removed, or 4 skinless, boneless chicken breast halves
> 1½ cups sliced fresh mushrooms
> 1 cup chopped onions
> 2 cloves garlic, minced
> 1 tablespoon snipped fresh parsley
> ½ teaspoon dried thyme
> ¼ teaspoon dried rosemary
> 1 (16-ounce) can recipe-style stewed tomatoes (with juices)
> ¼ cup dry white wine or nonalcoholic white wine
> 1 bay leaf
> Snipped fresh parsley (optional)

Lightly spray an unheated large skillet with no-stick spray. Add the chicken and brown lightly on all sides over medium-high heat. Remove the chicken.

Add the mushrooms, onions and garlic to the skillet. Cook and stir over medium heat until the onions are tender. Return the chicken to the skillet. Sprinkle with the parsley, thyme and rosemary. Then add the tomatoes (with juices), wine and bay leaf. Bring to a boil, then reduce the heat. Partially cover and gently simmer about 45 minutes for chicken pieces or about 25 minutes for boneless chicken, or until tender and no longer pink. Remove the bay leaf before serving. Sprinkle with the parsley.

Makes 4 servings.

Chicken à la King

This creamy dish is a great way to use up leftover chicken or turkey. It's also versatile—you can serve it as an elegant dinner-party entrée or as a homey main dish for a family supper. Calories, fat and cholesterol were reduced by:

• Using no-stick spray instead of oil to sauté the mushrooms

• Using evaporated skim milk instead of whole milk

• Replacing puff pastry shells with phyllo dough

• Removing the fat from the chicken broth

Nutrition Scorecard
(per serving)

	Before	After
Calories	614	323
Fat (g.)	36	6
% Calories from fat	53%	16%
Cholesterol (mg.)	108	67

PHYLLO TRIANGLES
    4 sheets phyllo dough

CHICKEN MIXTURE
    1 cup sliced fresh mushrooms
    ¼ teaspoon salt
    ¼ teaspoon ground black pepper
    1¾ cups evaporated skim milk
    3 tablespoons cornstarch
    1 cup chicken broth, defatted
    2 cups cooked and chopped chicken breasts
    ¼ cup chopped pimientos
    2 tablespoons dry sherry, dry white wine or nonalcoholic white wine

TO MAKE THE PHYLLO TRIANGLES: Preheat the oven to 375°. Place one sheet of the phyllo dough on a large piece of wax paper. (Cover the remaining sheets of phyllo with a damp cloth to prevent drying out.) Spray the sheet with no-stick spray. Then place another sheet on top and coat with more spray.

To form triangles, cut the stack lengthwise into four strips. Fold one end of each strip at a 45° angle. Continue folding each strip to form triangles, similar to folding a flag. Transfer the triangles to a cookie sheet.

Repeat the steps of stacking and forming triangles with the remaining two sheets of phyllo dough. Bake for 5 to 8 minutes or until golden brown. Transfer the phyllo triangles to a wire rack to cool.

TO MAKE THE CHICKEN MIXTURE: Lightly spray an unheated medium saucepan with no-stick spray. Add the mushrooms. Cook and stir over medium heat until tender. Stir in the salt and pepper.

In a custard cup, stir together ¼ cup of the milk and the cornstarch until smooth. Stir the cornstarch mixture into the mushrooms in the saucepan. Then stir in the remaining 1½ cups milk and the broth. Cook and stir until thickened and bubbly. Cook and stir for 1 minute more. Stir in the chicken, pimientos and sherry or wine. Cover and cook until heated through, stirring occasionally.

To serve, place two phyllo triangles on each dinner plate and spoon the chicken mixture on top.

Makes 4 servings.

Crispy Oven-Fried Chicken

Pictured on page 70

	Nutrition Scorecard *(per serving)*		
		Before	After
Calories		384	226
Fat (g.)		21	2
% Calories from fat		50%	6%
Cholesterol (mg.)		113	68

Just the simple step of switching to "oven frying" made this all-American favorite healthier. And a couple more tricks let me trim calories, fat and cholesterol even more. They were:

• Removing the skin from the chicken

• Using egg whites instead of melted butter to make the coating stick

> 2½–3 *pounds chicken pieces, skin removed,*
> *or 6 skinless, boneless chicken breast halves*
> ⅓ *cup all-purpose flour*
> 2 *egg whites, lightly beaten*
> 1 *cup cornflake crumbs*

Preheat the oven to 375°. Lightly spray a cookie sheet with no-stick spray. Set the cookie sheet aside.

To coat the chicken, first roll the pieces or breast halves in the flour to evenly cover all sides. Then dip the chicken in the egg whites and roll in the cornflake crumbs.

Place the coated chicken pieces on the prepared cookie sheet. Bake for 45 to 55 minutes for the chicken pieces or 20 to 30 minutes for the boneless breast halves, or until tender and no longer pink. (Do not turn the chicken over during baking.)

Makes 6 servings.

Turkey and Biscuit Turnovers

Here's an easy entrée I like to make when I'm short on time. It's also a delicious way to use up leftover poultry. I reduced calories, fat and cholesterol by:

- Replacing cream cheese with a combination of light cream cheese and reduced-fat cream of mushroom soup

- Replacing whole milk with evaporated skim milk

- Using an egg white instead of melted margarine to make the bread crumbs stick to the top of the turnovers

Nutrition Scorecard (per serving)	Before	After
Calories	549	366
Fat (g.)	31	9
% Calories from fat	51%	23%
Cholesterol (mg.)	97	77

3 tablespoons soft-style light cream cheese
2 tablespoons 99%-fat-free condensed cream of mushroom soup with ⅓ less salt
2 tablespoons evaporated skim milk
¼ teaspoon salt
⅛ teaspoon ground black pepper
3 cups cooked and diced turkey breast
1 tablespoon shredded onions
1 tablespoon chopped pimientos (optional)
1 (9-ounce) can whole-grain refrigerated biscuit dough (see note)
1 egg white, lightly beaten
2 tablespoons fine dry seasoned bread crumbs

Preheat the oven to 350°. Lightly spray a cookie sheet with no-stick spray and set aside.

In a medium bowl, stir together the cream cheese, condensed soup, milk, salt and pepper until smooth. Add the turkey, onions and pimientos, if desired. Mix until well combined.

Separate the refrigerated dough into eight biscuits. Roll two biscuits together to form a ball. Then use a rolling pin to roll the ball into a 6" circle. Repeat with the remaining biscuits.

To assemble the turnovers, spoon about ¾ cup of the turkey mixture onto half of each circle. Fold the other half of the circle over the filling to form a turnover. Seal the edges with the tines of a fork. Brush the tops with the egg white and sprinkle with the bread crumbs. Transfer the turnovers to the prepared cookie sheet. Bake for 20 to 25 minutes or until golden brown.

Makes 4 turnovers; 4 servings.

Note: If whole-grain refrigerated biscuit dough is unavailable, use 1 (10-ounce) can refrigerated pizza dough. Do not unroll the pizza dough. Cut the roll into four pieces. Roll each piece into a ball. Then use a rolling pin to roll each ball into a 6" circle.

Quick Reduced-Fat Gravies and Sauces

When I'm short on time yet still want to serve a reduced-fat gravy or sauce, I use one of these quick ideas:

- For a fast creamy gravy, mix 1 single-serving-size envelope of instant creamy soup mix and 1 tablespoon cornstarch in a small saucepan. Then stir in 1 cup evaporated skim milk. Cook and stir until thickened and bubbly. Cook and stir for 2 minutes more. Makes 1 cup; 4 servings. (Per ¼ cup: 68 calories, 1 g. fat, 5% calories from fat, 3 mg. cholesterol.)

- Mix 1 can (10¾ ounces) reduced-fat condensed cream of mushroom or chicken soup, ¼ cup evaporated skim milk and 1 teaspoon of a dried herb—such as basil, dill or tarragon—in a small saucepan. Heat and serve. Makes 1½ cups; 6 servings. (Per ¼ cup: 35 calories, 1 g. fat, 24% calories from fat, 0 mg. cholesterol.)

Chicken Sloppy Joes

Serve these hot sandwiches for a hearty lunch or as an on-the-go supper. When your family's schedule is hectic, keep a batch of this meat mixture in the refrigerator and reheat it in the microwave for a fast meal. I slashed calories, fat and cholesterol by:

- Replacing the ground beef with a combination of ground chicken breast, shredded carrots and rolled oats and reducing the total amount of meat

- Using tomato paste instead of ketchup

Nutrition Scorecard
(per serving)

	Before	After
Calories	365	217
Fat (g.)	17	6
% Calories from fat	42%	24%
Cholesterol (mg.)	66	55

12 ounces ground chicken breast
1 medium green pepper, chopped
½ cup chopped onions
1 medium tomato, chopped
1 medium carrot, coarsely shredded
1 clove garlic, minced
1 (8-ounce) can tomato sauce
2 tablespoons tomato paste
1 tablespoon rolled oats
2 teaspoons Worcestershire sauce
6 whole-wheat hamburger buns

Lightly spray an unheated large skillet with no-stick spray. Add the chicken; cook until no longer pink, stirring occasionally. Drain and discard the fat and juices.

Add the green peppers, onions, tomatoes, carrots and garlic. Cook over medium heat until tender, stirring occasionally.

Stir in the tomato sauce, tomato paste, oats and Worcestershire sauce. Bring to a boil, then reduce the heat. Cover and simmer for 10 minutes. Serve the mixture in the buns.

Makes 6 sandwiches; 6 servings.

Peppers Stuffed with Spanish Rice

For this recipe, I took a lightened-up version of Spanish rice and stuffed it into sweet green peppers. If you like, use one green pepper and one yellow pepper for a more colorful presentation. Calories, fat and cholesterol were cut by:

- Replacing the ground beef with ground turkey breast and reducing the total amount

- Reducing the amount of cheddar cheese and using its reduced-fat alternate (less than 5 grams of fat per ounce of cheese)

Nutrition Scorecard
(per serving)

	Before	After
Calories	381	171
Fat (g.)	22	3
% Calories from fat	51%	13%
Cholesterol (mg.)	89	31

2 large green peppers
8 ounces ground turkey breast (see note)
½ cup chopped onions
1 cup cooked brown rice
1 cup recipe-style stewed tomatoes (with juices)
2 tablespoons tomato paste
1 tablespoon Worcestershire sauce
½ teaspoon dried basil
¼ teaspoon salt
¼ teaspoon ground black pepper
¼ cup (1 ounce) finely shredded reduced-fat cheddar cheese

Bring water in a large saucepan to a boil. Meanwhile, cut the peppers lengthwise in half. Remove and discard the stems, seeds and membranes.

Carefully, place the peppers in the boiling water for 3 minutes. Using a slotted spoon, remove the peppers and invert them onto paper towels to drain well.

Preheat the oven to 375°. Lightly spray an unheated large skillet with no-stick spray. Add the turkey and onions. Cook over medium heat until the turkey is no longer pink, stirring occasionally.

Stir in the rice, tomatoes (with juices), tomato paste, Worcestershire sauce, basil, salt and pepper. Cover and simmer for 10 minutes, stirring occasionally.

Place the pepper halves in an 8" × 8" × 2" baking dish. Spoon the meat mixture into the pepper shells. Sprinkle the cheese on top. Bake about 10 minutes or until heated through.

Makes 4 servings.

Note: To make sure you're buying the leanest ground turkey available, check the label. Look for products made with only turkey breast meat. Many ground turkey products contain the dark meat and the fatty skin.

Italian Meat Loaf

My family loves this Italian version of a meat loaf that I make with ground turkey. Calories, fat and cholesterol were reduced by:

- Using egg whites instead of a whole egg

- Replacing ground beef with ground turkey breast

- Using shredded apples to add moisture that is lost by eliminating the beef fat

- Using a reduced-fat spaghetti sauce (less than 1 gram of fat per 4 ounces of sauce)

Nutrition Scorecard
(per serving)

	Before	After
Calories	445	227
Fat (g.)	26	3
% Calories from fat	53%	10%
Cholesterol (mg.)	156	54

2 egg whites, lightly beaten
2 cloves garlic, minced
¾ teaspoon dried basil
½ teaspoon salt
½ teaspoon dried rosemary
¼ teaspoon crushed red pepper
1 medium apple, peeled, cored and finely shredded
½ cup chopped onions
½ cup fine dry seasoned bread crumbs
1 pound ground turkey breast (see note)
⅔ cup reduced-fat spaghetti sauce
2 tablespoons grated Parmesan cheese

Preheat the oven to 350°. In a large bowl, stir together the egg whites, garlic, basil, salt, rosemary and red pepper. Then stir in the apples, onions and bread crumbs. Add the turkey and mix until well combined.

Spray a 7½" × 3½" × 2" or 8" × 4" × 2" loaf pan with no-stick spray. Pat the turkey mixture into the pan. Bake for 15 minutes.

Spread the spaghetti sauce over the top of the turkey. Bake about 25 minutes more or until the turkey is no longer pink. Let stand for 5 minutes. Transfer the loaf to a serving plate. Sprinkle the Parmesan cheese over the top. Slice and serve.

Makes 4 servings.

Note: To make sure you're buying the leanest ground turkey available, check the label. Look for products made with only turkey breast meat. Many ground turkey products contain the dark meat and the fatty skin.

Healthy Homestyle Country Sausage

Pictured on page 135

This breakfast sausage is almost fat-free and tastes so much like its fatty counterpart that my taste testers kept asking how I did it. Here's how: I cut calories, fat and cholesterol by:

- Replacing ground pork with ground turkey breast

- Using shredded apples and cooked brown rice to add moisture that is lost by eliminating the pork fat

Nutrition Scorecard (per serving)		
	Before	After
Calories	609	160
Fat (g.)	46	2
% Calories from fat	69%	8%
Cholesterol (mg.)	215	51

1 pound ground turkey breast (see note)
1 medium apple, peeled, cored and finely shredded
½ cup cooked brown rice
2 tablespoons shredded onions
2 cloves garlic, minced
1½ teaspoons ground sage
1 teaspoon salt
½ teaspoon ground red pepper
½ teaspoon ground black pepper
½ teaspoon dried thyme
¼ teaspoon ground allspice
Snipped fresh parsley (optional)

In a large bowl, stir together the turkey, apples, rice, onions and garlic.

In a small bowl, stir together the sage, salt, red and black peppers, thyme and allspice. Sprinkle the spice mixture over the turkey mixture. Using your hands, mix until well blended. Shape the turkey mixture into eight ½" thick patties.

Spray an unheated large skillet with no-stick spray. Add the patties and cook over medium heat for 4 minutes. Turn the patties over and cook about 4 minutes more or until they are no longer pink. Sprinkle with the parsley, if desired.

Makes 8 patties; 4 servings.

Note: To make sure you're buying the leanest ground turkey available, check the label. Look for products made with only turkey breast meat. Many ground turkey products contain the dark meat and the fatty skin.

Sole Stuffed with Broccoli and Cheese

Even though most fish is naturally low in fat, many recipes transform this good-for-you food into a high-calorie entrée. In this recipe makeover, I simply switched to reduced-fat ingredients to create a healthier version of this classic dish. Calories, fat and cholesterol were reduced by:

- Using egg whites instead of a whole egg

- Replacing cream cheese with a combination of Neufchâtel cheese and fat-free plain yogurt (5 grams of fat per ounce of Neufchâtel cheese)

- Using evaporated skim milk instead of whole milk

Nutrition Scorecard
(per serving)

	Before	After
Calories	394	258
Fat (g.)	24	8
% Calories from fat	57%	28%
Cholesterol (mg.)	174	73

4 (4-ounce) fresh or frozen sole fillets
1 cup broccoli florets, chopped
2 egg whites, lightly beaten
½ cup soft-style Neufchâtel cheese spread
½ cup fat-free plain yogurt
3 tablespoons grated Parmesan cheese
¾ cup herb-seasoned stuffing mix
1 tablespoon evaporated skim milk
1 tablespoon dry white wine or nonalcoholic white wine

Thaw the fish, if frozen. Set aside.

In a large saucepan with a tight-fitting lid, bring 1" of water to a boil. Place the broccoli in a steamer basket and set the basket in the saucepan, making sure the basket sits above the water. Cover the saucepan and steam about 8 minutes or until the broccoli is crisp-tender.

Meanwhile, preheat the oven to 350°.

In a medium bowl, stir together the egg whites, ¼ cup of the Neufchâtel cheese, ¼ cup of the yogurt and 2 tablespoons of the Parmesan cheese.

Add the steamed broccoli and stuffing mix to the cheese mixture. Stir until well combined. Lightly spray a 10" × 6" × 2" baking dish with no-stick spray. Assemble the fish rolls by spooning one-quarter of the stuffing onto one end of each fillet. Roll the fillets around the stuffing. Secure each with a toothpick. Place the rolls, seam side down, in the prepared baking dish. Cover with foil. Bake for 30 to 35 minutes or until the fish flakes easily when tested with a fork.

Meanwhile, in a small saucepan stir together the remaining ¼ cup of Neufchâtel cheese, milk and wine. Cook and stir until heated through. Remove the saucepan from the heat and stir in the remaining ¼ cup of yogurt. Cook and stir over low heat just until heated. (Do not overheat, otherwise the yogurt will separate.) Stir in the remaining Parmesan cheese and serve over the fish rolls.

Makes 4 servings.

Dilly Lemon Sauce for Fish

Whether you poach it, grill it or microwave it, fish is one food you can cook in a flash when you need a quick main dish. To transform it into an extra-special entrée while keeping its health benefits intact, I serve it with the following low-fat sauce. Calories, fat and cholesterol were reduced by:

• Eliminating the butter

• Using evaporated skim milk instead of heavy cream

• Removing the fat from the chicken broth

Nutrition Scorecard (per 2 tablespoons)

	Before	After
Calories	46	18
Fat (g.)	4	1
% Calories from fat	77%	2%
Cholesterol (mg.)	11	0

  1 *tablespoon cornstarch*
  1 *tablespoon lemon juice*
  ½ *cup chicken broth, defatted*
  ½ *cup evaporated skim milk*
  1 *teaspoon dillweed*
  1 *teaspoon finely shredded lemon peel*

In a small saucepan, stir together the cornstarch and lemon juice until smooth. Then stir in the broth and milk.

Cook and stir over medium heat until thickened and bubbly. Stir in the dillweed and lemon peel. Cook and stir for 2 minutes more.

Makes 1 cup; 8 servings.

Sunshine Halibut

Pictured on page 136

When I serve my family fresh halibut, I make sure its delicate flavor shines through. In this recipe, I do that by using only freshly squeezed orange and lemon juices. Calories, fat and cholesterol were reduced by:

• Using no-stick spray instead of butter to sauté the vegetables

Nutrition Scorecard
(per serving)

	Before	After
Calories	165	140
Fat (g.)	6	3
% Calories from fat	31%	18%
Cholesterol (mg.)	44	36

---

4 *(4-ounce) fresh halibut steaks, cut ¾" thick*
⅓ *cup finely chopped onions*
1 *clove garlic, minced*
2 *tablespoons snipped fresh parsley*
½ *teaspoon finely shredded orange peel*
⅛ *teaspoon ground black pepper*
¼ *cup fresh orange juice*
1 *tablespoon fresh lemon juice*

Preheat the oven to 400°. Arrange the fish in an 8" × 8" × 2" baking dish and set aside.

Lightly spray an unheated small skillet with no-stick spray. Add the onions and garlic. Cook and stir over medium heat until the onions are tender.

Remove the skillet from the heat. Stir in the parsley, orange peel and pepper. Spread the onion mixture on top of the fish.

In a custard cup, stir together the orange and lemon juices. Then pour the juice mixture over the fish. Cover with foil and bake for 10 to 15 minutes or until the fish flakes easily when tested with a fork.

Makes 4 servings.

Selecting the Best Catch

Fish, shellfish and other types of seafood are generally low in fat, high in protein and just swimming with vitamins and minerals. An easy way to guesstimate your calorie intake is to figure that 3½ ounces of most types has about 100 calories. A few of the lower-fat varieties include cod, haddock, scallops, yellowfin tuna, water-packed light tuna, crab and shrimp.

New England Crab Cakes

These crispy little cakes are usually pan-fried in half an inch of oil. Just eliminating that procedure allowed me to reduce the fat per serving from 12 grams to 2. As a bonus, these cakes are even tastier than usual because there's no oil to mask the delicate flavor of the crab. Calories, fat and cholesterol were reduced by:

• Using no-stick spray instead of oil to sauté the vegetables and pan-fry the crab cakes

• Using egg whites instead of whole eggs

Nutrition Scorecard
(per serving)

	Before	After
Calories	237	143
Fat (g.)	12	2
% Calories from fat	48%	10%
Cholesterol (mg.)	168	51

  1 stalk celery, finely chopped
  ¼ cup finely chopped onions
  1 tablespoon snipped fresh parsley
  6 egg whites, lightly beaten
  1 cup fine dry plain bread crumbs
  2 teaspoons Worcestershire sauce
  1 teaspoon dry mustard
  2 (6-ounce) cans crab meat, drained and flaked
     Lemon wedges

Spray an unheated large skillet with no-stick spray. Add the celery, onions and parsley. Cook and stir over medium heat until tender. Remove from the heat.

In a medium bowl, stir together the egg whites, ¾ cup of the bread crumbs, Worcestershire sauce and mustard. Stir in the celery mixture and crab meat.

Using about ⅓ cup of crab mixture for each, shape into ½" thick patties. Coat patties with the remaining ¼ cup bread crumbs.

Spray the skillet again with the no-stick spray. Add the crab patties. Cook over medium heat about 3 minutes or until golden brown. Turn the patties over and cook about 3 minutes more or until golden brown. Serve warm with lemon wedges.

Makes 6 servings.

Pot-Roasted Beef Dinner

Pictured on page 137

Leftovers never tasted so good! Here's a slimmed-down version of Mom's pot roast you can prepare on weekends when you have more time to cook. Then during the week, just pop the leftovers into the microwave—in minutes you can serve a nutritious home-cooked meal. Calories, fat and cholesterol were reduced by:

- Reducing the amount of beef and using a top round roast (25% calories from fat) instead of a chuck arm roast (35% calories from fat)

- Using no-stick spray instead of oil to brown the meat

- Increasing the amount of vegetables

Nutrition Scorecard
(per serving)

	Before	After
Calories	616	392
Fat (g.)	31	11
% Calories from fat	46%	26%
Cholesterol (mg.)	180	108

12	ounces tiny or medium potatoes
1	(1½-pound) beef top round roast, trimmed of all visible fat
1½	cups vegetable juice cocktail
2	tablespoons Worcestershire sauce
1	teaspoon dried basil
24	baby carrots
8	tiny boiling onions or 2 small onions, quartered
3	stalks celery, sliced diagonally into 1″ pieces

Preheat the oven to 325°. If using the tiny potatoes, peel a strip around the center of each. If using the medium potatoes, cut them into chunks. Set the potatoes aside.

Lightly spray an unheated Dutch oven with no-stick spray. Add the meat and brown it over medium-high heat. Drain and discard any pan drippings.

In a medium bowl, stir together the vegetable juice cocktail, Worcestershire sauce and basil. Pour the juice mixture over the meat. Cover and bake for 45 minutes. Add the potatoes, carrots, onions and celery. Bake, covered, for 45 to 60 minutes more or until the meat and vegetables are tender.

Makes 6 servings.

Steak and Spinach Slices

When you're trying to eat healthy, a hefty 10- or 12-ounce steak dinner is no longer in vogue. However, a more moderate 3-ounce portion looks skimpy on a dinner plate. To trick the eye, serve these tasty spinach-stuffed pinwheels. Each meat lover gets two plump roll-ups that, when served with a big baked potato, fill the plate as well as an empty stomach. Calories, fat and cholesterol were reduced by:

Nutrition Scorecard
(per serving)

	Before	After
Calories	529	242
Fat (g.)	33	9
% Calories from fat	58%	31%
Cholesterol (mg.)	134	70

• Reducing the amount of beef and using a top round steak (25% calories from fat) instead of a flank steak (44% calories from fat)

• Eliminating bacon inside the pinwheels

• Using reduced-fat Parmesan cheese (3 grams of fat per ounce of cheese)

1 (12-ounce) beef top round steak, cut ½"–¾" thick and trimmed of all visible fat
2 (10-ounce) packages frozen chopped spinach, thawed and well drained
¼ cup grated reduced-fat Parmesan cheese
2 teaspoons bottled minced garlic or 4 cloves garlic, minced

Preheat the oven to 350°. Score both sides of the steak by making shallow cuts in a diamond pattern. Use a meat mallet to pound the steak to a 12" × 8" rectangle.

In a medium bowl, toss together the spinach and cheese until combined. Spread the spinach mixture on top of the steak. Then sprinkle with the garlic. Roll up the steak, jelly-roll fashion, beginning at a short side. Keep the meat from unrolling by skewering it with eight wooden toothpicks placed 1" apart (starting ½" from an end). Then cut the roll between the toothpicks to form eight slices (each 1" thick).

Spray a cookie sheet with no-stick spray. Place the slices on the cookie sheet. Bake for 12 to 15 minutes for medium doneness.

Makes 4 servings.

Apple Stuffed Tenderloin
with Cinnamon Raisin Sauce

Pictured on page 138

This hearty entrée started out as stuffed pork chops. To make the dish leaner and still keep its character, I switched to stuffing a pork tenderloin. Calories, fat and cholesterol were reduced by:

• Using pork tenderloin (26% calories from fat) instead of rib chops (52% calories from fat)

• Using no-stick spray instead of butter to sauté the onions

• Eliminating the butter in the sauce

Nutrition Scorecard
(per serving)

	Before	After
Calories	472	245
Fat (g.)	24	4
% Calories from fat	46%	16%
Cholesterol (mg.)	143	74

STUFFED PORK TENDERLOIN
- 1 pork tenderloin (1–1½ pounds), trimmed of all visible fat
- 2 medium oranges
- 1 medium apple, cored and chopped
- 2 tablespoons finely chopped onions
- ⅔ cup fine dry plain bread crumbs

SAUCE
- 1 cup unsweetened apple juice
- 1 tablespoon cornstarch
- ¼ teaspoon ground cinnamon
- ¼ cup raisins

TO MAKE THE STUFFED PORK TENDERLOIN: Preheat the oven to 425°. Cut a pocket in the side of the tenderloin by cutting a lengthwise slit from one side to almost the other side and stopping about ½" from each of the tapered ends. Set the tenderloin aside.

Finely shred the peel from the oranges and set aside. Then squeeze 3 tablespoons of juice from the oranges. In a medium bowl, combine the orange juice and apples. Set the apple mixture aside.

Spray an unheated small skillet with no-stick spray. Add the onions. Cook and stir over medium heat until tender. Then add the onions and bread crumbs to the apple mixture. Toss until combined.

Spoon the bread mixture into the pocket of the tenderloin. Securely close the pocket with wooden toothpicks. Place the tenderloin on a rack in a shallow roasting pan. Insert a meat thermometer into the meat portion only. Bake for 25 to 30 minutes or until the thermometer registers 160°. Let stand about 5 minutes before slicing.

TO MAKE THE SAUCE: In a small saucepan, use a wire whisk to stir together 2 tablespoons of the apple juice and the cornstarch. Then stir in the remaining apple juice.

Cook and stir over medium heat until boiling. Stir in the reserved orange peel and cinnamon. Add the raisins and cook for 5 minutes, stirring occasionally.

To serve, slice the tenderloin. Spoon the sauce over the slices.

Makes 4 servings.

Meatless Cheese Burgers

Most of my clients love to occasionally sink their teeth into a big burger snuggled in a soft bun with lettuce, tomatoes and onions. So when my clients feel a burger urge coming on, I recommend this meatless version. They're easy to make and, take it from my husband, tasty too! Calories, fat and cholesterol were reduced by:

- Using egg whites instead of a whole egg

- Using fat-free cottage cheese

- Using no-stick spray instead of oil for cooking the burgers

Nutrition Scorecard
(per serving)

	Before	After
Calories	286	208
Fat (g.)	10	4
% Calories from fat	33%	18%
Cholesterol (mg.)	41	1

2 egg whites, lightly beaten
1 cup fat-free cottage cheese
1 envelope instant onion soup dip mix
1 cup rolled oats

In a medium bowl, stir together the egg whites, cottage cheese and soup mix until well combined. Then stir in the oats.

Using about ⅓ cup of mixture for each burger, shape the mixture into six ½" thick patties. Spray an unheated griddle or large skillet with no-stick spray. Heat the griddle or skillet over medium heat. Add the patties and cook about 3 minutes on each side or until golden brown.

Makes 6 patties; 6 servings.

FAMILY-FAVORITE ONE-DISH MEALS

If your schedule is anything like mine, you don't have time for fancy cooking. One-dish meals can be the key to serving your family nutritious, home-cooked meals on weekdays. Casseroles, skillet suppers and other such dishes combine protein with vegetables and pasta or grains.

One-dish meals became popular in the '50s and '60s, when more and more women began spending less and less time in the kitchen. Unfortunately, many of these dishes were built on high-fat, high-sodium ingredients like canned soup, hamburger and cheese. The basic idea behind these meals was good; the execution left something to be desired. That's why I considered them prime targets for makeovers.

Sprinkled throughout this chapter are lots of still-popular dishes that I've updated to today's nutrient standards. Let's face it, you can't beat such old-fashioned dinners as chicken and biscuits, tuna casserole and macaroni chili. I've also added some recent favorites, like Cheesy Chicken and Artichoke Bake and Turkey Sausage Spaghetti Pie, to round things out. The only thing missing from these filling dinners is the fat!

Chicken in a Packet

Pictured on page 139

Here's a barbecued chicken meal that's oh-so-easy to prepare—the chicken, potatoes and peppers all cook together in one big foil packet. Best of all, there's no messy cleanup! Calories, fat and cholesterol were reduced by:

• Removing the skin from the chicken

• Eliminating oil drizzled over the chicken and vegetables

Nutrition Scorecard (per serving)		
	Before	After
Calories	423	203
Fat (g.)	27	2
% Calories from fat	58%	11%
Cholesterol (mg.)	92	68

½ cup bottled barbecue sauce
4 (4-ounce) skinless, boneless chicken breast halves
1 green pepper, cut into strips
1 sweet red pepper, cut into strips
4 small baking potatoes or 12 new potatoes, thinly sliced
¼ teaspoon ground black pepper

Preheat the oven to 350°. Tear off two pieces of foil the size of a cookie sheet. Place one piece of the foil on a cookie sheet. Spoon half of the barbecue sauce on the center of the foil. Layer the chicken, green and red peppers and potatoes on top. Sprinkle with the black pepper. Top with the remaining barbecue sauce. Place the remaining piece of foil on top. Seal edges with double folds.

Bake for 50 minutes. Carefully open the packet and check the chicken for doneness. If the chicken is still pink, close the packet and bake about 5 minutes more or until done.

Makes 4 servings.

Note: To make individual packets, use four 18" × 14" pieces of foil. On one half of each piece of foil, layer the ingredients as directed above. Fold the other half of the foil over the top and seal each packet. Bake as directed.

Cheesy Chicken and Artichoke Bake

Pictured on page 140

In this dish, chicken and artichokes are smothered in a virtually fat-free Parmesan sauce. Calories, fat and cholesterol were reduced by:

- Removing the fat from the chicken broth

- Using no-stick spray instead of butter to sauté the onions and garlic

- Replacing half-and-half with evaporated skim milk

- Reducing the amount of Parmesan cheese

Nutrition Scorecard
(per serving)

	Before	After
Calories	616	351
Fat (g.)	30	5
% Calories from fat	44%	13%
Cholesterol (mg.)	207	110

1 (14-ounce) can chicken broth, defatted
1½ pounds skinless, boneless chicken breasts
¼ cup chopped onions
1 clove garlic, minced
¾ cup evaporated skim milk
2 tablespoons cornstarch
2 tablespoons dry white wine
⅓ cup grated Parmesan cheese
½ teaspoon dried rosemary
¼ teaspoon salt
⅛ teaspoon ground white pepper
1 (14-ounce) can artichoke hearts (with juices)
2 cups sliced fresh mushrooms

Bring the broth to a simmer in a large skillet. Carefully add the chicken. Cover and simmer for 15 to 20 minutes or until the chicken is no longer pink. Reserve ¾ cup chicken broth. Shred or cut the chicken into bite-size pieces and set aside.

Lightly spray an unheated medium saucepan with no-stick spray. Add the onions and garlic. Cook and stir over medium heat until the onions are tender and translucent.

Stir in the reserved broth and milk. Stir together the cornstarch and wine until smooth. Using a wire whisk, slowly stir the cornstarch mixture into the broth mixture. Cook and stir over medium heat until the mixture comes to a boil. Reduce the heat. Cook and stir for 1 minute more.

Stir in the Parmesan cheese, rosemary, salt and pepper. Cook and stir until the cheese is melted.

Preheat the oven to 350°. Lightly spray a 2-quart casserole with no-stick spray. Place the chicken in the dish. Drain the artichokes and reserve the juices. Cut the artichokes in half and arrange them around the chicken. Pour the cheese sauce over the chicken and artichokes. Bake for 25 to 30 minutes or until heated through.

Meanwhile, add 2 tablespoons of reserved artichoke liquid to a medium skillet. Add the mushrooms. Cook and stir until tender. Before serving the casserole, top with the mushrooms.

Makes 4 servings.

Curried Chicken Divan

This casserole was a childhood favorite of mine. To make it healthier over the years, I whittled away calories and fat until I came up with this latest version. My most recent change was switching to a reduced-fat condensed cream of chicken soup (it's a real find—saving you both fat and sodium). I also reduced calories, fat and cholesterol by:

- Using fat-free plain yogurt instead of a mixture of mayonnaise and lemon juice

- Reducing the amount of cheddar cheese and using its reduced-fat alternate (less than 5 grams of fat per ounce of cheese)

Nutrition Scorecard (per serving)	Before	After
Calories	567	318
Fat (g.)	35	9
% Calories from fat	55%	24%
Cholesterol (mg.)	113	99

1 pound broccoli florets, cut into bite-size pieces
2 (10¾-ounce) cans 99%-fat-free condensed cream of chicken soup with ⅓ less salt
1 cup fat-free plain yogurt (made without gelatin)
1 tablespoon curry powder
1½ pounds skinless, boneless chicken breasts, cooked and cut into bite-size pieces
1½ cups (6 ounces) finely shredded reduced-fat sharp cheddar cheese

In a large saucepan with a tight-fitting lid, bring 1" of water to a boil. Place the broccoli in a steamer basket and set the basket in the saucepan, making sure the basket sits above the water. Cover the saucepan and steam about 8 minutes or until the broccoli is crisp-tender.

Preheat the oven to 350°. In a large bowl, stir together the condensed soup, yogurt and curry powder.

Place the chicken in a 10" × 9" × 2" baking dish. Then layer the broccoli on top. Pour the yogurt mixture over the broccoli and chicken and top with the cheese. Bake, uncovered, about 30 minutes or until the cheese is bubbly and the mixture is heated through.

Makes 6 servings.

Weekday Chicken and Dumplings

This quick-and-healthy version of chicken and dumplings uses cooked chicken to speed up the preparation. And I put whole-wheat flour into the dumplings for added fiber. I cut calories, fat and cholesterol by:

- Replacing oil in the dumplings with finely sieved fat-free cottage cheese

- Using buttermilk in the dumplings instead of whole milk

- Removing the fat from the chicken broth

- Cooking the vegetables in chicken broth rather than sautéing them in margarine

- Replacing heavy cream in the chicken mixture with evaporated skim milk

- Using cornstarch as a thickener instead of a flour-and-butter roux

Nutrition Scorecard
(per serving)

	Before	After
Calories	420	253
Fat (g.)	26	4
% Calories from fat	56%	13%
Cholesterol (mg.)	88	61

DUMPLINGS
- ¼ cup fat-free cottage cheese
- ½ cup all-purpose flour
- ½ cup whole-wheat flour
- 1 tablespoon snipped fresh parsley
- 1 teaspoon baking powder
- ⅛ teaspoon dried thyme
- ¼ cup buttermilk

CHICKEN MIXTURE
- 2 cups canned chicken broth, defatted
- ½ cup finely chopped onions
- ½ cup finely chopped carrots
- ¼ cup finely chopped celery
- ½ cup evaporated skim milk
- 3 tablespoons cornstarch
- 1 teaspoon dry mustard
- 3 cups cooked and diced chicken breasts

To make the dumplings: Place the cottage cheese in a fine-mesh sieve. Using the back of a spoon, push the cottage cheese through the sieve. Set aside.

In a small bowl, stir together the all-purpose flour, whole-wheat flour, parsley, baking powder and thyme. Using the tines of a fork or pastry blender, cut in the cottage cheese until crumbly. Set the dumpling mixture aside while preparing the chicken mixture.

To make the chicken mixture: In a large skillet, combine the broth, onions, carrots and celery. Bring to a boil, then reduce the heat. Cover and simmer for 5 minutes or until the vegetables are tender.

In a small bowl, use a wire whisk to stir together the evaporated milk, cornstarch and dry mustard until smooth. Slowly stir the milk mixture into the broth mixture. Cook and stir over medium heat until the mixture comes to a boil. Reduce the heat. Cook and stir for 1 minute more. Stir in the chicken.

Use a fork to stir the buttermilk into the dumpling mixture until combined. Then spoon the mixture in six mounds on top of the bubbling chicken mixture. Cover and gently simmer for 10 to 12 minutes or until a toothpick comes out clean.

Makes 6 servings.

Label Savvy

Are you confused by the nutrition information on food labels? Don't be. All you need to do is to choose foods that contain:

- No more than 3 grams of total fat for every 100 calories

- No more than 800 milligrams of sodium for a main-dish food

- At least 3 grams of fiber for a good source of fiber

Southwest Chicken Lasagna

Pictured on page 141

When I want to cook once and eat twice, I make this chicken lasagna. The beauty of lasagna—even this Southwestern version—is that you can heat leftovers in the microwave. Calories, fat and cholesterol were reduced by:

- Using no-stick spray instead of oil to sauté the vegetables

- Using reduced-fat tomato soup

- Reducing the amount of cheddar and Monterey Jack cheeses and using their reduced-fat alternates (less than 5 grams of fat per ounce of cheese)

- Using egg whites instead of whole eggs

Nutrition Scorecard
(per serving)

	Before	After
Calories	553	410
Fat (g.)	28	12
% Calories from fat	45%	26%
Cholesterol (mg.)	165	86

NOODLES
    1 (10-ounce) package lasagna noodles

COTTAGE CHEESE MIXTURE
    4 egg whites, lightly beaten
    3 cups fat-free cottage cheese
    ⅓ cup chopped parsley
    3 tablespoons canned diced green chili peppers

LASAGNA
    1 cup chopped onions
    1 sweet red or green pepper, chopped
    2 cloves garlic, minced
    2 (10¾-ounce) cans 99%-fat-free condensed tomato soup with
        ⅓ less salt
    1 (10-ounce) can enchilada sauce
    1 tablespoon chili powder
    1 teaspoon ground cumin
    ¼ teaspoon ground black pepper
    4 cups cooked chicken breasts torn into bite-size pieces
    1½ cups (6 ounces) finely shredded reduced-fat sharp cheddar cheese
    1 cup (4 ounces) finely shredded reduced-fat Monterey Jack cheese
        Sweet purple or green pepper rings (optional)

TO MAKE THE NOODLES: Cook the noodles according to the directions on the package. Drain and set aside.

TO MAKE THE COTTAGE CHEESE MIXTURE: While the noodles are cooking, stir together the egg whites, cottage cheese, parsley and chili peppers in a medium bowl. Set aside.

To make the lasagna: Lightly spray an unheated large skillet with no-stick spray. Add the onions, chopped red or green peppers and garlic. Cook and stir over medium heat until tender.

Stir in the condensed soup, enchilada sauce, chili powder, cumin and black pepper. Bring to a boil, then reduce the heat. Simmer, uncovered, for 10 minutes, stirring often.

Preheat the oven to 375°. Lightly spray a 13" × 9" × 2" baking pan with no-stick spray. To assemble the lasagna, place four of the noodles in the pan. Then spread half of the cottage cheese mixture over the noodles. Top with half of the sauce mixture, 2 cups of the chicken and half each of the cheddar and Monterey Jack cheeses.

Repeat layers with the remaining noodles, cottage cheese mixture, sauce mixture, chicken, cheddar cheese and Monterey Jack cheese. Cover with foil. Bake about 50 minutes or until bubbly. Let stand 15 minutes before cutting. If desired, garnish with the pepper rings.

Makes 8 servings.

Carrot Power

To boost the beta-carotene content of my tomato sauces, rice dishes, stuffings and other recipes, I often toss in some shredded or grated carrots. Research has shown that beta-carotene (the plant form of vitamin A) may help prevent cancer, delay cataracts and reduce the risk of heart attack and lung cancer. Just one medium carrot provides twice your Recommended Dietary Allowance of this antioxidant.

Deep-Dish Turkey Pot Pie

Pot pies are usually not allowed in a healthy diet. But by making just a few simple changes, you can enjoy this family-style dish without the guilt. I slashed calories, fat and cholesterol by:

- Removing the fat from the chicken broth

- Cooking the vegetables in chicken broth rather than sautéing them in margarine

- Replacing heavy cream with evaporated skim milk

- Using a nearly fat-free phyllo crust instead of a typical fatty pastry crust

- Using cornstarch as a thickener instead of flour and margarine

Nutrition Scorecard
(per serving)

	Before	After
Calories	671	251
Fat (g.)	32	3
% Calories from fat	43%	9%
Cholesterol (mg.)	95	52

Turkey Mixture
2¼ cups chicken broth, defatted
½ cup chopped celery
¼ cup chopped onions
2 medium carrots, coarsely chopped
3 tablespoons cornstarch
1¾ cups evaporated skim milk
3 cups cooked and chopped turkey breast
1 cup frozen peas, thawed
¼ cup snipped fresh parsley
½ teaspoon dried sage

Pastry Crust
3 sheets phyllo dough

To make the turkey mixture: Preheat the oven to 350°. In a medium saucepan, combine 2 cups of the broth, the celery, onions and carrots. Bring to a boil, then reduce the heat. Cover and simmer about 5 minutes or until vegetables are tender.

In a custard cup, stir together the remaining ¼ cup of broth and the cornstarch until smooth. Slowly stir the cornstarch mixture into the broth-vegetable mixture. Then stir in the milk.

Cook and stir over medium heat until the mixture comes to a boil. Reduce the heat. Cook and stir for 1 minute more. Then stir in the turkey, peas, parsley and sage. Transfer the mixture to a shallow 2-quart casserole.

TO MAKE THE PASTRY CRUST: Lay one sheet of the phyllo dough on top of the turkey mixture. Spray the dough with no-stick spray. Repeat layering and spraying the phyllo two more times. Fold or crumple the edges of the dough and tuck them inside the casserole dish.

Bake for 35 to 40 minutes or until the crust is golden brown.

Makes 6 servings.

TO MAKE CHICKEN POT PIE: Use 3 cups cooked and chopped chicken breast instead of the turkey. (Per serving: 262 calories, 3 g. fat, 12% calories from fat, 62 mg. cholesterol.)

TO MAKE BEEF POT PIE: Use defatted canned beef broth instead of the chicken broth and 3 cups cooked and chopped beef round instead of the turkey. Replace the carrots with 1½ cups sliced fresh mushrooms; omit the sage. (Per serving: 298 calories, 8 g. fat, 24% calories from fat, 75 mg. cholesterol.)

Go for the Leanest

One way to create great-tasting main dishes that are low in fat is to start with the leanest cuts of meat and poultry available. Here are some of the items I recommend. All the figures are based on cooked, 3-ounce portions. (One note about the beef: Most of what's generally available at supermarkets fall into the "prime" and "choice" grades. These contain more fat than beef labeled "select." If your market doesn't carry select grade, try to create a demand by asking for it whenever you shop.)

CUT	CALORIES	FAT (g.)	CHOLESTEROL (mg.)
Beef eye of round with ¼" fat trim (select grade)	136	3.4	59
Beef eye of round with no-fat trim (select grade)	132	3.0	59
Beef eye of round with no-fat trim (choice grade)	150	4.8	59
Pork tenderloin	159	5.4	80
Chicken breast (skin removed)	140	3.0	72
Turkey breast (skin removed)	115	<1.0	70

Chicken and Biscuits

To create the crowning touch for this casserole, I use refrigerated whole-grain biscuits and a tasty yogurt topping. I reduced calories, fat and cholesterol by:

- Replacing mayonnaise with evaporated skim milk

- Using reduced-fat cream of chicken soup

- Reducing the amount of cheddar cheese and using its reduced-fat alternate (less than 5 grams of fat per ounce of cheese)

- Replacing homemade biscuits with lower-fat whole-grain refrigerated biscuits

Nutrition Scorecard
(per serving)

	Before	After
Calories	400	366
Fat (g.)	23	10
% Calories from fat	51%	24%
Cholesterol (mg.)	100	63

TOPPING
- 2 egg whites, lightly beaten
- ¼ cup fat-free plain yogurt
- ½ teaspoon celery seed
- ¼ teaspoon salt

CHICKEN MIXTURE
- 2 cups cooked and diced chicken breast
- 1 cup broccoli florets
- 1 (4-ounce can) sliced mushrooms, drained
- ¼ cup chopped onions
- 1 (10¾-ounce) can 99%-fat-free condensed cream of chicken soup with ⅓ less salt
- ¼ cup evaporated skim milk
- 1½ teaspoons Worcestershire sauce
- ¼ teaspoon curry powder
- ⅓ cup finely shredded reduced-fat sharp cheddar cheese
- 1 (9-ounce) can whole-grain refrigerated biscuit dough (see note)

TO MAKE THE TOPPING: In a small bowl, use a wire whisk to stir together the egg whites, yogurt, celery seed and salt until well combined. Set the topping aside.

TO MAKE THE CHICKEN MIXTURE: Preheat the oven to 375°. Lightly spray a flat 2-quart casserole with no-stick spray. In the casserole, combine the chicken, broccoli, mushrooms and onions.

In a small bowl, stir together the condensed soup, milk, Worcestershire sauce and curry powder. Add the soup mixture to the chicken mixture. Toss until well coated and combined. Bake for 20 minutes. Remove the casserole from the oven and sprinkle with the cheese.

Separate the refrigerated dough into eight biscuits. Using a serrated knife, cut each biscuit into 2 layers. Arrange the biscuit halves, cut sides down, on top of the chicken mixture.

Spread the topping mixture on top of the biscuits. Return the casserole to the oven and bake for 20 to 25 minutes or until the biscuits are golden brown.

Makes 6 servings.

Note: If the whole-grain refrigerated biscuit dough is unavailable, use 1 (10-ounce) can refrigerated pizza dough. Unroll the pizza dough onto a piece of wax paper. Press and form the dough into a 7½" square. Using a sharp 2½" biscuit cutter, cut the dough into eight rounds. Then cut each round into 2 layers.

Easy Chili

Pictured on page 142

Simple, hearty and healthy! Calories, fat and cholesterol were reduced by:

• Replacing ground beef with a combination of ground turkey breast and additional beans

Nutrition Scorecard *(per serving)*		
	Before	After
Calories	386	282
Fat (g.)	16	3
% Calories from fat	38%	9%
Cholesterol (mg.)	66	17

8 ounces ground turkey breast
1 cup chopped onions
1 medium green pepper, chopped
2 cloves garlic, minced
3 (15-ounce) cans pinto beans, rinsed and drained
1 (16-ounce) can recipe-style stewed tomatoes (with juices)
1 cup salsa
1 tablespoon ground cumin
2 teaspoons chili powder
Fat-free sour cream or plain yogurt (optional)

Lightly spray an unheated large saucepan with no-stick spray. Add the turkey, onions, green peppers and garlic. Cook until the turkey is no longer pink, stirring occasionally.

Add the beans, tomatoes (with juices), salsa, cumin and chili powder. Bring to a boil, then reduce the heat. Cover and simmer for 20 minutes to blend the flavors. If desired, top with the sour cream or yogurt.

Makes 6 servings.

Turkey and Rice Bake

Here's an easy dish I make when I have leftover turkey from Thanksgiving. I just prepare a quick reduced-fat white sauce, add some cooked rice and within 45 minutes I've got a delicious casserole on the table. Calories, fat and cholesterol were reduced by:

• Removing the fat from the chicken broth

• Cooking the vegetables in chicken broth rather than sautéing them in margarine

• Using evaporated skim milk instead of heavy cream

• Reducing the amount of almonds

• Eliminating the step of sautéing the almonds in margarine

Nutrition Scorecard
(per serving)

	Before	After
Calories	445	235
Fat (g.)	25	5
% Calories from fat	51%	21%
Cholesterol (mg.)	76	50

1 (14-ounce) can chicken broth, defatted
1 cup finely chopped onions
½ cup finely shredded carrots
¼ cup finely shredded celery
2 tablespoons snipped fresh parsley
½ cup evaporated skim milk
3 tablespoons cornstarch
1 teaspoon dry mustard
¼ teaspoon ground white pepper
3 cups cooked and diced turkey breast
1½ cups cooked brown rice
3 tablespoons chopped blanched almonds

Preheat the oven to 350°. In a medium saucepan, combine the broth, onions, carrots, celery and parsley. Bring to a boil, then reduce the heat. Cover and simmer about 5 minutes or until the vegetables are tender.

In a small bowl, use a wire whisk to stir together the milk, cornstarch, dry mustard and pepper until smooth. Slowly stir the milk mixture into the broth mixture. Cook and stir over medium heat until the mixture comes to a boil. Reduce the heat. Cook and stir for 1 minute more.

Stir in the turkey and rice, then transfer the mixture to a 1½-quart casserole. Sprinkle with the almonds. Bake about 35 minutes or until heated through.

Makes 6 servings.

Italian Eggplant and Rice Bake

This meatless casserole is best during the summer months, when eggplants and tomatoes are at their peak. (But you can enjoy it throughout the year if you select fully ripe but firm produce at its prime.) I cut calories, fat and cholesterol by:

- Using no-stick olive oil spray instead of olive oil

- Reducing the amount of mozzarella cheese and using its reduced-fat alternate (less than 5 grams of fat per ounce of cheese)

- Reducing the amount of Parmesan cheese

Nutrition Scorecard
(per serving)

	Before	After
Calories	505	260
Fat (g.)	35	9
% Calories from fat	61%	30%
Cholesterol (mg.)	67	24

1 cup brown rice
½ cup chopped onions
2 cloves garlic, minced
3 cups chopped tomatoes
1 tablespoon sugar
2 teaspoons dried basil
½ teaspoon ground allspice
¼ teaspoon dried thyme
1 (12-ounce) eggplant (with peel), thinly sliced
1⅓ cups (about 5½ ounces) finely shredded reduced-fat mozzarella cheese
1⅓ cups finely shredded Parmesan cheese

Cook the rice according to the directions on the package. Set aside.

Meanwhile, lightly spray an unheated large skillet with olive oil no-stick spray. Add the onions and garlic. Cook and stir over medium heat until the onions are tender and translucent. Stir in the tomatoes, sugar, basil, allspice and thyme. Cover and gently simmer for 20 minutes.

Preheat the oven to 350°. Lightly spray an 8" × 8" × 2" baking pan with olive oil no-stick spray. Spoon just enough of the tomato mixture into the pan to thinly cover the bottom.

In the following order, layer half each of: the eggplant, tomato mixture, rice, mozzarella cheese and Parmesan cheese. Repeat the layers with the remaining eggplant, tomato mixture, rice, mozzarella cheese and Parmesan cheese. Bake for 20 to 25 minutes or until bubbly. Cut into squares to serve.

Makes 4 servings.

Turkey Sausage Spaghetti Pie

Spaghetti makes a wonderful reduced-fat crust for this pie. (This recipe is also a great way to use up leftover cooked spaghetti—just use 2¼ cups.) I cut calories, fat and cholesterol by:

- Eliminating butter in the spaghetti crust

- Using fat-free cottage cheese

- Replacing whole eggs with egg whites

- Replacing the Italian sausage with turkey sausage and reducing the total amount

- Using reduced-fat spaghetti sauce (less than 1 gram of fat per 4 ounces of sauce)

- Reducing the amount of mozzarella cheese and using its reduced-fat alternate (less than 5 grams of fat per ounce of cheese)

Nutrition Scorecard
(per serving)

	Before	After
Calories	536	312
Fat (g.)	30	9
% Calories from fat	51%	27%
Cholesterol (mg.)	182	33

SPAGHETTI CRUST
4 ounces spaghetti
2 egg whites, lightly beaten
⅓ cup grated Parmesan cheese

CHEESE FILLING
1 cup fat-free cottage cheese
2 egg whites, lightly beaten

SAUSAGE FILLING
4 ounces diced turkey sausage links or ground turkey sausage
½ cup chopped onions
⅓ cup chopped green peppers
¾ cup reduced-fat spaghetti sauce
½ cup (2 ounces) finely shredded reduced-fat mozzarella cheese

TO MAKE THE SPAGHETTI CRUST: Lightly spray a 9" pie plate with no-stick spray and set aside.

Cook the spaghetti according to the directions on the package. Drain and rinse with hot water. Transfer the hot spaghetti to a medium bowl. Stir in the 2 egg whites and Parmesan cheese. Press the pasta mixture evenly into the bottom and up the sides of the prepared pie plate.

TO MAKE THE CHEESE FILLING: Place the cottage cheese in a sieve. Using the back of a spoon, push the cottage cheese through the sieve into a small bowl. Stir in the 2 egg whites until well combined. Spread the cheese mixture in the bottom of the spaghetti crust and set aside.

TO MAKE THE SAUSAGE FILLING: Preheat the oven to 350°. Lightly spray an unheated large skillet with no-stick spray. Add the sausage, onions and green peppers. Cook and stir until the sausage is no longer pink and the vegetables are tender.

Stir in the spaghetti sauce. Cook until heated through, stirring occasionally. Spoon the sausage filling on top of the cheese filling. Bake for 20 minutes. Top with the mozzarella cheese and bake about 5 minutes more or until melted. Let stand for 5 minutes before serving.

Makes 4 servings.

Zucchini Cornbread Pie

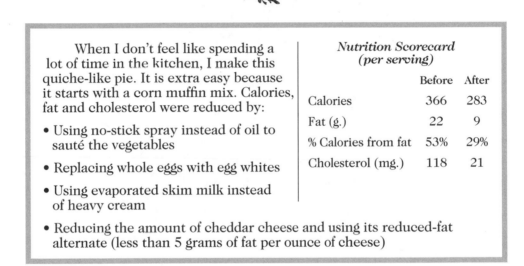

When I don't feel like spending a lot of time in the kitchen, I make this quiche-like pie. It is extra easy because it starts with a corn muffin mix. Calories, fat and cholesterol were reduced by:

- Using no-stick spray instead of oil to sauté the vegetables

- Replacing whole eggs with egg whites

- Using evaporated skim milk instead of heavy cream

- Reducing the amount of cheddar cheese and using its reduced-fat alternate (less than 5 grams of fat per ounce of cheese)

Nutrition Scorecard (per serving)

	Before	After
Calories	366	283
Fat (g.)	22	9
% Calories from fat	53%	29%
Cholesterol (mg.)	118	21

3 *zucchini, quartered and thinly sliced*
½ *cup chopped onions*
½ *cup evaporated skim milk*
3 *egg whites*
1 *(8½-ounce) package corn muffin mix*
¾ *cup (3 ounces) finely shredded reduced-fat sharp cheddar cheese*

Preheat the oven to 375°. Lightly spray an unheated large skillet with no-stick vegetable spray. Add the zucchini and onions. Cook and stir over medium-high heat until the zucchini is crisp-tender. Remove from the heat and set aside.

Lightly spray a 9" pie plate with no-stick spray.

In large bowl, beat together the milk and egg whites. Stir in the muffin mix just until combined. Then fold in the zucchini mixture and ½ cup of the cheese.

Transfer the mixture to the prepared pie plate. Sprinkle with the remaining cheese. Bake about 30 minutes until golden brown and a toothpick inserted in the center comes out clean.

Makes 6 servings.

Tamale Pie

This south-of-the-border meal uses both frozen and canned corn. Sometimes I use frozen corn in both the filling and the topping, but I make sure to cook it before blending it with the applesauce so I get the right texture. I reduced calories, fat and cholesterol by:

- Reducing the amount of ground beef and using a leaner variety (85% lean)

- Using no-stick spray instead of oil to sauté the vegetables

- Reducing the amount of olives

- Reducing the amount of cheddar cheese and using its reduced-fat alternate (less than 5 grams of fat per ounce of cheese)

- Replacing whole eggs with egg whites

- Using applesauce instead of oil in the topping

- Replacing canned cream-style corn with pureed corn

Nutrition Scorecard
(per serving)

	Before	After
Calories	732	458
Fat (g.)	43	15
% Calories from fat	51%	29%
Cholesterol (mg.)	161	48

FILLING
1½ cups chopped onions
  2 medium green peppers, chopped
  1 clove garlic, minced
12 ounces ground beef (85% lean)
  1 (10-ounce) package frozen corn
  1 (8-ounce) can tomato sauce
½ cup sliced, pitted ripe olives
  2 tablespoons tomato paste
  1 tablespoon cornmeal
  1 tablespoon ground cumin
  1 tablespoon Worcestershire sauce
1½ teaspoons chili powder
½ teaspoon ground allspice

   ¾ *cup all-purpose flour*
   ¾ *cup cornmeal*
   2 *teaspoons baking powder*
   1 *(8¾-ounce) can corn, drained, or 1 cup cooked corn*
   3 *tablespoons unsweetened applesauce*
   4 *egg whites*
   ½ *cup skim milk*
   ⅔ *cup finely shredded reduced-fat sharp cheddar cheese*
   2 *tablespoons canned diced green chili peppers*

TO MAKE THE FILLING: Lightly spray an unheated large skillet with no-stick spray. Add the onions, green peppers and garlic. Cook and stir over medium heat until tender.

Add the ground beef. Cook until browned, stirring occasionally. Stir in the corn, tomato sauce, olives, tomato paste, cornmeal, cumin, Worcestershire sauce, chili powder and allspice. Bring to a boil. Reduce the heat. Simmer, uncovered, for 30 minutes.

Lightly spray a 2½-quart casserole with no-stick spray. Transfer the meat mixture to the casserole and set aside. Preheat the oven to 375°.

TO MAKE THE TOPPING: In a medium bowl, stir together the flour, ¾ cup cornmeal and baking powder. Set the flour mixture aside.

In a blender or food processor, blend or process the canned or cooked corn and applesauce until the corn is pureed. Add the egg whites and milk. Blend or process until combined.

Add the corn mixture to the flour mixture. Stir just until combined. Fold in half of the cheese and all of the chili peppers.

Spread the topping over the filling. Sprinkle with the remaining cheese. Bake for 25 to 30 minutes or until golden brown. Let stand for 5 minutes before serving.

Makes 6 servings.

Wild Rice and Sausage Bake

For an easy yet elegant meal, serve this company-special casserole with a crispy romaine salad and crusty bread. Calories, fat and cholesterol were reduced by:

- Replacing heavy cream with evaporated skim milk

- Removing the fat from the chicken broth

- Replacing the pork sausage with turkey sausage and reducing the total amount

- Reducing the amount of cheddar cheese and using its reduced-fat alternate (less than 5 grams of fat per ounce of cheese)

Nutrition Scorecard
(per serving)

	Before	After
Calories	657	355
Fat (g.)	45	11
% Calories from fat	61%	27%
Cholesterol (mg.)	99	48

6 cups water
2 cups wild rice, rinsed and drained
12 ounces turkey sausage links or ground turkey sausage
1 cup chopped onions
12 ounces mushrooms, sliced
1 medium green pepper, chopped
½ cup evaporated skim milk
3 tablespoons cornstarch
2½ cups canned chicken broth, defatted
⅔ cup finely shredded reduced-fat sharp cheddar cheese
1 (2-ounce) jar chopped pimientos, drained
2 teaspoons dried thyme
2 teaspoons dried marjoram
⅛ teaspoon ground black pepper

In a large saucepan, bring the water and rice to a boil. Reduce the heat. Cover and simmer for 35 minutes. Drain and cover the rice to keep warm.

Meanwhile, preheat the oven to 350°. In a large skillet, cook the sausage until it is no longer pink. Drain and discard the fat and juices. Dice the sausage, if using links; break the sausage into large chunks, if using ground.

Spray the skillet with no-stick spray. Add the onions, mushrooms and green peppers. Cook and stir over medium heat until tender. Stir in the sausage and set aside.

In a medium saucepan, use a wire whisk to stir together the milk and cornstarch until smooth. Then stir in the chicken broth. Cook and stir over medium heat until the mixture comes to a boil. Reduce the heat. Cook and stir for 1 minute more.

Stir in the cheese, pimientos, thyme, marjoram and pepper. Cook and stir just until the cheese is melted. Then stir in the rice and sausage mixture.

Transfer the mixture to a 2-quart casserole. Cover and bake about 30 minutes or until bubbly.

Makes 6 servings.

Macaroni Chili

Pictured on page 143

Here's a well-loved skillet dinner that I trimmed down by using a leaner ground beef (85%) and reducing the amount of it. (And then draining off as much fat as possible after browning it.) To make this dish even lower in fat, you could use ground chicken or turkey breast in place of the beef. Just be sure to look at the label when selecting a ground poultry product. Some products contain skin and dark meat, making them higher in fat. Calories, fat and cholesterol were also reduced by:

Nutrition Scorecard (per serving)		
	Before	After
Calories	380	280
Fat (g.)	20	11
% Calories from fat	47%	33%
Cholesterol (mg.)	78	43

• Reducing the amount of cheddar cheese and using its reduced-fat alternate (less than 5 grams of fat per ounce of cheese)

    12 ounces ground beef (85% lean)
     ¾ cup chopped onions
      1 clove garlic, minced
      1 (15½-ounce) can red kidney beans, rinsed and drained
      1 (8-ounce) can tomato sauce
      1 (8-ounce) can stewed tomatoes (with juices), chopped
     ¾ cup macaroni
     ¼ cup water
      2 teaspoons chili powder
      1 teaspoon ground cumin
     ⅓ cup finely shredded reduced-fat sharp cheddar cheese

In a large skillet, cook the ground beef, onions and garlic until the beef is browned, stirring occasionally. Drain and discard the fat and juices.

Stir in the beans, tomato sauce, tomatoes (with juices), macaroni, water, chili powder and cumin. Bring to a boil, then reduce the heat. Cover and simmer for 10 minutes. Stir well, then cover and simmer about 10 minutes more or until the macaroni is tender but firm. Sprinkle with the cheese. Cover and heat over low heat just until the cheese is melted.

Makes 6 servings.

Easy Cheesy Chili Relleno Casserole

Often I'm asked to demonstrate my fat-cutting techniques on television. Here's a dish I show because it's simple to assemble and is always a big hit with my clients (not to mention my dinner guests). Calories, fat and cholesterol were reduced by:

- Replacing half-and-half with evaporated skim milk

- Replacing whole eggs with egg whites

- Using reduced-fat cheeses (less than 5 grams of fat per ounce of cheese)

Nutrition Scorecard
(per serving)

	Before	After
Calories	427	288
Fat (g.)	30	8
% Calories from fat	64%	25%
Cholesterol (mg.)	159	26

3 (4-ounce) cans whole green chili peppers, drained
1 cup evaporated skim milk
4 egg whites
⅓ cup all-purpose flour
2 cups (8 ounces) finely shredded reduced-fat Monterey Jack cheese
2 cups (8 ounces) finely shredded reduced-fat sharp cheddar cheese
1 (8-ounce) can tomato sauce

Preheat the oven to 350°. Lightly spray a 1½-quart casserole with no-stick spray and set aside.

Wearing disposable gloves or plastic bags over your hands, slit the chili peppers in half lengthwise. Remove and discard the seeds from the peppers. Rinse and drain the peppers on paper towels.

In a medium bowl, beat together the milk, egg whites and flour until smooth; set aside.

In another bowl, combine the Monterey Jack and cheddar cheeses. Set ½ cup of the cheese mixture aside for the topping.

To assemble the casserole, layer half each of the chili peppers, the cheese mixture and egg mixture. Repeat the layers with the remaining chili peppers, cheese mixture and egg mixture.

Pour the tomato sauce over the top, then bake for 30 minutes. Sprinkle with the reserved ½ cup cheese mixture and bake about 20 minutes more or until a knife inserted near the center comes out clean.

Makes 6 servings.

Healthy Homestyle Country Sausage (page 105)

Sunshine Halibut (page 108)

Pot-Roasted Beef Dinner (page 110)

Apple Stuffed Tenderloin with Cinnamon Raisin Sauce (page 112)

Chicken in a Packet (page 115)

Cheesy Chicken and Artichoke Bake (page 116)

Southwest Chicken Lasagna (page 120)

141

Easy Chili (page 125)

Macaroni Chili (page 133)

Homestyle Tuna Casserole (page 151)

Cream of Asparagus Soup (page 156)

Southwest Black Bean Soup (page 162)

Minestrone (page 166)

French Onion Soup (page 167)

New England Clam Chowder (page 169)

Beef Stroganoff (page 175)

Homestyle Tuna Casserole

Pictured on page 144

Remember Mom's tuna casserole? This version is just as satisfying, but it's made with today's health-conscious moms in mind. Calories and fat were reduced by:

• Using no-stick spray instead of butter to sauté the vegetables

• Using reduced-fat cream of mushroom soup

• Replacing whole milk with evaporated skim milk

• Using water-packed canned tuna instead of the oil-packed variety

• Using reduced-fat Parmesan cheese (3 grams of fat per ounce of cheese)

Nutrition Scorecard (per serving)	Before	After
Calories	404	263
Fat (g.)	20	2
% Calories from fat	44%	8%
Cholesterol (mg.)	36	39

1 *cup bow tie pasta or macaroni*
1 *cup chopped celery*
⅓ *cup chopped onions*
1 *(10¾-ounce) can 99%-fat-free condensed cream of mushroom soup with ⅓ less salt*
¾ *cup evaporated skim milk*
1 *(9¼-ounce) can water-packed tuna, drained*
¼ *cup drained and chopped pimientos*
2 *tablespoons grated reduced-fat Parmesan cheese*
Snipped fresh parsley

Cook the pasta according to the directions on the package. Drain and set aside.

Meanwhile, preheat the oven to 375°. Lightly spray an unheated medium saucepan with no-stick spray. Add the celery and onions. Cook and stir over medium heat until tender.

Stir in the condensed soup and milk. Then gently stir in the pasta, tuna and pimiento. Transfer the mixture to a 1½-quart casserole. Sprinkle with the Parmesan cheese. Bake for 25 to 30 minutes or until heated through. Sprinkle with the parsley to garnish.

Makes 4 servings.

Garden Frittata

Eggs can easily fit into a healthy diet as long as you attack their main culprit—cholesterol, which is found in the yolks only. In this egg dish, I used egg whites in place of whole eggs. I further reduced calories and fat by:

• Using no-stick spray instead of oil to sauté the vegetables

• Replacing whole milk with evaporated skim milk

Nutrition Scorecard (per serving)		
	Before	After
Calories	238	118
Fat (g.)	16	1
Calories from fat	58%	8%
Cholesterol (mg.)	322	2

12 egg whites
2 tablespoons evaporated skim milk
1 teaspoon dry mustard
1 teaspoon dried basil
¼ teaspoon salt
¼ teaspoon ground black pepper
1 cup peeled and diced potatoes
1 cup shredded zucchini
1 green pepper, cut into thin 1½" strips
1 sweet red pepper, cut into thin 1½" strips
1 cup sliced fresh mushrooms
½ cup chopped onions
2 tablespoons finely shredded Parmesan cheese

In a medium bowl, beat together the egg whites, milk, dry mustard, basil, salt and pepper until well combined. Set aside.

Preheat the broiler. Lightly spray a 10" ovenproof skillet with no-stick spray. Add the potatoes, zucchini, green and red peppers, mushrooms and onions. Cook and stir over medium heat for 7 to 10 minutes or until the vegetables are tender. Then evenly spread the vegetables in the skillet.

Pour the egg mixture over the vegetable mixture. Cook over medium heat. As the mixture sets, run a spatula around the edge of the skillet, slightly lifting the egg mixture to allow the uncooked portions to flow underneath. (Do not stir.) When eggs are almost set, cover and cook over low heat 8 to 10 minutes or until eggs are set.

If necessary, cover the handle of the skillet with a double thickness of heavy foil to protect it from the heat of the broiler.

Sprinkle the Parmesan cheese on top of the eggs. Broil the eggs about 3" from the heat for 3 to 5 minutes or until the top is lightly browned. Cut into wedges to serve.

Makes 4 servings.

Fiesta Cheese Strata

When I need a special brunch entrée or a quick breakfast for my family, I turn to this soufflé-like dish. I can assemble it the night before and just pop it into the oven in the morning. Calories, fat and cholesterol were reduced by:

- Eliminating the step of buttering the bread

- Reducing the amount of cheddar cheese and using its reduced-fat alternate (less than 5 grams of fat per ounce of cheese)

- Using egg whites instead of whole eggs

- Using evaporated skim milk instead of whole milk

Nutrition Scorecard
(per serving)

	Before	After
Calories	442	285
Fat (g.)	28	7
% Calories from fat	57%	23%
Cholesterol (mg.)	187	30

6 slices sourdough bread, crusts removed
2 cups (8 ounces) finely shredded reduced-fat sharp cheddar cheese
2 cups evaporated skim milk
6 egg whites
1 teaspoon dry mustard
¼ teaspoon salt
1 (4-ounce) can diced green chili peppers (with juices)

Lightly spray a 10" × 6" baking dish with no-stick spray. Cut the bread into ½" cubes.

Place half of the bread cubes in the baking dish, then top with half of the cheese. Repeat layers with the remaining bread and cheese.

In a medium bowl, beat together the milk, egg whites, dry mustard and salt until well combined. Stir in the chili peppers (with juices). Pour the milk mixture over the cheese and bread in the dish. Cover and refrigerate overnight.

Preheat the oven to 350°. Remove the cover from the strata and bake about 45 minutes or until puffy. Serve immediately.

Makes 6 servings.

HEARTWARMING SOUPS AND STEWS

Soups and stews are the ultimate comfort foods. Whether they're teamed with a sandwich, crusty bread or a salad, they're the foundation of soul-satisfying meals. And many of us instinctively turn to them when we want a really healthy lunch or dinner.

That's why it's so ironic that many traditional soups and stews are bursting with fat. Many start with a butter-and-flour roux or are "enriched" with heavy cream, egg yolks, butter or cheese just before being served. These fatty additions undermine the nutritional value of otherwise very healthy fare. Fortunately, there are many simple, basic methods for cutting the fat while keeping flavor and texture intact. And I use them liberally throughout this chapter.

One thing I always do is start with defatted broth or stock. It's quite easy. If you're using canned broth, simply spoon off the fat that's risen to the top. If you're making your own stock, cook and strain it as usual, then chill the stock until the fat that's risen to the top congeals. Remove it with a spoon or pour the liquid through a fine-mesh strainer.

Cream of Mushroom Soup

This soup is so creamy my taste testers couldn't believe there was no cream in it. I achieved that and also cut calories, fat and cholesterol by:

- Using white wine instead of butter to sauté the mushrooms and onions

- Removing the fat from the chicken broth

- Using evaporated skim milk instead of heavy cream

- Using a cornstarch-and-milk mixture instead of a flour-and-butter roux to thicken the soup

Nutrition Scorecard
(per serving)

	Before	After
Calories	293	111
Fat (g.)	26	1
% Calories from fat	78%	6%
Cholesterol (mg.)	90	3

1 pound sliced fresh mushrooms
½ cup chopped onions
2 tablespoons dry white wine or nonalcoholic white wine
1½ cups chicken broth, defatted
1 cup evaporated skim milk
2 tablespoons cornstarch

Lightly spray an unheated medium saucepan with no-stick spray. Add the mushrooms, onions and wine. Cook and stir over medium heat until tender.

Stir in the broth. Then transfer the mixture to a blender or food processor. Blend or process until smooth. Return the mixture to the saucepan and set aside.

In a custard cup, stir together ¼ cup of the milk and the cornstarch until smooth. Stir the cornstarch mixture into the mushroom mixture, then stir in the remaining ¾ cup milk. Cook and stir over medium heat until thickened and bubbly. Cook and stir for 2 minutes more.

Makes 4 side-dish servings.

Cream of Asparagus Soup

Pictured on page 145

In this soup, I use a fat-busting technique developed by Julia Child— rice is added to the soup and the mixture is then pureed to produce a creamy texture. Calories, fat and cholesterol were also reduced by:

- Using no-stick spray instead of butter to sauté the onions and celery

- Removing the fat from the chicken broth

- Using evaporated skim milk instead of whole milk

- Replacing sour cream with fat-free sour cream

Nutrition Scorecard
(per serving)

	Before	After
Calories	362	135
Fat (g.)	32	1
% Calories from fat	79%	3%
Cholesterol (mg.)	100	4

½ cup chopped onions
½ cup chopped celery
1 (10½-ounce) can chicken broth, defatted
¼ cup white rice
1 pound asparagus spears
2 cups evaporated skim milk
½ cup fat-free sour cream

Lightly spray an unheated large saucepan with no-stick spray. Add the onions and celery. Cook and stir over medium heat until the onions are tender.

Stir in the broth and rice. Bring to a boil. Reduce the heat. Cover and simmer about 20 minutes or until the rice is tender.

Meanwhile, in a large saucepan with a tight-fitting lid, bring 1" of water to a boil. Place the asparagus in a steamer basket and set the basket in the saucepan, making sure the basket sits above the water. Cover the saucepan and steam for 10 to 15 minutes or until tender.

Cut the tips from the asparagus and set aside. Chop the spears. Add the spears and ½ cup of the milk to the rice mixture. Bring to a boil. Reduce the heat and simmer for 5 minutes.

Transfer the asparagus-rice mixture to a blender or food processor. Blend or process until smooth. While the blender or food processor is still running, slowly pour in the remaining 1½ cups of milk. The final consistency should be smooth and slightly thickened.

Return the mixture to the saucepan. Heat the soup to a simmer. Remove from the heat and stir in the sour cream. Garnish each serving with the reserved asparagus tips. If desired, drizzle with additional fat-free sour cream slightly thinned with water.

Makes 5 side-dish servings.

Note: Sometimes fat-free plain yogurt is used to replace sour cream in recipes. I didn't use it here, however, because I found the yogurt to be too tart.

Creamy Celery Soup

This cream of celery soup is a taste winner and lower in fat and sodium than the canned variety. Serve it as a first course at dinner or with a tuna salad or chicken salad sandwich for a light lunch. I cut calories, fat and cholesterol by:

- Removing the fat from the chicken broth

- Using chicken broth instead of butter for cooking the celery

- Using evaporated skim milk instead of heavy cream

- Using a cornstarch-and-milk mixture to thicken the soup instead of a flour-and-butter roux

Nutrition Scorecard
(per serving)

	Before	After
Calories	184	116
Fat (g.)	14	1
% Calories from fat	67%	3%
Cholesterol (mg.)	41	4

5 *cups sliced celery*
3 *cups chicken broth, defatted*
2 *cups evaporated skim milk*
¼ *cup cornstarch*
½ *teaspoon dried basil*

In a large saucepan, combine the celery and 1 cup of the broth. Bring to a boil, then reduce the heat. Cover and simmer for 8 to 10 minutes or until tender, stirring occasionally.

Transfer the celery mixture to a blender or food processor. Blend or process until nearly smooth (the celery will be in tiny pieces).

In a custard cup, stir together ¼ cup of the milk and the cornstarch until smooth. Then stir the cornstarch mixture into the celery mixture. Add the remaining 1¾ cups milk and remaining 2 cups broth. Cook and stir until thickened and bubbly. Stir in the basil. Cook and stir for 2 minutes more.

Makes 6 side-dish servings.

Cream of Broccoli Soup

The percent of calories from fat plunged from 48 to 15 when I made just a few basic changes to this rich-tasting, creamy soup. Calories, fat and cholesterol were reduced by:

- Removing the fat from the chicken broth

- Using evaporated skim milk instead of heavy cream

- Using a cornstarch-and-milk mixture instead of a flour-and-butter roux to thicken the soup

Nutrition Scorecard
(per serving)

	Before	After
Calories	258	213
Fat (g.)	14	3
% Calories from fat	48%	15%
Cholesterol (mg.)	45	15

6 *cups broccoli florets*
3 *cups chicken broth, defatted*
2 *cups evaporated skim milk*
¼ *cup cornstarch*
½ *teaspoon dried thyme*

In a large saucepan, combine the broccoli and 1 cup of the broth. Bring to a boil. Reduce the heat. Cover and simmer for 8 to 10 minutes or until the broccoli is tender.

Transfer the broccoli mixture to a blender or food processor. Blend or process until nearly smooth (the broccoli will be in tiny pieces). Return the mixture to the saucepan and set aside.

In a custard cup, stir together ¼ cup of the milk and the cornstarch until smooth. Then stir the cornstarch mixture into the broccoli mixture. Add the remaining 1¾ cups milk and remaining 2 cups broth. Cook and stir until thickened and bubbly. Add the thyme. Cook and stir for 2 minutes more.

Makes 4 main-dish servings.

Less Sodium in Your Bowl

Soups are notoriously high in sodium. Canned varieties can easily cost you more than 800 milligrams a serving, putting a large dent in the 2,400 milligrams that some health experts recommend as a daily limit. And the plain canned broth that you might use to make your own soup also tends to be quite salty. Here are some ways to keep a lid on the sodium when preparing soup at home.

• Use reduced-sodium canned broths as the base for your soups. Or prepare homemade stock without adding any salt.

• Opt for fresh garlic instead of garlic salt. It's got superior flavor and is basically sodium free.

• Likewise, flavor your soup with fresh onions or onion powder instead of onion salt.

• Read food labels and compare the sodium levels of different products and different brands. Canned tomato products, for instance, are often very high in sodium; so look for the no-salt-added brands. Canned vegetables have more sodium than fresh or frozen ones.

• Choose reduced-sodium soy sauce instead of regular soy sauce.

• Use lots of herbs to flavor your soup. Experiment with different salt-free herb seasonings.

• Boost the flavor of your soup with some lemon zest, lemon juice, balsamic vinegar or another flavored vinegar.

• If you feel you must add some salt to your soup, use only half the amount called for in the recipe. You won't miss the extra.

Leek Vichyssoise

Potatoes and leeks are a classic combination. Here I blend them together for a thick and creamy soup. This soup is usually served chilled as a first course, but it's also delicious warm as an entrée. Calories, fat and cholesterol were reduced by:

- Using no-stick spray instead of butter to sauté the leeks

- Removing the fat from the chicken broth

- Using evaporated skim milk instead of heavy cream

Nutrition Scorecard
(per serving)

	Before	After
Calories	297	151
Fat (g.)	23	1
% Calories from fat	68%	2%
Cholesterol (mg.)	76	4

3 medium leeks (about 1 pound)
3 medium potatoes, peeled and diced
3 cups chicken broth, defatted
2 cups evaporated skim milk
¼ teaspoon ground white pepper

Cut and discard the roots and tough leaves from the leeks. Cut the leeks lengthwise in half and rinse under cold water to remove the dirt. Then cut the leeks crosswise into ¼"-thick slices (you should have 2 cups).

Lightly spray an unheated medium saucepan with no-stick spray. Heat the saucepan over medium heat. Add the leeks. Cook and stir for 5 minutes. Then add the potatoes and broth. Bring to a boil. Reduce the heat to low. Cover and simmer for 30 minutes.

Transfer the leek mixture to a blender or food processor. Blend or process until smooth. Stir in the milk and pepper. If desired, chill the soup before serving. Or, return the mixture to the saucepan. Cook over low heat just until heated through.

Makes 6 main-dish servings.

Cheesy Potato Soup

Cheddar cheese adds a unique flavor to this potato soup, which has become a favorite of mine. By using a combination of reduced-fat and fat-free cheeses, I get the melting advantages of the reduced-fat cheese and the fat savings of the fat-free variety. Calories, fat and cholesterol were reduced by:

- Removing the fat from the chicken broth

- Using evaporated skim milk instead of whole milk

- Using a combination of fat-free and reduced-fat (less than 5 grams of fat per ounce) cheddar cheeses

Nutrition Scorecard
(per serving)

	Before	After
Calories	258	213
Fat (g.)	14	3
% Calories from fat	48%	15%
Cholesterol (mg.)	45	15

1¾ cups chicken broth, defatted
1 cup peeled and diced potatoes
½ cup finely shredded carrots
¼ cup finely chopped onions
¼ cup finely chopped celery
1¾ cups evaporated skim milk
3 tablespoons cornstarch
½ cup (2 ounces) finely shredded fat-free cheddar cheese
½ cup (2 ounces) finely shredded reduced-fat sharp cheddar cheese

In a medium saucepan, combine the broth, potatoes, carrots, onions and celery. Bring to a boil, then reduce the heat. Cover and simmer about 10 minutes or until the vegetables are tender. Using the back of a fork, slightly mash the potatoes against the side of the saucepan.

In a custard cup, stir together ¼ cup of the milk and the cornstarch until smooth. Then stir the cornstarch mixture into the broth mixture. Add the remaining 1½ cups milk. Cook and stir until thickened and bubbly. Cook and stir for 1 minute more. Slowly stir in the cheeses. Cook and stir just until melted.

Makes 4 main-dish servings.

Southwest Black Bean Soup

Pictured on page 146

This rich and thick meatless soup is one of my favorites—it's both hearty and full of flavor. For a special treat and pretty presentation, I top it with sieved egg whites and thin lime slices. Calories, fat and cholesterol were reduced by:

- Removing the fat from the chicken broth

- Using dry sherry instead of oil to sauté the onions and garlic

- Replacing the flavor of ham hocks with liquid smoke

- Using hard-cooked egg whites instead of whole eggs

- Using reduced-fat Monterey Jack cheese (less than 5 grams of fat per ounce of cheese)

Nutrition Scorecard (per serving)

	Before	After
Calories	422	322
Fat (g.)	15	3
% Calories from fat	34%	7%
Cholesterol (mg.)	67	6

1 cup dried black beans, sorted and rinsed
5½ cups chicken broth, defatted
⅓ cup dry sherry or nonalcoholic red wine
1 cup chopped onions
4 cloves garlic, minced
1 carrot, coarsely chopped
2 stalks celery, coarsely chopped
1 bay leaf
1 tablespoon snipped fresh parsley
1–1¼ teaspoons ground cumin
½ teaspoon ground black pepper
¼ teaspoon liquid smoke
2 hard-cooked egg whites (discard yolks)
½ cup (2 ounces) shredded reduced-fat Monterey Jack cheese
Lime slices (optional)
Red chili peppers (optional)

In a large saucepan, combine the beans and broth. Bring to a boil, then reduce the heat. Cover and simmer for 30 to 40 minutes or until the beans are fork-tender.

Meanwhile, in a large skillet, combine the sherry or wine, onions and garlic. Cook and stir until the onions are tender.

Add the onion mixture to the beans. Then add the carrots, celery, bay leaf, parsley, cumin, pepper and liquid smoke. Bring to a boil, then reduce the heat. Cover and simmer for 20 to 30 minutes or until the vegetables are tender. Remove and discard the bay leaf.

Transfer half of the bean mixture to a blender or food processor. Blend or process until smooth. Return the mixture to the saucepan with the remaining bean mixture. Heat through.

To serve, press the egg whites through a sieve. Ladle the soup into individual bowls. Top with the egg whites and cheese. If desired, top with lime slices and chili peppers.

Makes 4 main-dish servings.

Split Pea Soup

I remember when my grandmother used to boil ham hocks to develop the flavor of pea soup. Today, I just use turkey ham along with a small amount of liquid smoke. It tastes just as good as Grandmother's but has a lot fewer calories, fat and cholesterol were also reduced by:

• Removing the fat from the chicken broth

Nutrition Scorecard *(per serving)*		
	Before	After
Calories	336	228
Fat (g.)	11	2
% Calories from fat	30%	6%
Cholesterol (mg.)	54	4

4 cups chicken broth, defatted
1 cup dried split peas, sorted and rinsed
½ cup chopped carrots
½ cup chopped onions
½ cup chopped celery
2 ounces turkey ham, finely chopped
¼ teaspoon dried marjoram
⅛ teaspoon liquid smoke
1 bay leaf

In a large saucepan, combine the broth and peas. Bring to a boil, then reduce the heat. Cover and simmer for 1 hour, stirring occasionally.

Add the carrots, onions, celery, turkey ham, marjoram, liquid smoke and bay leaf. Return to a boil, then reduce the heat. Cover and simmer for 30 minutes to blend the flavors. Remove and discard the bay leaf before serving.

Makes 4 main-dish servings.

Navy Bean Soup

On chilly days, I accompany this soup with warm crusty bread for a simple, tummy-warming meal. Calories, fat and cholesterol were reduced by:

- Removing the fat from the chicken broth

- Replacing ham hocks with turkey ham (and enhancing the flavor with liquid smoke)

Nutrition Scorecard
(per serving)

	Before	After
Calories	371	262
Fat (g.)	12	1
% Calories from fat	29%	5%
Cholesterol (mg.)	55	9

5½ cups chicken broth, defatted
1 cup dried small white beans, sorted and rinsed
1½ cups chopped celery
1 cup chopped onions
2 ounces turkey ham, finely chopped
¾ teaspoon dried thyme
¼ teaspoon ground black pepper
¼ teaspoon liquid smoke
1 bay leaf

In a large saucepan, combine the broth and beans. Bring to a boil, then reduce the heat. Cover and simmer about 1¼ hours or until the beans are tender.

Add the celery, onions, turkey ham, thyme, pepper, liquid smoke and bay leaf. Cover and simmer about 30 minutes or until the vegetables are tender. Remove and discard the bay leaf.

Transfer half of the soup to a blender or food processor. Blend or process until smooth. Return the mixture to the saucepan with the remaining bean mixture. Heat through.

Makes 4 main-dish servings.

Italian Bean and Pasta Soup

Chock-full of beans, pasta and veggies, this is a nourishing, well-seasoned soup. Calories and fat were reduced by:

- Using olive oil no-stick spray instead of olive oil to sauté the vegetables

- Removing the fat from the chicken broth

Nutrition Scorecard
(per serving)

	Before	After
Calories	318	230
Fat (g.)	12	1
% Calories from fat	32%	4%
Cholesterol (mg.)	10	10

1 cup chopped onions
1 cup coarsely chopped carrots
1 stalk celery, chopped
3 cloves garlic, minced
7 cups chicken broth, defatted
1 cup dried white beans, sorted and rinsed
1 cup canned recipe-style stewed tomatoes (with juices)
1 teaspoon dried rosemary
1 teaspoon dried basil
¼ teaspoon crushed red pepper
¼ teaspoon dried sage
1 cup tiny shell pasta

Lightly spray an unheated large saucepan with olive oil no-stick spray. Heat the saucepan over medium heat. Add the onions, carrots, celery and garlic. Cook and stir over medium heat until the onions are tender.

Add the broth, beans, tomatoes (with juices), rosemary, basil, red pepper and sage. Bring to a boil, then reduce the heat. Cover and simmer, stirring occasionally, for 1 to 1½ hours or until the beans are tender.

Transfer about half of the bean mixture to a blender or food processor. Blend or process until smooth. Return the mixture to the saucepan with the remaining bean mixture.

Stir in the pasta. Bring to a boil, then reduce the heat. Cover and simmer about 7 minutes until the pasta is tender but firm.

Makes 6 main-dish servings.

Minestrone

Pictured on page 147

So full of beans, pasta and veggies—this Italian soup is a complete meal in a bowl. I like to use spaghettini (thin spaghetti) as the pasta in this soup, but almost any pasta will do. Calories, fat and cholesterol were reduced by:

- Using olive oil no-stick spray instead of a combination of olive oil and bacon drippings to sauté the vegetables

- Replacing the bacon with turkey bacon and reducing the total amount

- Eliminating the Italian pork sausage

Nutrition Scorecard
(per serving)

	Before	After
Calories	280	131
Fat (g.)	16	2
% Calories from fat	50%	15%
Cholesterol (mg.)	37	5

> 1 cup chopped onions
> ¼ cup chopped celery
> 3 slices turkey bacon, chopped
> 1 clove garlic, minced
> 3 cups water
> 1 (14-ounce) can stewed tomatoes (with juices), chopped
> ½ cup canned chick-peas (garbanzo beans) or small white beans, rinsed and drained
> ½ cup finely shredded cabbage
> ½ cup coarsely chopped carrots
> 2 tablespoons minced fresh parsley
> ½ teaspoon dried basil
> ½ teaspoon dried oregano
> ¼ cup broken spaghettini

Lightly spray an unheated medium saucepan with olive oil no-stick spray. Add the onions, celery, bacon and garlic. Cook and stir over medium heat until the onions and celery are tender.

Add the water, tomatoes (with juices), chick-peas, cabbage, carrots, parsley, basil and oregano. Bring to a boil, then reduce the heat. Cover and simmer for 20 to 30 minutes or until the cabbage and carrots are tender.

Add the spaghettini. Return to a boil, then reduce the heat. Cover and simmer about 10 minutes or until the spaghettini is tender but firm.

Makes 6 main-dish servings.

French Onion Soup

Pictured on page 148

This lightened version of the classic soup became a favorite with my taste testers. For a delicious light meal or lunch, serve it with a tossed spinach or Caesar salad. Calories, fat and cholesterol were reduced by:

- Using sherry instead of butter to sauté the onions

- Removing the fat from the beef broth

- Using reduced-fat cheese (4 grams of fat per ounce of cheese)

Nutrition Scorecard
(per serving)

	Before	After
Calories	314	231
Fat (g.)	16	6
% Calories from fat	46%	21%
Cholesterol (mg.)	42	11

2 cups thinly sliced onions
2 tablespoons dry sherry, dry wine or nonalcoholic wine
4 cups beef broth, defatted
1 teaspoon Worcestershire sauce
8 slices baguette or 4 slices French bread, toasted
4 ounces reduced-fat Jarlsberg cheese, cut into 4 slices, or
1 cup (4 ounces) finely shredded reduced-fat Swiss cheese
Sliced green onion tops (optional)

In a large saucepan, combine the onions and sherry or wine. Cook and stir until the onions are tender.

Add the broth and Worcestershire sauce. Bring to a boil, then reduce the heat. Cover and simmer for 10 minutes to blend the flavors.

Meanwhile, place the bread slices on a cookie sheet. If necessary, cut the cheese slices in half to fit the bread. Place the cheese on top of the bread. Broil just until the cheese melts.

To serve, ladle the soup into bowls and float the bread on top of each. If desired, sprinkle with the green onion tops.

Makes 4 main-dish servings.

Corn Chowder

Here's a Southwestern-style corn chowder that's virtually fat-free. Enjoy this soup as it is or stir in chopped cooked chicken breast for a low-fat chicken-corn chowder. Calories, fat and cholesterol were reduced by:

- Removing the fat from the chicken broth

- Using no-stick spray instead of butter to sauté the vegetables

- Using evaporated skim milk instead of heavy cream

- Using a cornstarch-and-milk mixture to thicken the chowder instead of a flour-and-butter roux

Nutrition Scorecard
(per serving)

	Before	After
Calories	325	216
Fat (g.)	23	1
% Calories from fat	61%	2%
Cholesterol (mg.)	68	5

1¾ cups frozen whole kernel corn, thawed
¾ cup chicken broth, defatted
1 small potato (4 ounces), peeled and diced
1 stalk celery, chopped
½ green pepper or sweet red pepper, finely chopped
¼ cup chopped onions
2 cups evaporated skim milk
2 tablespoons cornstarch

In a blender or food processor, blend or process ½ cup of the corn and ¼ cup of the broth until smooth. Set the corn mixture aside.

Lightly spray an unheated medium saucepan with no-stick spray. Add the potatoes, celery, green peppers and onions. Cook and stir over medium heat until the onions are tender.

Stir in the remaining ½ cup broth. Bring to a boil. Reduce the heat. Cover and simmer about 10 minutes or until the potatoes are tender. Using the back of a fork, slightly mash the potatoes against the side of the saucepan.

In a custard cup, stir together 2 tablespoons of the milk and the cornstarch until smooth. Then stir the cornstarch mixture into the corn mixture. Add the remaining milk and the remaining 1¼ cups corn. Cook and stir until bubbly and thickened. Cook and stir for 2 minutes more.

Makes 4 side-dish servings.

New England Clam Chowder

Pictured on page 149

Here's a regional favorite made healthy. I used canned rather than shucked clams because they're easy to have on hand. I cut back on calories, fat and cholesterol by:

- Using evaporated skim milk instead of heavy cream

- Replacing whole milk with 1% milk

- Replacing the flavor of bacon with liquid smoke

Nutrition Scorecard (per serving)	Before	After
Calories	322	259
Fat (g.)	14	2
% Calories from fat	39%	8%
Cholesterol (mg.)	74	40

2 (6½-ounce) cans minced clams (with juices)
2½ cups peeled and finely chopped potatoes
1 cup chopped onions
1 teaspoon instant chicken bouillon granules
1 teaspoon Worcestershire sauce
¼ teaspoon dried thyme
⅛ teaspoon ground black pepper
1½ cups 1% milk
3 tablespoons cornstarch
1½ cups evaporated skim milk
¼ teaspoon liquid smoke
Crushed pink peppercorns (optional)
Snipped fresh thyme (optional)

Drain the clams, reserving the juices. If necessary, add enough water to the clam juice to make 1 cup.

In a medium saucepan, combine the juice mixture, potatoes, onions, bouillon granules, Worcestershire sauce, thyme and black pepper. Bring to a boil, then reduce the heat. Cover and simmer about 5 minutes or until the potatoes are tender. Using the back of a fork, slightly mash the potatoes against the side of the saucepan.

In a small bowl, stir together the 1% milk and cornstarch. Add the cornstarch mixture, evaporated skim milk and liquid smoke to the potato mixture. Cook and stir until slightly thickened and bubbly. Stir in the clams. Return to a boil, then reduce the heat. Cook for 1 minute, stirring frequently. If desired, garnish with the peppercorns and thyme.

Makes 4 main-dish servings.

Old-Fashioned Beef Stew

Pictured on the cover

With just a few simple changes, I dramatically reduced the calories and fat in this classic stew. You can easily adapt my techniques to your own favorite stew recipe. Calories, fat and cholesterol were reduced by:

- Reducing the amount of beef stew meat and replacing the remainder with a leaner cut of beef

- Using no-stick spray instead of oil to brown the beef

- Removing the fat from the beef broth

- Using evaporated skim milk instead of heavy cream

Nutrition Scorecard
(per serving)

	Before	After
Calories	687	315
Fat (g.)	39	9
% Calories from fat	52%	24%
Cholesterol (mg.)	201	82

12 ounces boneless beef round roast, cut into bite-size pieces
½ cup chopped onions
1 green pepper, chopped
2 cloves garlic, minced
2 medium potatoes, peeled and diced
4 medium carrots, sliced
1 (14-ounce) can beef broth, defatted
¼ cup evaporated skim milk
1 teaspoon paprika
2 tablespoons cornstarch
2 tablespoons dry sherry or dry red wine or
  nonalcoholic red wine

Spray an unheated large skillet with no-stick spray. Heat the skillet over medium-high heat. Add the beef, onions, green peppers and garlic. Cook and stir until the beef is browned.

Stir in the potatoes, carrots and broth. Bring to a boil, then reduce the heat. Cover and simmer about 30 minutes or until the meat is nearly tender. (Do not boil.)

Stir in the milk and paprika. In a custard cup, stir together the cornstarch and sherry or wine until smooth. Then stir the cornstarch mixture into the beef mixture. Cook until slightly thickened and bubbly. Cook and stir for 2 minutes more.

Makes 4 main-dish servings.

Country Chicken Gumbo

By eliminating the traditional flour-and-oil roux and using no-stick spray instead of oil to cook the flour, I was able to slash the fat in this Louisiana favorite. But I retained the good down-home taste. Calories and fat were also reduced by:

• Removing the fat from the chicken broth

Nutrition Scorecard (per serving)		
	Before	After
Calories	293	161
Fat (g.)	16	1
% Calories from fat	48%	6%
Cholesterol (mg.)	35	35

⅓ cup all-purpose flour
3 cups chicken broth, defatted
2 skinless, boneless chicken breast halves (8 ounces total), diced
1 (10-ounce) package frozen cut okra, thawed
½ cup chopped onions
⅓ cup chopped celery
4 cloves garlic, minced
¼ teaspoon ground black pepper
¼ teaspoon ground red pepper
2 bay leaves
2 cups hot cooked rice (optional)

Lightly spray an unheated large skillet with no-stick spray. Heat the skillet over medium heat. Add the flour. Cook and stir until the flour turns reddish brown.

Slowly stir in the broth. Then add the chicken, okra, onions, celery, garlic, black and red peppers and bay leaves. Bring to a boil, then reduce the heat. Cover and simmer for 20 to 30 minutes or until the chicken is tender and no longer pink. Remove and discard the bay leaves. If desired, serve the gumbo over the rice.

Makes 4 main-dish servings.

Lentil Stew with Turkey Sausage

Lentils and turkey sausage make a really delicious stew that's very low in fat. Calories, fat and cholesterol were reduced by:

- Using no-stick spray instead of oil to brown the sausage and sauté the onions

- Replacing pork sausage with a combination of turkey sausage and spinach

Nutrition Scorecard
(per serving)

	Before	After
Calories	486	271
Fat (g.)	23	3
% Calories from fat	43%	11%
Cholesterol (mg.)	39	20

1 medium onion, chopped
4 ounces smoked turkey sausage, chopped
2 cloves garlic, minced
4 cups chicken broth, defatted
1 cup lentils, sorted and rinsed
1 cup chopped canned stewed tomatoes (with juices)
1 tablespoon Worcestershire sauce
¼ teaspoon dried oregano
¼ teaspoon ground black pepper
⅛ teaspoon ground cumin
1 bay leaf
1 medium carrot, sliced
1 stalk celery, chopped
1 cup spinach, chopped

Lightly spray an unheated large saucepan with no-stick spray. Add the onions, sausage and garlic. Cook over medium heat until the sausage is browned, stirring occasionally.

Stir in the broth, lentils, tomatoes (with juices), Worcestershire sauce, oregano, pepper, cumin and bay leaf. Bring to a boil, then reduce the heat. Cover and simmer for 15 minutes.

Add the carrots, celery and spinach. Return to a boil, then reduce the heat. Cover and simmer about 20 minutes or until the lentils and vegetables are tender. Remove and discard the bay leaf before serving.

Makes 4 main-dish servings.

THE POWER OF PASTA

Pasta is low in fat and high in hunger-appeasing complex carbohydrates. And it comes in countless varieties, so you can enjoy a different pasta every night. No wonder this glorious food has risen in popularity among those committed to healthy eating.

There's just one trap to avoid when eating pasta, and it's a big one. Too many people sabotage pasta's health benefits by ladling on a fatty sauce. Sometimes it's easy to recognize a fatty sauce. Fettuccine Alfredo, for instance, usually comes with a creamy cheese sauce that just screams "calories." But even a tomato or vegetable sauce can contain lots of fat without looking like it does.

The main culprit in many sauces is oil. Even olive oil, which contains heart-healthy monounsaturated fat, is still 100 percent fat and quickly piles on the fat calories. Other fatty additions, such as cheese, excess butter, sausage and pine nuts, contribute their unfair share of fat to the equation. Fortunately, there are ways to minimize the fat in delicious sauces without sacrificing their unique flavor. In this chapter, I'll show you how it's done.

Turkey Tetrazzini

When I was growing up, my mother reserved this rich, creamy pasta dish for special occasions. But over the years, I've significantly lightened it and turned it into anytime fare. I reduced calories, fat and cholesterol by:

- Using a cornstarch-and-sherry mixture to thicken the sauce instead of a flour-and-butter roux

- Using chicken broth instead of butter to cook the mushrooms

- Replacing heavy cream with evaporated skim milk

- Removing the fat from the chicken broth

Nutrition Scorecard
(per serving)

	Before	After
Calories	524	315
Fat (g.)	30	4
% Calories from fat	53%	11%
Cholesterol (mg.)	128	44

8 ounces spaghetti
1 (14½-ounce) can chicken broth, defatted
8 ounces sliced fresh mushrooms
1 cup evaporated skim milk
3 tablespoons cornstarch
3 tablespoons dry sherry, dry white wine or nonalcoholic white wine
¼ teaspoon salt
¼ teaspoon ground black pepper
2½ cups cooked chopped turkey breast
3 tablespoons grated Parmesan cheese

Cook the pasta according to the directions on the package. Drain and set aside.

Meanwhile, preheat the oven to 375°. Bring the broth to a boil in a medium saucepan. Add the mushrooms. Simmer, uncovered, about 4 minutes or until tender.

Stir the milk into the mushroom mixture. In a custard cup stir together the cornstarch and sherry or wine until smooth. Stir the cornstarch mixture into the mushroom mixture. Bring to a boil over medium heat, stirring constantly. Cook and stir for 1 minute more.

Remove the saucepan from heat. Stir in the salt and pepper. Then stir in the turkey. Add the pasta and toss until well coated.

Transfer the pasta mixture to a shallow 3-quart casserole or a 13" × 9" × 2" baking dish. Sprinkle with the Parmesan cheese. Bake for 20 to 30 minutes or until golden brown and bubbly.

Makes 6 servings.

Beef Stroganoff

Pictured on page 150

Here's one of the recipes my readers loved from my column "Recipe Makeovers" in *Shape* magazine. This dish shows how well fat-free plain yogurt substitutes for sour cream without changing the flavor of the dish. Calories, fat and cholesterol were also reduced by:

- Reducing the amount of beef

- Using no-stick spray instead of oil to brown the meat

- Replacing canned cream of mushroom soup with a combination of evaporated skim milk, cornstarch and instant onion-mushroom soup

Nutrition Scorecard
(per serving)

	Before	After
Calories	599	398
Fat (g.)	34	9
% Calories from fat	57%	20%
Cholesterol (mg.)	112	69

Sauce
- 1 cup evaporated skim milk
- 1 tablespoon cornstarch
- 1 envelope instant onion-mushroom soup dip mix

Beef Mixture
- 12 ounces beef sirloin steak, trimmed of all visible fat and cut into thin bite-size strips
- ½ medium onion, sliced and separated into rings
- 1 clove garlic, minced
- 1½ cups sliced fresh mushrooms
- 1 (8-ounce) container fat-free plain yogurt
- 2 cups hot cooked noodles
- Fresh parsley (optional)

To make the sauce: In a medium saucepan, use a wire whisk to stir together the milk and cornstarch until smooth. Then stir in the soup mix. Bring to a boil over medium heat, stirring constantly. Remove from the heat. Cover to keep warm.

To make the beef mixture: Lightly spray an unheated large skillet with no-stick spray. Add the beef, onions and garlic. Cook and stir over medium-high heat for 2 minutes. Add the mushrooms. Cook and stir about 1 minute more or until the onions and mushrooms are tender. Reduce the heat to low.

Stir the sauce mixture into the beef mixture. Then stir in the yogurt. Cook and stir just until heated through. (Do not overheat because the yogurt will curdle.) Serve over the hot noodles. If desired, top with the parsley to garnish.

Makes 4 servings.

Spaghetti with Spicy Italian Meat Sauce

Pictured on page 215

Here's an old-fashioned, slow-cooking spaghetti sauce that's well worth the wait as it simmers. It's great to make on a weekend, when you have more time to cook, or to put in a crockpot in the morning before you go to work. Calories, fat and cholesterol were reduced by:

• Using olive oil no-stick spray instead of olive oil to sauté the vegetables

• Replacing Italian pork sausage with turkey sausage

• Replacing the ground beef with ground turkey breast and reducing the total amount

Nutrition Scorecard
(per serving)

	Before	After
Calories	626	371
Fat (g.)	30	7
% Calories from fat	43%	17%
Cholesterol (mg.)	95	42

¾ cup sliced fresh mushrooms
½ cup chopped onions
½ cup chopped celery
½ cup chopped green peppers
2 tablespoons snipped fresh parsley
2 cloves garlic, minced
8 ounces ground turkey sausage
8 ounces ground turkey breast (see note)
1 (28-ounce) can tomatoes (with juices), cut up
1 (8-ounce) can tomato sauce
1 (6-ounce) can tomato paste
1½ teaspoons dried basil
½ teaspoon salt
½ teaspoon dried oregano
¼ teaspoon paprika
¼ teaspoon crushed red pepper
⅛ teaspoon ground red pepper
1 bay leaf
12 ounces spaghetti
Parmesan cheese (optional)

Lightly spray a 4-quart saucepan or Dutch oven with olive oil no-stick spray. Add the mushrooms, onions, celery, green peppers, parsley and garlic. Cook and stir about 5 minutes over medium heat or until the vegetables are tender.

Add the turkey sausage and turkey breast. Cook about 5 minutes or until no longer pink, stirring occasionally. If desired, sprinkle with Parmesan cheese.

Stir in the tomatoes (with juices), tomato sauce, tomato paste, basil, salt, oregano, paprika, crushed and ground red peppers and bay leaf. Bring to a gentle boil. Reduce the heat to low. Cover and gently simmer for 1½ hours.

Before serving, cook the pasta according to the directions on the package and drain. Remove and discard the bay leaf from the meat mixture. Serve the meat mixture on top of the spaghetti.

Makes 6 servings.

Note: To make sure you're buying the leanest ground turkey available, check the label. Look for products made with only turkey breast meat. Many ground turkey products contain the dark meat and the fatty skin.

Fettuccine Alfredo

The hallmark of this classic dish is its rich sauce of butter, fresh Parmesan cheese and heavy cream. Here's a much lighter version that preserves its distinctive characteristics—and gives you only a third of the fat. Calories, fat and cholesterol were reduced by:

- Replacing heavy cream with a combination of evaporated skim milk and half-and-half

- Reducing the amount of butter

Nutrition Scorecard (per serving)		
	Before	After
Calories	644	397
Fat (g.)	44	13
% Calories from fat	62%	30%
Cholesterol (mg.)	139	35

  12 *ounces fettuccine*
    1 *cup evaporated skim milk*
  ½ *cup half-and-half*
    2 *tablespoons butter, cut into small pieces*
1½ *cups grated fresh Parmesan cheese*
    2 *tablespoons snipped fresh chives*

Cook the pasta according to the directions on the package.

Meanwhile, in a medium saucepan, heat the milk, half-and-half and butter over medium heat just until the butter is melted and the mixture is hot.

Gradually stir in 1¼ cups of the Parmesan cheese. Cook and stir just until the cheese has melted. Drain the pasta and add the hot pasta to the cheese mixture. Toss until well coated.

To serve, transfer the pasta to plates. Sprinkle with the remaining ¼ cup of Parmesan cheese and the chives to garnish.

Makes 6 servings.

Creamy Seafood Linguine

You'll receive rave reviews when you serve this creamy seafood dish. To dress up the meal, I serve it with steamed fresh asparagus or a tossed romaine salad and French bread. Calories, fat and cholesterol were reduced by:

- Using olive oil no-stick spray and a reduced amount of olive oil to sauté the onions and garlic

- Using evaporated skim milk instead of heavy cream

Nutrition Scorecard
(per serving)

	Before	After
Calories	642	425
Fat (g.)	35	6
% Calories from fat	49%	13%
Cholesterol (mg.)	186	107

8 ounces linguine
1 tablespoon olive oil
½ cup finely chopped onions
5 cloves garlic, minced
3 tablespoons dry white wine or nonalcoholic white wine
1 tablespoon cornstarch
1 cup evaporated skim milk
½ teaspoon ground coriander
8 ounces large shrimp, peeled and deveined
8 ounces bay scallops
3 tablespoons snipped fresh parsley
½ teaspoon salt
⅛ teaspoon ground black pepper

Cook the pasta according to the directions on the package. Drain and set aside. If necessary, cover to keep warm.

Meanwhile, lightly spray an unheated large skillet with olive oil no-stick spray. Add the oil and heat over medium-high heat. Add the onions and garlic. Cook and stir about 5 minutes or until the onions are golden brown.

In a small custard cup, stir together the wine and cornstarch until smooth. Stir the wine mixture and milk into the onion mixture.

Bring the mixture to a simmer over medium heat, stirring constantly. Reduce the heat. Stir in the coriander and cook for 1 minute. Then add the shrimp and scallops. Return to a simmer. Simmer, uncovered, for 3 to 5 minutes or until the shrimp turn pink and the scallops are opaque.

Stir in the parsley, salt and pepper. Serve on top of the hot pasta.

Makes 4 servings.

Linguine with Clam Sauce

Just keep a few cans of clams on hand in your cupboard and you'll have what it takes to prepare a healthful, savory main dish on a moment's notice. Calories, fat and cholesterol were reduced by:

- Reducing the amount of olive oil

- Using olive oil no-stick spray instead of butter to sauté the garlic

- Eliminating the butter from the clam sauce

Nutrition Scorecard (per serving)

	Before	After
Calories	632	440
Fat (g.)	29	7
% Calories from fat	42%	14%
Cholesterol (mg.)	99	76

8 ounces linguine
1 tablespoon olive oil
6 large cloves garlic, minced
3 (10-ounce) cans whole baby clams (with juices)
⅓ cup dry white wine or nonalcoholic white wine
⅓ cup chicken broth, defatted
1 large carrot, shredded
½ teaspoon dried oregano
½ cup snipped and loosely packed fresh Italian parsley
½ teaspoon salt
⅛ teaspoon ground black pepper

Cook the pasta according to the directions on the package. Drain and set aside. If necessary, cover to keep warm.

Meanwhile, lightly spray an unheated large skillet with olive oil no-stick spray. Add the oil and heat over medium heat. Add the garlic. Cook and stir for 1 minute.

Drain the clams, reserving the juices. Set the clams aside. Add the juices, wine, broth, carrots and oregano to the skillet. Bring to a boil over high heat. Boil about 15 minutes or until the mixture reduces to about 1⅓ cups.

Stir in the clams and all but 1 tablespoon of the parsley. Simmer about 1 minute or just until heated through. Then stir in the salt and pepper.

To serve, transfer the hot pasta to a large bowl. Pour the clam sauce over the pasta and gently toss until well combined. Sprinkle with the remaining 1 tablespoon parsley to garnish.

Makes 4 servings.

Spaghetti with Red Sauce
and Fresh Mushrooms

For the best tasting sauce, I always try to purchase the freshest mushrooms. When selecting mushrooms, look for those with caps that are white or creamy and closed around the stem (or only moderately open with light tan gills). Calories and fat were reduced by:

• Using olive oil no-stick spray and a reduced amount of olive oil to sauté the onions and garlic

• Reducing the amount of sugar

Nutrition Scorecard *(per serving)*	Before	After
Calories	365	302
Fat (g.)	11	4
% Calories from fat	26%	12%
Cholesterol (mg.)	0	0

1 *tablespoon olive oil*
½ *cup chopped onions*
2 *cloves garlic, minced*
2 *pounds mushrooms*
1 *(16-ounce) can tomatoes (with juices), crushed*
1 *tablespoon tomato paste*
1 *tablespoon snipped fresh basil*
1 *tablespoon snipped fresh parsley*
1 *teaspoon sugar*
1 *teaspoon dried oregano*
½ *teaspoon dried thyme*
½ *teaspoon salt*
12 *ounces spaghetti*

Lightly spray an unheated large skillet with olive oil no-stick spray. Add the oil and heat over medium heat. Add the onions and garlic. Cook and stir about 3 minutes or until tender.

Meanwhile, coarsely chop 1 pound of the mushrooms and slice the remaining mushrooms.

Add the chopped and sliced mushrooms to the onion mixture. Cook and stir for 15 to 20 minutes or until their liquid evaporates and they begin to brown.

Stir in the tomatoes (with juices), tomato paste, basil, parsley, sugar, oregano, thyme and salt. Bring to a gentle boil. Reduce the heat. Simmer, uncovered, for 10 to 15 minutes or until the sauce is slightly thickened.

Meanwhile, cook the pasta according to the directions on the package and drain. Serve the sauce on top of the hot pasta.

Makes 6 servings.

Pasta Primavera

Pictured on page 216

Here's a dish that's colorful, tasty and hearty. My family likes the vegetable combination of broccoli, zucchini, carrots and sweet red peppers. But any fresh spring or summer vegetable would be delightful in this dish. Calories and fat were reduced by:

- Using olive oil no-stick spray and a reduced amount of olive oil to sauté the onions and garlic

- Reducing the amount of olive oil and replacing most of it with white wine

Nutrition Scorecard (per serving)

	Before	After
Calories	508	297
Fat (g.)	30	6
% Calories from fat	53%	17%
Cholesterol (mg.)	5	5

12 ounces linguine or spaghetti
1 tablespoon olive oil
3 cloves garlic, minced
1½ cups small broccoli florets
1½ cups zucchini julienne strips
1 cup carrot julienne strips
1 sweet red pepper, cut into thin 1" long strips
¼ cup dry white wine or nonalcoholic white wine
1 teaspoon dried thyme
¼ teaspoon ground black pepper
½ cup finely shredded fresh Parmesan cheese (optional)
¼ cup snipped and loosely packed fresh Italian parsley (optional)

Cook the pasta according to the directions on the package. Drain and set aside. If necessary, cover to keep warm.

Meanwhile, lightly spray an unheated large skillet with olive oil no-stick spray. Add the oil and heat over medium-high heat. Add the garlic. Cook and stir for 30 seconds. Then add the broccoli, zucchini, carrots and red peppers. Cook and stir for 3 to 5 minutes or until crisp-tender.

Stir in the wine, thyme and pepper. Reduce the heat to medium. Cover and cook for 1 minute more.

Transfer the vegetable mixture to a large bowl. Add the hot pasta. If desired, sprinkle with the Parmesan cheese and parsley. Gently toss until well mixed. Serve immediately.

Makes 6 servings.

Angel Hair Pasta with Fresh Tomato and Basil Sauce

When my family craves pasta with a fresh tomato sauce, I quickly pull out this recipe because it's so easy to make. I always use plum—sometimes called Roma or Italian—tomatoes because they're meaty, juicy and rich in flavor. And if I don't have time to peel the tomatoes, that's okay. The sauce just has bits of skin in it. Calories and fat were reduced by:

- Using olive oil no-stick spray and a reduced amount of olive oil to sauté the garlic and tomatoes

Nutrition Scorecard
(per serving)

	Before	After
Calories	475	384
Fat (g.)	16	6
% Calories from fat	29%	13%
Cholesterol (mg.)	0	0

1½ pounds plum tomatoes
12 ounces angel hair pasta
1 tablespoon olive oil
2 cloves garlic, minced
¼ cup loosely packed fresh basil, snipped
½ teaspoon salt
½ teaspoon sugar (optional)

To prepare the tomatoes, bring water to a boil in a large saucepan. Carefully immerse the tomatoes into the boiling water for 30 to 45 seconds. Drain the tomatoes in a colander. Then immediately immerse the tomatoes into a bowl of cold water.

Using a sharp knife, pull the skin off of the tomatoes. Cut each tomato in half and use your fingers or a spoon to remove the seeds. Discard the seeds and coarsely chop the pulp. Set the tomato pulp (with juices) aside.

Cook the pasta according to the directions on the package. Drain and set aside. If necessary, cover to keep warm.

Meanwhile, lightly spray an unheated large skillet with olive oil no-stick spray. Add the oil and heat over medium heat. Add the garlic. Cook and stir for 1 minute. Then add the tomato pulp (with juices). Cook, uncovered, over medium-high heat about 5 minutes or until slightly thickened.

Stir in the basil and salt. If necessary, adjust flavor with the sugar. Bring the sauce to a gentle boil. Reduce heat. Simmer, uncovered, for 1 minute. Serve on top of the hot pasta.

Makes 4 servings.

Angel Hair Pasta with Italian Spinach

This was one of my first recipe makeovers. Over the years, it has become one of my family's favorites for a quick meal. Calories, fat and cholesterol were reduced by:

- Using olive oil no-stick spray and a reduced amount of olive oil to sauté the garlic and spinach

- Using fat-free cottage cheese

Nutrition Scorecard (per serving)	Before	After
Calories	520	412
Fat (g.)	23	10
% Calories from fat	38%	22%
Cholesterol (mg.)	125	118

1 (9-ounce) package fresh angel hair pasta
1 tablespoon olive oil
2 cloves garlic, minced
1 (10-ounce) package frozen chopped spinach, thawed and well drained
1 cup fat-free cottage cheese
½ cup grated Parmesan cheese

Cook the pasta according to the directions on the package. Drain and set aside. If necessary, cover to keep warm.

Meanwhile, lightly spray an unheated large skillet with olive oil no-stick spray. Add the oil and heat over medium heat. Add the garlic. Cook and stir for 30 seconds.

Add the spinach. Cook and stir for 2 minutes. Then stir in the cottage cheese and Parmesan cheese. Cook and stir until the Parmesan cheese melts. Add the hot pasta. Gently toss until well combined.

Makes 4 servings.

Green and White Lasagna Bundles

Pictured on page 217

Broccoli and cheese are snugged together in these easy-to-assemble lasagna roll-ups. For a change of pace, I sometimes substitute frozen chopped spinach for the broccoli. Calories, fat and cholesterol were reduced by:

- Using olive oil no-stick spray instead of olive oil to cook the broccoli and chives

- Using egg whites instead of a whole egg

- Using reduced-fat ricotta cheese (1 gram of fat per ounce of cheese)

- Using reduced-fat spaghetti sauce (less than 1 gram of fat per 4 ounces of sauce)

- Reducing the amount of mozzarella cheese and using its reduced-fat alternate (less than 5 grams of fat per ounce of cheese)

Nutrition Scorecard
(per 2 roll-ups)

	Before	After
Calories	634	427
Fat (g.)	31	9
% Calories from fat	44%	18%
Cholesterol (mg.)	133	39

    8 *lasagna noodles*
    2 *egg whites, lightly beaten*
    1 *(15-ounce) container reduced-fat ricotta cheese (see note)*
    ¼ *cup grated Parmesan cheese*
    ½ *teaspoon salt*
    1 *(10-ounce) package frozen chopped broccoli, thawed and drained*
    ¼ *cup snipped fresh chives*
    1½ *cups reduced-fat spaghetti sauce*
    ½ *cup (2 ounces) finely shredded reduced-fat mozzarella cheese*
       Snipped fresh chives (optional)

Cook the lasagna noodles according to the directions on the package. Drain and set aside.

Meanwhile, in a large bowl, stir together the egg whites, ricotta cheese, Parmesan cheese and salt. Set the cheese mixture aside.

Lightly spray an unheated large skillet with olive oil no-stick spray. Add the broccoli and chives. Cook and stir over medium heat for 5 minutes. Add the broccoli mixture to the cheese mixture. Stir until well combined.

Preheat the oven to 350°. Spread a thin layer of the spaghetti sauce in the bottom of a 12" × 7½" × 2" baking dish.

To assemble, place one noodle on a piece of wax paper. Then place ¼ cup of the broccoli mixture in a mound ¼" from a short end. Roll the noodle around the broccoli mixture. Place the roll-up, seam side down, in the baking dish. Repeat making roll-ups with the remaining noodles and broccoli mixture.

Pour the remaining spaghetti sauce over the roll-ups in the baking dish. Sprinkle the mozzarella cheese on top and cover with foil. Bake for 35 to 45 minutes until bubbly. If desired, garnish with the chives.

Makes 8 roll-ups; 4 servings.

Note: Use reduced-fat rather than fat-free ricotta cheese, because the fat-free cheese becomes too runny when heated.

Tomato Mac 'n' Cheese

Pictured on page 218

Here is my favorite way of making macaroni and cheese—I just layer the ingredients in a casserole. It's much quicker and easier than preparing a cheese sauce. I slashed calories, fat and cholesterol by:

- Replacing the typical cheese sauce with a reduced-fat tomato-based sauce

- Using reduced-fat cheddar cheese (less than 5 grams of fat per ounce of cheese)

Nutrition Scorecard
(per serving)

	Before	After
Calories	555	327
Fat (g.)	33	11
% Calories from fat	53%	29%
Cholesterol (mg.)	104	41

    2   cups macaroni
    1   (16-ounce) can tomato sauce
    3   tablespoons chopped onions
    2½ cups (10 ounces) finely shredded reduced-fat
        sharp cheddar cheese
        Tomato slices (optional)
        Cracked pepper (optional)

Cook the macaroni according to the directions on the package. Drain and set aside.

Meanwhile, preheat the oven to 350°. In a medium bowl, stir together the tomato sauce and onions.

Lightly spray a 2-quart casserole with no-stick spray. Spread a thin layer of the tomato sauce mixture in the bottom of the casserole. Place one-third of the macaroni in the dish. Top with one-third of the remaining sauce mixture and one-third of the cheese. Repeat layering remaining macaroni, sauce mixture and cheese two more times. Bake for 30 to 35 minutes or until bubbly and heated through. If desired, garnish with the tomatoes and cracked pepper.

Makes 6 servings.

Easy Cheesy Lasagna

This tasty lasagna has a two-for-one advantage: It's easy to assemble, and it's a whole lot leaner than its traditional counterpart. I reduced calories, fat and cholesterol by:

- Replacing the fatty sausage with chopped vegetables

- Using olive oil no-stick spray instead of olive oil to sauté the vegetables

- Using egg whites instead of a whole egg

- Using reduced-fat mozzarella and ricotta cheeses (3 grams of fat per ounce of mozzarella; 1 gram of fat per ounce of ricotta cheese)

- Using reduced-fat spaghetti sauce (less than 1 gram of fat per 4 ounces of sauce)

Nutrition Scorecard
(per serving)

	Before	After
Calories	586	321
Fat (g.)	33	9
% Calories from fat	515	27%
Cholesterol (mg.)	120	39

½ *cup chopped onions*
½ *cup coarsely chopped carrots*
1 *sweet red pepper, chopped*
2 *cloves garlic, minced*
1½ *cups reduced-fat spaghetti sauce*
1 *(8-ounce) can stewed tomatoes (with juices)*
½ *teaspoon dried basil*
½ *teaspoon dried oregano*
6 *lasagna noodles*
2 *egg whites*
1 *(15-ounce) container reduced-fat ricotta cheese (see note)*
½ *cup grated Parmesan cheese*
2 *cups (8 ounces) finely shredded reduced-fat mozzarella cheese*

Lightly spray an unheated large skillet or saucepan with olive oil no-stick spray. Add the onions, carrots, red peppers and garlic. Cook and stir over medium heat for 5 minutes.

Stir in the spaghetti sauce, stewed tomatoes (with juices), basil and oregano. Bring to a boil, then reduce the heat. Simmer, uncovered, about 15 minutes or until the vegetables are tender.

Meanwhile, cook the lasagna noodles according to the directions on the package. Drain and set aside.

In a medium bowl, stir together the egg whites, ricotta cheese and ¼ cup of the Parmesan cheese until well combined.

Preheat the oven to 375°. To assemble, spread a thin layer of the spaghetti sauce mixture in the bottom of a 12" × 7½" × 2" baking dish. Place three of the noodles in a single layer in the dish. Spread with half of the cheese mixture. Top with half of the remaining sauce. Sprinkle half of the mozzarella cheese. Repeat layers using the remaining noodles, cheese mixture, sauce and mozzarella cheese. Sprinkle the remaining ¼ cup of Parmesan cheese on top. Bake for 30 to 35 minutes. Let stand for 10 minutes before cutting and serving.

Makes 6 servings.

Note: Use reduced-fat rather than fat-free ricotta cheese, because the fat-free cheese becomes too runny when heated.

Be Eggs-tra Safe!

By following a few simple precautions, you can protect yourself from salmonella, the food-poison bacteria that may be present in raw or undercooked eggs. To avoid it, always:

- Avoid tasting foods that contain raw eggs, like cookie doughs and batters.

- Use a pasteurized egg substitute in recipes that traditionally use uncooked eggs, such as mayonnaise and Caesar dressing.

- Use an egg separator when separating the yolks from the whites. That will prevent any bacteria that might be present on the shell from contaminating the yolk or white.

- Fully cook foods that contain eggs. Salmonella is killed at a temperature of 160°. If you're making fried or poached eggs, it means the yolks will be firm.

- Do not wash eggs prior to storage, because that will remove their protective coating.

- Buy eggs that are refrigerated. Store raw eggs in their original carton in a colder section of the refrigerator, not on the door.

- Store hard-cooked eggs in the refrigerator for no longer than one week

My Favorite Manicotti

These reduced-fat manicotti are one of my dinner choices when my schedule is busy. I can stuff the shells and assemble the dish ahead of time, then just pop it into the oven just before serving. Calories, fat and cholesterol were reduced by:

- Using egg whites instead of a whole egg

- Using reduced-fat ricotta cheese (1 gram of fat per ounce of cheese)

- Reducing the amount of mozzarella cheese and using its reduced-fat alternate (3 grams of fat per ounce of cheese)

- Using reduced-fat spaghetti sauce (less than 1 gram of fat per 4 ounces of sauce)

Nutrition Scorecard
(per 2 manicotti)

	Before	After
Calories	661	479
Fat (g.)	30	11
% Calories from fat	41%	22%
Cholesterol (mg.)	127	44

10 *manicotti shells*
2 *cups reduced-fat spaghetti sauce*
2 *lightly beaten egg whites*
1 *(15-ounce) container reduced-fat ricotta cheese (see note)*
1 *tablespoon snipped fresh parsley*
¼ *teaspoon salt*
¼ *teaspoon ground black pepper*
⅛ *teaspoon ground nutmeg*
1¾ *cups (7 ounces) finely shredded reduced-fat mozzarella cheese*
½ *cup grated Parmesan cheese*

Cook the manicotti shells according to the directions on the package. (Do not overcook the shells.) Drain, rinse with cold water and drain again. Arrange the shells in a single layer and set aside.

Spread ½ cup of the spaghetti sauce evenly in bottom of a 13" × 9" × 2" baking dish or pan. Set the baking dish aside.

For the filling, in a large bowl, stir together the egg whites, ricotta cheese, parsley, salt, pepper and nutmeg until well combined. Stir in 1¼ cup of the mozzarella cheese and ¼ cup of the Parmesan cheese.

Preheat the oven to 350°. To assemble, spoon the cheese mixture into manicotti shells and place the filled shells in a single layer in the baking dish. Spread the remaining 1½ cups of spaghetti sauce on top. Sprinkle with the remaining ½ cup of mozzarella cheese and ¼ cup of Parmesan cheese. Bake about 35 minutes or until bubbly.

Makes 10 manicotti; 5 servings.

Note: Use reduced-fat rather than fat-free ricotta cheese because the fat-free cheese becomes too runny when heated.

Old-Fashioned Macaroni and Cheese

Now you can enjoy this ultimate comfort food with less than half the fat of its original counterpart. Calories, fat and cholesterol were reduced by:

- Using no-stick spray instead of butter to sauté the onions

- Replacing whole milk with a combination of regular skim milk and evaporated skim milk

- Using a cornstarch-and-milk mixture instead of a flour-and-butter roux to thicken the sauce

- Reducing the amount of cheddar cheese and using its reduced-fat alternate (less than 5 grams of fat per ounce of cheese)

Nutrition Scorecard
(per serving)

	Before	After
Calories	555	393
Fat (g.)	33	13
% Calories from fat	53%	28%
Cholesterol (mg.)	104	50

2 cups macaroni
⅓ cup chopped onions
1½ cups skim milk
1 tablespoon cornstarch
1 cup evaporated skim milk
Dash of ground white or black pepper
3½ cups (14 ounces) finely shredded reduced-fat sharp cheddar cheese

Cook the macaroni according to the directions on the package. Drain and set aside.

Meanwhile, lightly spray a 2-quart casserole with no-stick spray and set aside.

Preheat the oven to 350°. Lightly spray a large saucepan with no-stick spray. Add the onions. Cook and stir over medium heat about 3 minutes or until tender.

In a custard cup, stir together 2 tablespoons of the skim milk and the cornstarch until smooth. Stir the remaining skim milk, evaporated milk, pepper and cornstarch mixture into the onions. Cook and stir over medium heat until thick and bubbly. Cook and stir for 1 minute more. Remove the saucepan from the heat. Slowly stir in the cheese until melted.

Stir the macaroni into the cheese sauce. Transfer the mixture to the prepared casserole. Bake for 25 to 30 minutes or until bubbly. Let stand for 10 minutes before serving.

Makes 6 servings.

Romanoff Bow Ties

Although egg noodles are fairly low in fat, they still contain much more fat than other types of dried pasta. So I replaced them in this dish with bow tie noodles (but almost any pasta will do). Calories, fat and cholesterol were reduced by:

- Replacing egg noodles with bowtie pasta

- Using fat-free cottage cheese

- Replacing sour cream with fat-free plain yogurt

- Using no-stick spray instead of butter to sauté the onions

- Replacing whole milk with a combination of regular skim milk and evaporated skim milk

- Using reduced-fat cheddar cheese (less than 5 grams of fat per ounce of cheese)

Nutrition Scorecard
(per serving)

	Before	After
Calories	388	245
Fat (g.)	20	2
% Calories from fat	46%	7%
Cholesterol (mg.)	92	7

8 ounces bow tie pasta
1 cup fat-free cottage cheese
1 cup fat-free plain yogurt
¼ cup chopped onions
½ cup skim milk
1 tablespoon cornstarch
½ cup evaporated skim milk
½ teaspoon dry mustard
½ teaspoon Worcestershire sauce
Dash of ground red pepper
Dash of hot-pepper sauce
¼ cup (1 ounce) finely shredded reduced-fat sharp cheddar cheese
3 tablespoons fine dry seasoned bread crumbs

Cook the pasta according to the directions on the package. Drain and set aside.

Meanwhile, lightly spray a 2-quart casserole with no-stick spray and set aside. Press the cottage cheese through a strainer or sieve into a large bowl. Add the yogurt and stir until well combined. Set the yogurt mixture aside.

Preheat the oven to 350°. Lightly spray a medium saucepan with no-stick spray. Add the onions. Cook and stir over medium heat about 3 minutes or until tender.

In a custard cup, stir together 2 tablespoons of the skim milk and the cornstarch until smooth. Stir the remaining skim milk, evaporated milk and cornstarch mixture into the onions. Cook and stir over medium heat until thickened and bubbly. Then stir in the dry mustard, Worcestershire sauce, red pepper and hot-pepper sauce. Cook and stir for 1 minute more.

Stir in the cheddar cheese and cook until melted. Slowly stir the cheese mixture into the yogurt mixture. Fold in the pasta. Transfer to the prepared casserole. Sprinkle the bread crumbs on top. Bake about 15 minutes or until bubbly.

Makes 6 servings.

Three-Pepper Pesto Pasta

This is a fancier version of the Reduced-Fat Pesto Pasta on page 192, adding a sautéed pepper-and-onion sauce to that recipe. The topping is also wonderful on plain pasta, grilled chicken breasts or poached fish. Calories and fat were reduced by:

• Using no-stick olive oil spray instead of olive oil to sauté the peppers

• Using reduced-fat pesto

Nutrition Scorecard (per serving)	Before	After
Calories	490	350
Fat (g.)	27	11
% Calories from fat	48%	28%
Cholesterol (mg.)	5	5

> 1 *large sweet red pepper, coarsely chopped*
> 1 *large yellow pepper, coarsely chopped*
> 1 *large green pepper, coarsely chopped*
> ⅓ *cup chopped onions*
> 2 *cloves garlic, minced*
> 1 *cup drained and chopped canned Italian-style plum tomatoes*
> *Reduced-Fat Pesto Pasta (page 192)*

Spray an unheated large skillet with olive oil no-stick spray. Add the red, yellow and green peppers. Stir in the onions and garlic. Cook over medium heat about 6 minutes or until tender.

Stir in the tomatoes. Cover and simmer for 7 minutes.

To serve, divide the Reduced-Fat Pesto Pasta among six dinner plates. Spoon the pepper topping over each serving.

Makes 6 servings.

Reduced-Fat Pesto Pasta

If you thought great-tasting pesto had to be full of fat, have I got a surprise for you: a flavorful pesto with only half the usual amount of fat! I cut calories and fat by:

- Reducing the amount of olive oil and replacing most of it with chicken broth

- Reducing the amount of pine nuts and toasting them to enhance their flavor

Nutrition Scorecard (per serving)		
	Before	After
Calories	422	322
Fat (g.)	22	11
% Calories from fat	46%	31%
Cholesterol (mg.)	5	5

12 ounces angel hair pasta, vermicelli or spaghettini
3 tablespoons pine nuts
½ cup fresh basil (leaves only)
2 cloves garlic, minced
2 tablespoons olive oil
⅓ cup chicken broth, defatted
½ cup grated Parmesan cheese

Cook the pasta according to the directions on the package. Drain and set aside. If necessary, cover to keep warm.

Meanwhile, preheat the oven to 400°. Place the pine nuts on a cookie sheet. Bake for 2 to 3 minutes or until lightly golden. (Watch carefully to prevent overtoasting.)

Transfer the pine nuts to a blender or food processor. Add the basil and garlic. Blend or process until finely chopped. With the machine running, slowly add the olive oil in a thin stream. Then slowly pour in the chicken broth and gradually add the Parmesan cheese until paste forms.

Add the pesto to the hot pasta. Toss until well coated.

Makes 6 servings.

Greek Penne

Pictured on page 219

Here's an easy dish I always get compliments on. The feta cheese and pine nuts give this pasta its Greek nature. And because feta's strong flavor goes a long way, I find I can reduce the amount and extend its flavor by mixing in fat-free cottage cheese. Calories, fat and cholesterol were also reduced by:

- Reducing the amount of olive oil

- Eliminating tossing the pasta with butter

- Reducing the amount of pine nuts and toasting them to enhance their flavor

Nutrition Scorecard (per serving)		
	Before	After
Calories	646	365
Fat (g.)	41	12
% Calories from fat	55%	28%
Cholesterol (mg.)	55	17

12 ounces penne
5 teaspoons olive oil
2 tablespoons pine nuts
5 cloves garlic, minced
1 (10-ounce) package frozen chopped spinach, thawed and well-drained
4 large plum tomatoes, chopped (about 8 ounces)
½ cup fat-free cottage cheese
4 ounces feta cheese
½ teaspoon salt
⅛ teaspoon ground black pepper

Cook the pasta according to the directions on the package. Drain and set aside. If necessary, cover to keep warm.

Meanwhile, spray an unheated large skillet with olive oil no-stick spray. Add 3 teaspoons of the oil. Heat the oil over medium heat. Add the pine nuts and garlic. Cook and stir about 5 minutes or until the pine nuts are lightly golden. Then stir in the spinach and tomatoes and cook about 3 minutes or until heated through, stirring occasionally.

Meanwhile, press the cottage cheese through a strainer or sieve into a small bowl. Add the feta cheese. Using a pastry blender, combine the cheeses.

To serve, place half of the hot pasta in a bowl. Drizzle with 1 teaspoon of the remaining olive oil. Gently toss until coated. Add the remaining pasta, drizzle with the remaining 1 teaspoon of oil and gently toss. Then add the spinach mixture and toss. Finally add the feta mixture, salt and pepper. Toss until well combined.

Makes 6 servings.

Cheese Ravioli
with Rosemary and Lemon

Pictured on page 220

Here's a savory cheese sauce that doesn't require any cooking—the creamy mixture is heated by the hot ravioli. Calories, fat and cholesterol were reduced by:

• Replacing the heavy cream with a combination of pureed fat-free cottage cheese and evaporated skim milk

Nutrition Scorecard *(per serving)*		
	Before	After
Calories	466	321
Fat (g.)	30	8
% Calories from fat	59%	23%
Cholesterol (mg.)	154	75

    1 (16-ounce) package cheese ravioli
    1 cup fat-free cottage cheese
    ½ cup evaporated skim milk
    1 teaspoon dried rosemary
    ¼ teaspoon salt
    ¼ teaspoon ground black pepper
    2 teaspoons fresh lemon juice
    ¼ cup finely shredded fresh Parmesan cheese
    3 tablespoons snipped fresh chives
    1 teaspoon finely shredded lemon peel
       Lemon wedges (optional)

Cook the pasta according to the directions on the package. Drain and set aside. If necessary, cover to keep warm.

Meanwhile, in a blender or food processor, blend or process the cottage cheese, milk, rosemary, salt and pepper until smooth. Set the cottage cheese mixture aside.

Drain the ravioli and transfer it to a bowl. Drizzle the lemon juice over the hot ravioli and gently toss. Then pour the cottage cheese mixture on top and gently toss until coated.

To serve, transfer the ravioli to plates. In a custard cup, combine the Parmesan cheese, chives and lemon peel. Sprinkle the mixture on top of each serving. If desired, serve with lemon wedges.

Makes 4 servings.

ENTRÉES FROM AROUND THE WORLD

Italian, Mexican and Chinese are a few of the most popular ethnic cuisines in America. Their pasta entrées, tortilla dishes and stir-fries make frequent, much-appreciated appearances on our tables. Unfortunately, these foods are not always as healthy as we give them credit for being.

Sure, Italian dishes are most often centered around pasta, a filling, reduced-fat carbohydrate that nutritionists laud. But what often tops the pasta is a sauce full of oil, cheese, cream or meat. And need I mention the sour cream, guacamole and shredded cheese that seems to accompany most Mexican dishes? Then there are the stir-fries brimming with lightly cooked vegetables and served over another excellent complex carbohydrate, rice. Yet, too many stir-fries drown their healthy ingredients in a sea of oil.

To lighten up these three cuisines—and other ethnic favorites—I did what comes naturally. I simply switched to reduced-fat ingredients and used healthier cooking techniques. What shines through is the flavor that has made each of these cuisines an all-American favorite.

Chicken Cacciatore

Pictured on page 221

The original version of this dish just screamed "fat"! The main culprit: browning the chicken in oil. So I drastically reduced the amount of oil and supplemented it with no-stick spray. The result: a low-calorie, reduced-fat entrée that's indistinguishable from its fatty former self. I also cut calories, fat and cholesterol by:

- Using skinless chicken breasts instead of chicken pieces with the skin on

Nutrition Scorecard
(per serving)

	Before	After
Calories	503	133
Fat (g.)	32	2
% Calories from fat	59%	13%
Cholesterol (mg.)	187	44

4 (4-ounce) skinless, boneless chicken breast halves
½ teaspoon salt
¼ teaspoon ground black pepper
1 teaspoon olive oil
1 cup finely chopped onions
1 large green pepper, chopped
4 cloves garlic, minced
½ cup dry red wine or nonalcoholic red wine
1 (14-ounce) can peeled Italian tomatoes, drained and chopped
1 teaspoon dried oregano
½ teaspoon dried basil
2 tablespoons snipped fresh parsley (optional)

Season the chicken with the salt and pepper. Lightly spray a large skillet with olive oil no-stick spray. Add the oil and heat the skillet over medium heat. Add the chicken and cook about 4 minutes on each side or until browned.

Add the onions and green peppers to the skillet. Cook and stir about 2 minutes or until softened. Add the garlic. Cook and stir about 30 seconds.

Stir in the wine, tomatoes, oregano and basil. Bring to a boil, then reduce the heat to medium-low. Cover and simmer for 30 minutes. If desired, sprinkle with parsley just before serving.

Makes 4 servings.

Chicken Tostadas

Pictured on page 222

Serving this make-your-own meal lets your family members or guests customize their entrées. Simply put the toppings in separate dishes and let people help themselves. I reduced calories, fat and cholesterol by:

• Baking the tortillas instead of frying them

• Using fat-free refried beans

• Using reduced-fat cheddar cheese (less than 5 grams of fat per ounce of cheese)

Nutrition Scorecard (per serving)

	Before	After
Calories	350	196
Fat (g.)	20	6
% Calories from fat	51%	25%
Cholesterol (mg.)	43	27

    3 cups water
    ¼ medium onion, coarsely chopped
    ¼ teaspoon salt
    2 bay leaves
    1 pound skinless, boneless chicken breasts
   12 corn tortillas
    2 cups canned fat-free refried beans
    3 cups shredded lettuce
    ½ cup finely chopped onions
    2 tomatoes, chopped
    1 medium avocado, halved, seeded, peeled and sliced
    ¾ cup (3 ounces) finely shredded reduced-fat cheddar cheese
    1 cup salsa

Preheat the oven to 400°. In a medium saucepan, combine the water, coarsely chopped onions, salt and bay leaves. Bring to a boil, then add the chicken. Reduce the heat to medium. Cover and simmer for 10 to 15 minutes or until the chicken is no longer pink and is very tender. Remove the chicken from the saucepan. Using two forks, shred it into small pieces.

Meanwhile, spray two cookie sheets with no-stick spray. Place the tortillas on the cookie sheets in a single layer. Lightly spray the tortillas with the no-stick spray. Bake for 5 minutes. Turn the tortillas over and bake for 3 to 4 minutes more or until golden brown. Transfer the tortillas to a wire cooling rack.

To assemble the tostadas, spread about 2 tablespoons of the beans on each tortilla. Then top each with the chicken, lettuce, finely chopped onions, tomatoes, avocado and cheese. Drizzle each with the salsa.

Makes 12 tostadas; 6 servings.

Szechuan Chicken

Garlicky chili paste and hoisin sauce add a delightful spicy flavor to the chicken in this dish. Look for these ingredients in the ethnic section of your supermarket or in a food-specialty store. Calories, fat and cholesterol were reduced by:

• Removing the fat from the chicken broth

• Using no-stick spray for stir-frying rather than oil

• Replacing some of the chicken with additional vegetables

Nutrition Scorecard
(per serving)

	Before	After
Calories	347	195
Fat (g.)	13	2
% Calories from fat	34%	8%
Cholesterol (mg.)	98	65

1 pound skinless, boneless chicken breasts
1 egg white, lightly beaten
1½ tablespoons cornstarch
¼ teaspoon salt
¼ cup chicken broth, defatted
2 tablespoons hoisin sauce
1 tablespoon reduced-sodium soy sauce
1 tablespoon dry sherry or nonalcoholic wine
1 tablespoon chili paste with garlic
2 cloves garlic, minced
½ teaspoon grated ginger root
1 large sweet red pepper, cut into thin strips
1 large green pepper, cut into thin strips
½ cup fresh chives cut into ½" pieces
½ cup coarsely chopped fresh bean sprouts
⅓ cup finely sliced fresh or canned bamboo shoots
4 ounces fresh mushrooms, sliced

Cut the chicken into very thin strips. In a medium bowl, stir together the egg white, cornstarch and salt. Add the chicken and toss until well coated. Set the chicken aside.

In a small bowl, stir together the broth, hoisin sauce, soy sauce, sherry or wine, chili paste, garlic and ginger. Set the broth mixture aside.

Spray an unheated wok or large skillet with no-stick spray. Heat over medium-high heat. Add the chicken mixture and stir-fry about 3 minutes or until no longer pink. Remove the chicken and set aside.

Add the red and green peppers, chives, bean sprouts, bamboo shoots and mushrooms. Stir-fry for 2 minutes. Return the chicken to the wok or skillet. Then add the broth mixture. Cook and stir for 1 to 2 minutes.

Makes 4 servings.

Chicken Parmigiana

This is a quick-and-easy dish to fix during the week when you don't have a lot of time to cook. While the chicken is baking, I toss a salad and slice some whole wheat sourdough bread for a healthy, hearty supper that's on the table within 30 minutes. Calories, fat and cholesterol were reduced by:

Nutrition Scorecard (per serving)		
	Before	After
Calories	529	291
Fat (g.)	23	5
% Calories from fat	39%	16%
Cholesterol (mg.)	147	76

- Using reduced-fat spaghetti sauce (less than 1 gram of fat per 4 ounces of sauce)

- Using egg whites instead of a whole egg

- Using olive oil no-stick spray instead of olive oil to brown the chicken

- Reducing the amount of mozzarella cheese and using its reduced-fat alternate (less than 5 grams of fat per ounce of cheese)

- Reducing the amount of Parmesan cheese

1¾ cups reduced-fat spaghetti sauce
½ cup fine dry bread crumbs
2 egg whites, lightly beaten
4 skinless, boneless chicken breast halves (1 pound total)
⅓ cup finely shredded reduced-fat mozzarella cheese
2 tablespoons grated Parmesan cheese

Preheat the oven to 350°. Place ¾ cup of the spaghetti sauce in a 12" × 7½" × 2" baking dish. Set the baking dish aside.

Place the bread crumbs in a shallow dish. Place the egg whites in another shallow dish. Dip the chicken in the egg whites, then roll it in the bread crumbs to coat.

Lightly spray an unheated large skillet with olive oil no-stick spray. Heat the skillet over medium heat. Add the chicken and cook about 4 minutes on each side or until browned.

Transfer the chicken to the prepared baking dish. Top with the remaining spaghetti sauce. Sprinkle with the mozzarella and Parmesan cheeses. Bake about 20 minutes or until the chicken is no longer pink and the cheeses are melted and bubbly.

Makes 4 servings.

Chicken Paprikash

The paprika sauce in this Hungarian dish is typically made with sour cream. I used fat-free yogurt to get the same creamy, tangy results without a lot of fat. Serve this chicken with hot cooked noodles or rice to soak up its delicious rich sauce. Calories, fat and cholesterol were also reduced by:

• Using skinless chicken breasts instead of chicken pieces with the skin on

• Removing the fat from the chicken broth

• Eliminating the butter from the roux for the sauce

Nutrition Scorecard
(per serving)

	Before	After
Calories	619	206
Fat (g.)	41	2
% Calories from fat	61%	9%
Cholesterol (mg.)	187	69

1 cup fat-free plain yogurt
3 tablespoons all-purpose flour
¾ teaspoon salt
4 (4-ounce) skinless, boneless chicken breast halves
½ cup finely chopped onions
½ medium green pepper, finely chopped
1 clove garlic, minced
1 tablespoon paprika
¾ cup chicken broth, defatted
Fresh snipped parsley

Remove the yogurt from the refrigerator and let it stand at room temperature.

Meanwhile, in a large heavy plastic bag, combine 2 tablespoons of the flour and ½ teaspoon of the salt. Add the chicken and shake to coat evenly.

Lightly spray an unheated large skillet with no-stick spray. Heat the skillet over medium heat. Add the chicken and cook about 4 minutes on each side or until browned. Remove the chicken from the skillet and set aside.

Add the onions, green peppers and garlic to the skillet. Cook and stir until tender. Stir in the remaining 1 tablespoon flour, the paprika and the remaining ¼ teaspoon salt. Cook and stir for 1 minute.

Stir in the broth. Cook and stir about 2 minutes or until thickened.

Return the chicken to the skillet. Cover and simmer about 20 minutes or until tender. Transfer the chicken to an 8" × 8" × 2" baking pan.

Stir the yogurt into the liquid in the skillet. Then spoon the mixture over the chicken.

Preheat the broiler. Broil the chicken 4" from the heat about 2 minutes or just until the sauce begins to bubble (do not overheat or the sauce will curdle). Sprinkle with the parsley.

Makes 4 servings.

Yogurt Know-How

When I shop for yogurt, I always look for a brand made without gelatin. It seems to taste richer and thicker and to hold up better when heated. When adding yogurt to hot mixtures, like the reduced-fat sauces for Chicken Paprikash (opposite page) and Beef Stroganoff (page 175), stir it into the sauce at the very end of the cooking time. Then *briefly* warm it through. Take care not to overheat the yogurt or it will separate and curdle.

Teriyaki Breasts of Chicken

A fat-free marinade is the perfect way to add flavor to poultry or meat without using a lot of fat. To come up with the marinade used here, I substituted pineapple juice for the standard amount of oil. And I further reduced calories, fat and cholesterol by:

• Using skinless chicken breasts instead of chicken pieces with the skin on

Nutrition Scorecard (per serving)	Before	After
Calories	342	202
Fat (g.)	18	1
% Calories from fat	48%	6%
Cholesterol (mg.)	72	65

6 (4-ounce) skinless, boneless chicken breast halves
½ cup reduced-sodium soy sauce
⅓ cup packed brown sugar
⅓ cup dry sherry or nonalcoholic wine
2 tablespoons pineapple juice
1 teaspoon grated ginger root
1 clove garlic, minced

Place the chicken in a large resealable plastic bag. In a small bowl, stir together the soy sauce, brown sugar, sherry or wine, pineapple juice, ginger and garlic. Pour the mixture over the chicken in the bag. Seal the bag and marinate in the refrigerator for 3 to 6 hours, turning the bag occasionally.

Preheat the broiler. Remove the chicken from the bag. Discard the marinade. Broil the chicken 4" from the heat for 6 minutes. Turn the chicken over and broil for 4 to 6 minutes more or until the chicken is no longer pink.

Makes 6 servings.

Safe Marinating

Marinating is an excellent way to give flavor to reduced-fat seafood, meat and poultry. For the best—safest—results, follow a few rules: Always marinate these foods in the refrigerator, even if it's just for 15 minutes, because bacteria can quickly multiply at room temperature. If you intend to serve the marinade as a sauce, set some of it aside so it never comes in contact with the seafood, meat or poultry, or bring any that does come in contact to a full boil to kill any bacteria that might be present (this includes any marinade "contaminated" by a brush used to baste the meat, poultry or fish).

Chicken Fajitas

Lime juice and ground cumin accent the chicken and vegetables in this healthy version of a Mexican favorite. Calories and fat were reduced by:

- Using chicken broth instead of oil in the marinade

- Using no-stick spray instead of oil to cook the chicken and vegetables

Nutrition Scorecard
(per serving)

	Before	After
Calories	409	309
Fat (g.)	18	6
% Calories from fat	38%	18%
Cholesterol (mg.)	44	44

3 tablespoons fresh lime juice
2 tablespoons chicken broth, defatted
½ teaspoon ground cumin
⅛ teaspoon ground red pepper
1 pound skinless, boneless chicken breast halves, cut into thin strips
1 large yellow pepper, cut into thin strips
1 large sweet red pepper, cut into thin strips
1 large green pepper, cut into thin strips
1 onion, thinly sliced
1 clove garlic, minced
¼ teaspoon ground black pepper
12 small flour tortillas, warmed

In a medium bowl, stir together the lime juice, broth, cumin and ground red pepper. Add the chicken and toss until coated.

Lightly spray an unheated large skillet with no-stick spray. Heat over medium-high heat. Add the chicken mixture; yellow, red and green peppers; onions; garlic and black pepper. Cook and stir about 3 minutes or until the chicken is no longer pink and the vegetables are crisp-tender. Serve the warm vegetable mixture with the tortillas.

Makes 6 servings.

TO MAKE BEEF FAJITAS: Use 1 pound of boneless beef round steak instead of the chicken. Trim all visible fat from the beef before cutting it into thin strips. (Per serving: 373 calories, 12 g. fat, 27% calories from fat, 62 mg. cholesterol.)

Mu Shu Chicken

Pictured on page 223

This Beijing classic is made by tucking a spicy-sweet filling of shredded vegetables and chicken inside a thin pancake. To save time and effort, I use flour tortillas rather than make the traditional Mandarin pancakes. I cut calories, fat and cholesterol by:

• Using egg whites instead of a whole egg

• Using no-stick spray instead of oil to stir-fry the chicken and vegetables

Nutrition Scorecard (per serving)		
	Before	After
Calories	579	358
Fat (g.)	32	7
% Calories from fat	49%	17%
Cholesterol (mg.)	86	33

3 tablespoons reduced-sodium soy sauce
1 tablespoon cornstarch
¼ teaspoon ground black pepper
8 ounces skinless, boneless chicken breasts, cut into very thin strips
3 tablespoons hoisin sauce
2 tablespoons dry sherry or nonalcoholic wine
1 teaspoon chicken bouillon granules
½ teaspoon sugar
½ teaspoon oriental sesame oil
1 clove garlic, minced
2 cups finely shredded cabbage
1 medium carrot, shredded
⅓ cup bean sprouts
⅓ cup shredded green onions
3 tablespoons shredded canned bamboo shoots
2 egg whites, lightly beaten
8 small flour tortillas, warmed

In a small bowl, stir together 1 tablespoon of the soy sauce, the cornstarch and pepper. Add the chicken and toss until coated. Set the chicken aside.

In another small bowl, stir together the remaining 2 tablespoons soy sauce, 1 tablespoon of the hoisin sauce, the sherry or wine, bouillon granules, sugar and sesame oil. Set the soy mixture aside.

Lightly spray an unheated wok or large skillet with no-stick spray. Heat over medium-high heat. Add the garlic. Stir-fry for 30 seconds.

Add the chicken mixture. Stir-fry about 3 minutes or until no longer pink. Add the cabbage, carrots, bean sprouts, green onions and bamboo shoots. Stir-fry for 2 minutes. Add egg whites and stir-fry for 1 to 1½ minutes or until cooked. Then add the soy sauce mixture and stir-fry for 1 minute more.

Brush the remaining 2 tablespoons of the hoisin sauce onto the centers of the tortillas. Spoon the chicken mixture down the centers. Fold the bottom quarter of the tortilla up over the filling. Then fold in the sides of the tortilla. Serve immediately.

Makes 8 roll-ups; 4 servings.

TO MAKE MU SHU PORK: Use 8 ounces of pork tenderloin instead of the chicken. Trim all visible fat from the pork before cutting it into thin strips. (Per serving: 386 calories, 9 g. fat, 20% calories from fat, 36 mg. cholesterol)

All-Purpose Oriental Ginger Sauce

Use this sauce as a marinade or brush-on sauce when barbecuing chicken, pork or fish. Calories and fat were reduced by:

- Replacing peanut oil with defatted chicken broth

Nutrition Scorecard (per 2 tablespoons)	Before	After
Calories	104	26
Fat (g.)	10	0
% Calories from fat	81%	1%
Cholesterol (mg.)	0	0

> ¼ cup chicken broth, defatted
> 2 tablespoons dry sherry, dry white wine or nonalcoholic white wine
> 2 tablespoons hoisin sauce
> 2 tablespoons reduced-sodium soy sauce
> 1½ teaspoons minced ginger root
> 1 clove garlic, minced
> 1–2 drops hot chili sauce

In a small bowl, use a wire whisk to stir together the broth, sherry or wine, hoisin sauce, soy sauce, ginger, garlic and chili sauce until well combined. Use as a marinade or sauce when grilling or broiling chicken, fish or lean pork.

TO USE THE SAUCE AS A MARINADE: Place the chicken, fish or pork in a large resealable plastic bag. Add the sauce. Seal the bag and place it in the refrigerator; marinate fish for 1 hour and chicken or pork for at least 2 hours, turning the bag occasionally.

TO USE THE SAUCE AS A BRUSH-ON SAUCE: If the sauce was used as a marinade, bring it to a boil before using. During grilling or broiling, frequently brush the chicken, fish or pork with the sauce.

Makes ¾ cup; 6 servings.

Chicken Chow Mein

This old standby is always popular. (And it's a tasty way to use leftover chicken and pasta whenever you have them on hand.) Calories and fat were reduced by:

• Reducing the amount of sesame oil

• Removing the fat from the chicken broth

• Using no-stick spray instead of oil to stir-fry

Nutrition Scorecard
(per serving)

	Before	After
Calories	577	326
Fat (g.)	33	4
% Calories from fat	51%	12%
Cholesterol (mg.)	33	33

8 ounces spaghettini or angel hair pasta
2 teaspoons oriental sesame oil
3 tablespoons chicken broth, defatted
3 tablespoons reduced-sodium soy sauce
1 teaspoon cornstarch
⅛ teaspoon ground black pepper
1 clove garlic, minced
8 ounces skinless, boneless chicken breasts, cut into thin strips
2 cups finely shredded cabbage
2 medium carrots, coarsely shredded
1 cup sliced fresh mushrooms
½ cup chopped onions
½ cup canned bamboo shoots, thinly sliced
⅓ cup chopped fresh chives

Cook the pasta according to the directions on the package. Drain, rinse with cold water and drain again. Transfer the pasta to a medium bowl. Add the sesame oil and toss until coated.

In a small bowl, stir together the broth, soy sauce, cornstarch and pepper. Set the broth mixture aside.

Lightly spray an unheated wok or large skillet with no-stick spray. Heat over medium-high heat. Add the garlic and stir-fry for 30 seconds.

Add the chicken and stir-fry about 3 minutes or until no longer pink. Remove the chicken from the wok or skillet and cover to keep warm.

Add the cabbage, carrots, mushrooms, onions, bamboo shoots and chives to the wok or skillet. Stir-fry for 2 minutes. Remove from the wok or skillet and set aside. Then add the pasta to the wok or skillet and stir-fry for 3 minutes.

Add the broth mixture, vegetables and chicken to the pasta. Stir-fry for 2 minutes more.

Makes 4 servings.

Chicken Enchiladas

Here's an easy reduced-fat trick: Use enchilada sauce instead of hot oil to soften the tortillas for enchiladas. I'll admit this technique is a little messy, but the calorie and fat savings are well worth it. I further reduced calories, fat and cholesterol by:

- Reducing the amount of Monterey Jack and cheddar cheeses and using their reduced-fat alternates (less than 5 grams of fat per ounce of cheese)

- Reducing the amount of olives

- Eliminating the sour cream

Nutrition Scorecard
(per serving)

	Before	After
Calories	304	181
Fat (g.)	18	6
% Calories from fat	52	28
Cholesterol (mg.)	54	35

---

  3 cups cooked and shredded chicken breast
1¼ cups (5 ounces) finely shredded reduced-fat Monterey Jack cheese
  1 cup snipped fresh chives
  ½ teaspoon minced garlic
  ½ teaspoon ground cumin
  ¼ teaspoon ground black pepper
  1 (29-ounce) can enchilada sauce
 12 corn tortillas, warmed
  ½ cup (2 ounces) finely shredded reduced-fat cheddar cheese
  1 (2-ounce) can sliced, pitted ripe olives, drained

Preheat the oven to 350°. In a large bowl, combine the chicken, ¾ cup of the Monterey Jack cheese, ½ cup of the chives, the garlic, cumin and pepper. Set the chicken mixture aside.

Spread ½ cup of the enchilada sauce in a 13" × 9" × 2" baking pan. Transfer the remaining sauce to a large skillet. Heat the sauce until warm.

To soften each tortilla, completely submerge it in the sauce. Shake off the excess sauce and transfer the tortilla to a plate. Spoon about ¼ cup of the chicken filling down the center and roll up to enclose. Place, seam side down, in the prepared baking pan. Repeat softening and filling the remaining tortillas.

Pour the remaining sauce over the filled tortillas. Top with the remaining ½ cup of Monterey Jack cheese, the cheddar cheese, the remaining ½ cup of chives and the olives. Cover with foil and bake about 30 minutes or until bubbly.

Makes 12 enchiladas; 6 servings.

Layered Mexican Chicken Pie

With my busy schedule, easy dinner dishes are essential. This tortilla pie requires only a few ingredients and can be assembled the night before. Calories, fat and cholesterol were reduced by:

- Replacing sour cream with a mixture of fat-free yogurt and reduced-fat cream of mushroom soup

- Eliminating the step of softening the tortillas in hot oil

- Reducing the amount of cheddar cheese and using its reduced-fat alternate (less than 5 grams of fat per ounce of cheese)

Nutrition Scorecard
(per serving)

	Before	After
Calories	809	569
Fat (g.)	54	17
% Calories from fat	60%	27%
Cholesterol (mg.)	208	162

1 (10¼-ounce) can 99%-fat-free condensed cream of mushroom soup with ⅓ less salt
1 cup fat-free plain yogurt
1 (4-ounce) can diced green chili peppers, drained
⅓ cup finely chopped green peppers
¼ cup finely chopped onions
2 cloves garlic, minced
6 corn tortillas
4 cups cut or shredded cooked chicken breast
2 cups (8 ounces) finely shredded reduced-fat sharp cheddar cheese

Preheat the oven to 350°. In a medium bowl, stir together the condensed soup and yogurt until well combined. Then stir in the chili peppers, green peppers, onions and garlic.

Lightly spray a 9" pie plate with no-stick spray. Spoon a thin layer of the soup mixture on the bottom of the pie plate. Top with three of the tortillas, overlapping the tortillas to fit. Layer with half each of the soup mixture, chicken, and cheese. Place the remaining tortillas on top and repeat layering with the remaining soup mixture, chicken and cheese. Bake about 35 minutes or until heated through.

Makes 4 servings.

No-Fry Chimichangas

Chimichangas are simply deep-fried burritos. I slimmed down this popular Mexican entrée by lightly coating the filled tortillas with no-stick spray and pan-frying them until crisp. I also cut calories, fat and cholesterol by:

• Replacing the seasoned chicken filling with a combination of ground turkey breast and turkey sausage

• Using reduced-fat cheddar cheese (less than 5 grams of fat per ounce of cheese)

Nutrition Scorecard
(per serving)

	Before	After
Calories	400	260
Fat (g.)	22	8
% Calories from fat	49%	28%
Cholesterol (mg.)	56	30

12 ounces ground raw turkey breast
 8 ounces ground turkey sausage
 1 medium onion, chopped
 1 clove garlic, minced
 ½ teaspoon chili powder
 ¾ cup (3 ounces) finely shredded reduced-fat cheddar cheese
 1 (4-ounce) can diced green chili peppers, drained
 ½ cup snipped and loosely packed fresh cilantro
12 large flour tortillas
 Salsa (optional)

Lightly spray an unheated large skillet with no-stick spray. Add the turkey breast and sausage, onions, garlic and chili powder. Cook until the turkey is no longer pink, stirring occasionally. Drain and discard the liquid.

Stir in the cheese, chili peppers and cilantro.

To assemble, spoon about ¼ cup of the poultry mixture onto each tortilla just below its center. Fold in the sides of the tortillas. Then fold the bottom quarter of tortilla up over the filling and roll up to enclose. Secure with wooden toothpicks. Spray both sides of each stuffed tortilla with no-stick spray.

In a large skillet or on a griddle, cook three or four of the stuffed tortillas at a time over medium heat for 3 to 4 minutes on each side or until golden brown. Remove from the skillet or griddle and loosely cover to keep warm while cooking the remaining stuffed tortillas. If desired, serve with salsa.

Makes 12 chimichangas; 6 servings.

Moussaka

This classic one-dish Greek meal is typically made with ground beef or lamb. Just by switching to ground turkey breast, I made major calorie savings—without compromising the flavor or ethnic characteristics of this dish. Calories, fat and cholesterol were also reduced by:

- Using egg whites instead of a whole egg

- Using skim milk instead of whole milk

- Using a cornstarch-and-milk mixture to thicken the sauce instead of a flour-and-butter roux

Nutrition Scorecard
(per serving)

	Before	After
Calories	429	278
Fat (g.)	25	3
% Calories from fat	53%	11%
Cholesterol (mg.)	148	45

FILLING
12 ounces ground raw turkey breast or ground beef (85% lean)
½ cup chopped onions
2 cloves garlic, minced
1 (8-ounce) can tomato sauce
¼ cup dry red wine or nonalcoholic red wine
2 tablespoons snipped fresh parsley
½ teaspoon dried oregano
¼ teaspoon salt
¼ teaspoon ground cinnamon
¼ teaspoon ground black pepper
2 egg whites, lightly beaten

EGGPLANT
1 large eggplant, peeled and cut into ½" slices

SAUCE
1½ cups skim milk
4 teaspoons cornstarch
¼ cup grated Parmesan cheese
¼ cup fine dry seasoned bread crumbs

TO MAKE THE FILLING: Spray an unheated large skillet with no-stick spray. Add the turkey or beef, onions and garlic. Cook until the turkey is no longer pink or the beef is browned, stirring occasionally. Drain and discard the liquid.

Stir in the tomato sauce, wine, parsley, oregano, salt, cinnamon and pepper. Bring to a boil. Reduce the heat. Cover and simmer for 10 minutes, stirring occasionally.

Remove the filling mixture from the heat. Slowly stir some of the mixture into the egg whites. Then stir the egg white mixture into the remaining filling mixture. Set the mixture aside.

To make the eggplant: Preheat the broiler. Broil the eggplant slices 3" to 4" from the heat about 4 minutes or until tender. Move the oven rack to the center of the oven and preheat the oven to 350°.

To make the sauce: In a medium saucepan, use a wire whisk to stir together ¼ cup of the milk and the cornstarch to make a smooth mixture free of lumps. Then stir in the remaining milk. Cook and stir over medium heat until thickened and bubbly. Cook and stir for 1 minute more. Then stir in the Parmesan cheese.

In an 8" × 8" × 2" baking dish, layer half of the eggplant slices and all of the filling mixture. Top with the remaining eggplant and all of the sauce. Sprinkle with the bread crumbs.

Bake for 30 to 35 minutes or until set. Let stand for 5 minutes before serving.

Makes 6 servings.

One Small Step for a Big Savings

Doing *nothing* more than cutting just 1 teaspoon of oil, margarine or butter from your diet every day for one year will leave you four pounds lighter.

South-of-the-Border Tamales

Pictured on page 224

Many traditional Mexican dishes contain lard, which is used in part because it contributes a certain flavor. In this recipe, the full flavor of the pureed corn combined with a small amount of corn oil eliminates the need for lard. Calories, fat and cholesterol were also reduced by:

- Replacing the lard with a combination of corn oil and water

- Reducing the amount of cheddar cheese and using its reduced-fat alternate (less than 5 grams of fat per ounce of cheese)

Nutrition Scorecard
(per 2 tamales)

	Before	After
Calories	357	258
Fat (g.)	21	11
% Calories from fat	52%	36%
Cholesterol (mg.)	45	10

2 (8-ounce) cans whole kernel corn, drained
2 tablespoons water
2 cups masa harina (corn tortilla mix)
¾ cup warm water
¼ cup corn oil
2 tablespoons sugar
8 large dried corn husks
1 cup (4 ounces) finely shredded reduced-fat cheddar cheese
1 (4-ounce) can diced green chili peppers, drained

In a blender or food processor, pulse blend or process the corn and 2 tablespoons water until coarsely pureed.

In a large bowl, stir together the pureed corn, masa harina, ¾ cup water, oil and sugar until a soft, moist dough forms. (The dough should look like a soft cookie dough.) If the dough is too dry, add additional warm water, 1 tablespoon at a time. Set aside.

Bring a large saucepan of water to a boil. Add the husks and reduce the heat. Simmer, uncovered, about 5 minutes or until soft. Drain.

To assemble the tamales, place each husk on a flat surface with its shorter, tapered point towards you. Spread 3 to 4 tablespoons of the dough on each husk, beginning ¾" from the top and ending at least 1½" from the bottom point, leaving a 1½" border at the sides.

Sprinkle 2 tablespoons of the cheese and 2 teaspoons of the chili peppers down the center of each. Fold the sides of the husk up and over the filling. Then fold in half to bring the top and bottom ends together and tie them closed with a piece of string (see photo on page 224).

In a large skillet with a tight-fitting lid, place the tamales on an opened steamer basket or on a wire rack. Add enough water to the skillet to cover the bottom of the skillet, making sure the water sits below the basket or rack.

Bring the water to a boil. Then cover the skillet and steam for 35 to 40 minutes or until the tamales easily pull away from the husks when unwrapped. (If necessary, add more water to the skillet during steaming.)

Makes 8 tamales; 4 servings.

Garlic Scampi

Pictured on page 225

In Italian, "scampi" means large shrimp. In this recipe, I marinate them in a wine and garlic mixture to give them robust flavor, instead of sautéing them in a large amount of garlic-flavored oil. Although this is basically a main course, you can serve the shrimp as an elegant party appetizer. Calories and fat were reduced by:

- Reducing the amount of olive oil and replacing most of it with defatted chicken broth and white wine

Nutrition Scorecard (per serving)		
	Before	After
Calories	410	223
Fat (g.)	29	7
% Calories from fat	64%	30%
Cholesterol (mg.)	332	332

 3 tablespoons chicken broth, defatted
 2 tablespoons white wine, dry sherry or nonalcoholic white wine
1½ tablespoons olive oil
 ½ teaspoon salt
 ½ teaspoon dried oregano
 ¼ teaspoon ground black pepper
 3 cloves garlic, minced
1½ pounds jumbo shrimp, peeled and deveined
 2 lemons, cut into wedges

In a large shallow dish, stir together the broth, wine or sherry, olive oil, salt, oregano, pepper and garlic. Add the shrimp and turn them to coat them well. Cover with plastic wrap. Marinate in the refrigerator for 1½ to 2 hours. (Do not marinate for longer than 2 hours or shrimp will become tough.)

Preheat the broiler. Remove the shrimp from the dish, reserving the marinade. Thread the shrimp onto skewers, leaving a small space between each. Brush the shrimp with the reserved marinade. Broil 4" from the heat for 2 minutes. Turn the shrimp over, brush with the marinade and broil for 1 to 3 minutes more or until the shrimp are no longer pink. Serve with the lemon wedges.

Makes 4 servings.

Note: These shrimp also are delicious grilled. Grill them directly over medium-hot coals for about 8 minutes, or until they are no longer pink.

Pork Chop Suey

There are many versions of this popular Chinese-American dish. I serve my lean rendition with brown rather than white rice for a more fiber-rich meal. Calories, fat and cholesterol were reduced by:

- Reducing the amount of pork and using pork tenderloin (26% calories from fat) instead of ground pork (63% calories from fat)

- Removing the fat from the chicken broth

- Using no-stick spray instead of oil to stir-fry the vegetables and pork

Nutrition Scorecard
(per serving)

	Before	After
Calories	696	326
Fat (g.)	35	5
% Calories from fat	46%	12%
Cholesterol (mg.)	82	55

12 ounces pork tenderloin
3 tablespoons chicken broth, defatted
2 tablespoons reduced-sodium soy sauce
1 teaspoon cornstarch
½ teaspoon salt
⅛ teaspoon ground black pepper
½ teaspoon grated ginger root
2 cups thinly sliced bok choy or spinach
2 cups fresh or canned bean sprouts
2 stalks celery, chopped
½ cup very finely shredded carrots
½ cup snipped fresh chives
4 cups hot cooked brown rice

Cut the pork into very thin strips. Then cut the strips into 1" × ½" pieces and set aside.

In a small bowl, stir together the broth, soy sauce, cornstarch, salt and pepper. Set the broth mixture aside.

Lightly spray an unheated wok or large skillet with no-stick spray. Heat over medium-high heat. Add the ginger and stir-fry for 30 seconds.

Add the pork and stir-fry about 3 minutes or until no longer pink. Remove the pork from the pan and set aside. Add the bok choy or spinach, bean sprouts, celery, carrots and chives. Stir-fry for 3 minutes. Then add the broth mixture and cooked pork. Stir-fry for 2 minutes more. Serve with the rice.

Makes 4 servings.

Spaghetti with Spicy Italian Meat Sauce (page 176)

Pasta Primavera (page 181)

Green and White Lasagna Bundles (page 184)

217

Tomato Mac 'n' Cheese (page 185)

Greek Penne (page 193)

Cheese Ravioli with Rosemary and Lemon (page 194)

Chicken Cacciatore (page 196)

Chicken Tostadas (page 197)

Mu Shu Chicken (page 204)

South-of-the-Border Tamales (page 212)

Garlic Scampi (page 213)

Garden Vegetable Pizza (page 232)

Falafel (page 233) with Hummus (page 71)

Chinese Chicken Salad (page 236)

Cobb Salad (page 238)

Creamy Shrimp Salad on Romaine (page 246)

Chili Verde Burritos

These burritos are so full of flavor that my taste testers didn't even miss the sour cream. Calories, fat and cholesterol were reduced by:

- Using pork tenderloin (26% calories from fat) instead of ground pork (63% calories from fat)

- Eliminating the sour cream

Nutrition Scorecard
(per serving)

	Before	After
Calories	646	380
Fat (g.)	25	10
% Calories from fat	35%	21%
Cholesterol (mg.)	137	49

1 pound pork tenderloin, cut into 1" pieces
1 pound fresh or canned tomatillos, drained
2 medium carrots, coarsely chopped
1 large onion, chopped
1 large potato, peeled and cut into 1" pieces
4 cloves garlic, minced
2 (7-ounce) jars or cans green chili salsa
1 (7-ounce) can diced green chili peppers, drained
½ teaspoon salt
¼ teaspoon ground red pepper
12 (8") whole-wheat tortillas, warmed
2 medium tomatoes, chopped
1 cup snipped fresh chives
½ cup snipped and loosely packed fresh cilantro

Spray a Dutch oven with no-stick spray. Heat over medium-high heat. Add the pork. Cook and stir until the pork is no longer pink.

Add the tomatillos, carrots, onions, potatoes and garlic. Cook and stir about 7 minutes or until tender. Add the salsa, chili peppers, salt and red pepper. Bring to a boil, then reduce the heat. Cover and simmer for 30 minutes.

To serve, let guests assemble their own burritos. To assemble, spoon about ½ cup of the pork mixture onto each tortilla just below its center. Top with a small amount of tomatoes, chives and cilantro. Fold in the sides of the tortillas. Then roll up from the bottom to enclose the filling.

Makes 12 burritos; 6 servings.

Garden Vegetable Pizza

Pictured on page 226

When I'm in the mood for a casual dinner, I like to whip up this quick and healthy pizza. Its whole-wheat crust doesn't require any rising time, and it's topped with plenty of fresh vegetables so the traditional fatty toppings aren't even missed. Calories, fat and cholesterol were reduced by:

• Eliminating the oil in the crust

• Replacing fatty meat toppings with fresh vegetables

• Using reduced-fat mozzarella cheese (5 grams of fat per ounce of cheese)

Nutrition Scorecard
(per serving)

	Before	After
Calories	710	433
Fat (g.)	39	12
% Calories from fat	49%	24%
Cholesterol (mg.)	105	33

CRUST

   2 *cups all-purpose flour*
   1 *cup whole-wheat flour*
   1 *package active dry yeast*
   1 *cup warm water (120° to 130°)*
   2 *teaspoons cornmeal*

TOPPING

   1 *cup pizza sauce*
   3 *cups (12 ounces) finely shredded reduced-fat mozzarella cheese*
   1 *cup chopped sweet red peppers*
   1 *cup chopped green peppers*
   1 *cup sliced fresh mushrooms*
   ¼ *cup snipped fresh basil (optional)*

TO MAKE THE CRUST: In a large bowl, stir together 1 cup of the all-purpose flour, ¼ cup of the whole-wheat flour and the yeast. Add the warm water. Beat with an electric mixer on low speed for 30 seconds, scraping the sides of the bowl constantly. Then beat on high speed for 3 minutes.

Using a spoon, stir in the remaining ¾ cup of whole-wheat flour. Then stir in as much of the remaining 1 cup of all-purpose flour as you can.

Turn the dough out onto a lightly floured surface. Knead in enough of the remaining all-purpose flour to make a moderately stiff dough that is smooth and elastic. (This kneading step will take a total of 6 to 8 minutes.) Divide the dough in half. Cover and let rest for 10 minutes.

Meanwhile, preheat the oven to 425°. Lightly spray two 12" round pizza pans with no-stick spray. Sprinkle each pan with 1 teaspoon of the cornmeal.

On a lightly floured surface, roll each portion of the dough into a 13" circle. Transfer the dough to the pans. Build up the edges slightly. (Do not let rise.) Bake about 12 minutes or until lightly browned.

TO MAKE THE TOPPING: Spread the pizza sauce on top of the hot crusts. Sprinkle with the red and green peppers, mushrooms and basil. Then top with the cheese. Bake for 10 to 15 minutes more or until the cheese is melted and bubbly.

Makes 2 (12″) pizzas; 6 servings.

Falafel

Pictured on page 227

	Falafel are spicy Middle Eastern chick-pea patties usually deep-fat fried and served in pita breads. To scale down the calories and fat, I opt to pan-fry the patties and use no-stick spray instead of oil.		

Nutrition Scorecard (per serving)		
	Before	After
Calories	486	387
Fat (g.)	17	6
% Calories from fat	30%	12%
Cholesterol (mg.)	0	0

2 (15-ounce) cans chick-peas (garbanzo beans), rinsed and drained
½ cup grated onions
½ cup snipped fresh parsley
1 egg white
1 clove garlic, minced
1 teaspoon ground cumin
¼ teaspoon salt
¼ teaspoon ground black pepper
Dash of ground red pepper
3 large whole-wheat pita breads, heated and halved
2 cups shredded leaf lettuce
¾ cup Hummus (page 71)
Tomato slices (optional)

In a blender or food processor, combine the chick-peas, onions, parsley, egg white, garlic, cumin, salt, black pepper and red pepper. Pulse blend or process until the mixture resembles coarse cornmeal. Cover and refrigerate for 30 minutes.

Shape the mixture into small patties, about 2″ wide and ½″ thick. Set aside.

Spray an unheated large skillet with no-stick spray. Heat the skillet over medium heat. Add the patties and cook about 3 minutes on each side or until crispy and golden.

To serve, open the pocket of each pita half. Line each pocket with some of the lettuce, then place two or three patties in each. Top each with 2 tablespoons of hummus. If desired, serve with tomato slices.

Makes 6 servings.

Greek Spinach Pie

Feta cheese, with its sharp, salty flavor, is commonly used in Greek dishes. To keep the traditional flavor of this dish yet cut the fat, I replaced some of the feta cheese with fat-free cottage cheese. Calories, fat and cholesterol were also reduced by:

- Replacing the traditional fat-laden pastry crust with a pizza dough crust

- Using olive oil no-stick spray instead of olive oil to sauté the onions, garlic and basil

- Using egg whites instead of whole eggs

- Replacing heavy cream with evaporated skim milk

Nutrition Scorecard
(per serving)

	Before	After
Calories	373	274
Fat (g.)	25	7
% Calories from fat	59%	23%
Cholesterol (mg.)	181	22

1 (10-ounce) can refrigerated pizza crust dough
2 (10-ounce) packages frozen chopped spinach, thawed
½ cup chopped onions
1 clove garlic, minced
½ teaspoon dried basil
¾ cup fat-free cottage cheese
4 ounces feta cheese, crumbled
¾ cup evaporated skim milk
8 egg whites

Preheat the oven to 350°. Lightly spray a 9" pie plate with olive oil no-stick spray. Unroll the pizza dough. Form the dough into a ball. On a lightly floured surface, slightly flatten the dough with your hands. Then roll the dough from the center to the edges to form a 12" circle. Gently ease the dough into the prepared pie plate. Set the pie shell aside.

Drain and squeeze the spinach to remove excess moisture. Set the spinach aside.

Lightly spray an unheated small skillet with olive oil no-stick spray. Add the onions, garlic and basil. Cook and stir over medium heat until the onions are tender and translucent.

In a large bowl, beat together the cottage cheese and feta cheese until creamy and well blended. Then beat in the milk and egg whites until combined. Stir in the onion mixture and spinach.

Transfer the mixture to the pie shell. Bake for 45 to 60 minutes or until a knife inserted in the center comes out clean. Let stand for 15 minutes before serving.

Makes 6 servings.

SENSATIONAL SALADS AND DRESSINGS

When you think of healthy eating, the first thing that comes to mind is a salad: a colorful mixture of vibrant greens and crisp, raw vegetables. It's low in calories, low in fat and bursting with vital nutrients. Or at least it should be.

The downfall of most salads is the dressing—not to mention the fatty toppings that we somehow feel entitled to bury our greens under. When all is said and done, such a salad can easily have as many calories and grams of fat as a double cheeseburger with fries and a milk shake!

In this chapter, I've gathered my favorite reduced-fat salads and dressings. Some of the salads are main courses; others are side dishes. All fit beautifully into a healthy diet. And all were surprisingly easy to keep lean—the notes with each recipe detail how I did it.

One note about greens selection: You'll get more nutrients for your money by choosing rich-colored varieties. Romaine lettuce, red and green cabbage, bok choy, spinach, kale, radicchio, watercress, Swiss chard, beet greens and arugula give a salad extra pizzazz and lots of vitamins. Choose them instead of plain old iceberg lettuce.

Chinese Chicken Salad

Pictured on page 228

Sesame oil is the secret ingredient that gives this savory Chinese salad its characteristic flavor. The way I retained that flavor is by using only a small amount to marinate already-cooked chicken. I also reduced calories and fat by:

- Baking wonton wrappers instead of frying them

- Using a reduced-fat ginger sesame dressing instead of oil and vinegar

Nutrition Scorecard (per serving)	Before	After
Calories	495	360
Fat (g.)	26	6
% Calories from fat	47%	15%
Cholesterol (mg.)	65	65

CHICKEN
- 4 skinless, boneless chicken breast halves (1 pound total), cooked
- 3 tablespoons honey
- 2 tablespoons reduced-sodium soy sauce
- 1½ teaspoons oriental sesame oil

WONTON CRISPS
- 6 wonton wrappers

SALAD
- 8 cups torn romaine lettuce
- ½ cup loosely packed fresh cilantro, snipped
- 1 sweet red pepper, chopped
- 1 (11-ounce) can water-packed mandarin oranges, drained
- 1 cup Ginger Sesame Dressing (opposite page)

TO MAKE THE CHICKEN: Cut the chicken into bite-size strips. In a medium bowl, stir together the honey, soy sauce and oil. Add the chicken, then stir until coated. Cover and marinate in the refrigerator for at least 30 minutes, stirring often.

TO MAKE THE WONTON CRISPS: Preheat the oven to 350°. Stack the wonton wrappers, then cut them into narrow strips. Spray a cookie sheet with no-stick spray. Arrange the strips in a single layer so the edges are not touching. Lightly spray the strips with no-stick spray. Bake for 6 to 8 minutes or until lightly browned and crisp. Remove the crisps from the cookie sheet and let cool. Set aside.

TO MAKE THE SALAD: In a large bowl, combine the romaine, cilantro, peppers and wonton crisps. Divide the romaine mixture among four dinner plates. Place the chicken and oranges on top. Serve with the Ginger Sesame Dressing.

Makes 4 main-dish servings.

Ginger Sesame Dressing

This oriental dressing is one of my long-time favorites. It has a slightly sweet yet tangy flavor. Calories and fat were reduced by:

- Replacing the salad oil with a mixture of pineapple juice and chicken broth

- Reducing the amount of sesame oil

Nutrition Scorecard
(per 2 tablespoons)

	Before	After
Calories	160	42
Fat (g.)	15	1
% Calories from fat	84%	24%
Cholesterol (mg.)	0	0

3 tablespoons seasoned rice vinegar
1 tablespoon reduced-sodium soy sauce
4 teaspoons ground arrowroot
2 tablespoons honey
⅓ cup chicken broth, defatted
¼ cup pineapple juice
2 teaspoons oriental sesame oil
1 teaspoon grated ginger root
1 clove garlic, minced

In a small saucepan, use a wire whisk to combine the vinegar, soy sauce and arrowroot. Stir in the honey until smooth. Then stir in the broth, juice, oil, ginger and garlic.

Cook and stir over medium heat until thickened and translucent (maximum thickening occurs *before* boiling). Remove from the heat and let cool. Refrigerate to store. Stir before serving.

Makes 1 cup; 8 servings.

Cobb Salad

Pictured on page 229

The original version of this salad is a good example of how fat-laden toppings can transform a healthy salad into something that's not good for you. I slimmed down this California classic by modifying the toppings and using a lighter dressing. You can choose virtually any fat-free or reduced-fat commercial dressing, but more authentic choices include Dijon and Tarragon Dressing, Creamy Pesto Dressing or Creamy Blue Cheese Dressing (see pages 239 to 241). Calories, fat and cholesterol were reduced by:

Nutrition Scorecard (per serving)		
	Before	After
Calories	724	304
Fat (g.)	59	9
% Calories from fat	73%	27%
Cholesterol (mg.)	225	80

• Reducing the amount of cooked turkey

• Replacing some of the blue cheese with fat-free cottage cheese

• Replacing the bacon with turkey bacon and reducing the total amount

• Replacing hard-cooked egg yolks with additional hard-cooked egg whites

8 *cups torn romaine lettuce*
1 *small bunch chicory (curly endive), finely chopped*
12 *ounces cooked turkey breast, cut into bite-size pieces*
½ *cup crumbled blue cheese*
¼ *cup fat-free cottage cheese*
1 *large tomato, chopped (optional)*
½ *green or sweet red pepper, chopped*
½ *yellow pepper, chopped*
1 *small red onion, chopped*
4 *hard-cooked egg whites, coarsely chopped*
4 *slices turkey bacon, cooked, drained and crumbled*
1 *cup fat-free or reduced-fat salad dressing*

In a large bowl, combine the romaine and chicory. Divide the mixture among four salad plates. Top each with the turkey, mounding it in the center of the romaine mixture.

In a small bowl, use a fork to stir together the blue cheese and cottage cheese. Mound the cheese mixture on top of the romaine near the turkey. Then attractively arrange small mounds of the tomatoes (if desired), peppers, onions and egg whites on top of the romaine. Sprinkle with turkey bacon. Serve with desired dressing.

Makes 4 main-dish salads.

Dijon and Tarragon Dressing

This creamy dressing is virtually fat free. I reduced calories, fat and cholesterol by:

- Replacing salad oil with chicken broth
- Using fat-free yogurt instead of sour cream

Nutrition Scorecard
(per 2 tablespoons)

	Before	After
Calories	189	23
Fat (g.)	20	<1
% Calories from fat	95%	6%
Cholesterol (mg.)	3	0

⅔ *cup fat-free plain yogurt*
½ *cup chicken broth, defatted*
2 *tablespoons Dijon mustard*
2 *tablespoons honey*
2 *teaspoons dried tarragon*
2 *cloves garlic, minced*
½ *teaspoon salt*

In a medium bowl, use a wire whisk to stir together the yogurt, broth, mustard, honey, tarragon, garlic and salt. Refrigerate to store. Stir before serving.

Makes 1½ cups; 12 servings.

Note: You can easily cut this dressing in half to make ¾ cup (6 servings).

Creamy Pesto Dressing

Garlic lovers will go crazy over this dressing! To save time, I sometimes use minced fresh garlic from a jar (a teaspoon is about right). Calories, fat and cholesterol were reduced by:

- Replacing salad oil with a mixture of white grape juice and chicken broth

- Using reduced-fat Parmesan cheese (3 grams of fat per ounce of cheese)

Nutrition Scorecard
(per 2 tablespoons)

	Before	After
Calories	133	31
Fat (g.)	14	1
% Calories from fat	95%	25%
Cholesterol (mg.)	16	0

¼ cup grated reduced-fat Parmesan cheese
¼ cup white vinegar
2 tablespoons snipped fresh basil
2 tablespoons white grape juice
1 tablespoon chicken broth, defatted
1 teaspoon olive oil
2 cloves garlic, minced
½ cup fat-free plain yogurt

In a blender or small food processor, blend or process the cheese, vinegar, basil, juice, broth, oil and garlic until the basil is finely chopped and the mixture is well combined.

Transfer the mixture to a small bowl. Using a wire whisk, stir in the yogurt. Refrigerate to store. Stir before serving.

Makes 1 cup; 8 servings.

Creamy Blue Cheese Dressing

I prefer this reduced-fat version of blue cheese dressing to most commercial dressings because it's got more chunks of blue cheese and a stronger flavor. I reduced calories, fat and cholesterol by:

- Using less blue cheese

- Using a mixture of fat-free yogurt and fat-free ricotta cheese instead of the usual mayonnaise-and-cream mixture

- Replacing salad oil with additional fat-free ricotta cheese

Nutrition Scorecard (per 2 tablespoons)

	Before	After
Calories	245	54
Fat (g.)	26	3
% Calories from fat	96%	50%
Cholesterol (mg.)	21	10

3 ounces blue cheese
6 tablespoons fat-free plain yogurt
½ cup fat-free ricotta cheese
2 teaspoons white vinegar
⅛ teaspoon ground black pepper

Working in a small bowl, use a fork to crumble the blue cheese. Stir in 2 tablespoons of the yogurt until smooth and creamy. Add the ricotta cheese, vinegar, pepper and the remaining 4 tablespoons yogurt. Using a hand beater or an electric mixer, beat together until well combined. Refrigerate to store. Stir before serving.

Makes 1 cup; 8 servings.

Taco Salad

Taco salads are notoriously high in fat. But with a little whittling here and there, I was able to shave away many of the calories and much of the fat while maintaining the delicious south-of-the-border flavor. Calories, fat and cholesterol were reduced by :

- Using a mixture of ground turkey breast and turkey sausage instead of ground beef and reducing the total amount

- Reducing the amount of cheese and increasing the cheese flavor by using reduced-fat sharp cheddar cheese (5 grams of fat per ounce of cheese)

- Reducing the amount of olives

- Serving baked corn tortilla strips instead of corn chips

Nutrition Scorecard (per serving)		
	Before	After
Calories	671	352
Fat (g.)	40	13
% Calories from fat	54%	33%
Cholesterol (mg.)	106	40

MEAT MIXTURE
6 ounces ground turkey breast (see note)
6 ounces ground turkey sausage
3 cloves garlic, minced
1 (16-ounce) can red kidney beans
1 cup salsa
1 tablespoon chili powder
½ teaspoon ground cumin

TORTILLA CHIPS
6 corn tortillas, cut into ½"-wide strips

SALAD
3 cups torn iceberg lettuce
3 cups torn romaine lettuce
4 medium tomatoes, chopped
1¼ cups (5 ounces) finely shredded reduced-fat sharp cheddar cheese
1 green pepper, chopped
½ cup loosely packed snipped fresh cilantro
⅓ cup sliced pitted ripe olives
3 tablespoons snipped fresh chives
Salsa (optional)

TO MAKE THE MEAT MIXTURE: In a large skillet, cook the turkey breast, sausage and garlic over medium heat about 5 minutes or until no longer pink, stirring occasionally. Drain the turkey in a strainer or colander, then transfer it to a large plate lined with three layers of paper towels. Blot the top of the turkey with additional paper towels. Return the meat to the skillet.

Stir in the undrained kidney beans, salsa, chili powder and cumin. Bring to a boil, then reduce the heat. Cover and simmer for 10 minutes. Remove the mixture from the heat and chill in the refrigerator while preparing the chips and salad.

TO MAKE THE TORTILLA CHIPS: Preheat the oven to 400°. Spray a cookie sheet with no-stick spray. Arrange the tortilla strips in a single layer so the edges are not touching. Then lightly spray the tortilla strips with no-stick spray. Bake for 10 to 12 minutes or until golden brown. Transfer the strips to a wire rack to cool.

TO MAKE THE SALAD: In a large bowl, combine the iceberg lettuce, romaine, tomatoes, cheddar cheese, green peppers, cilantro, olives and chives. Add the chilled turkey mixture and toss until combined.

To serve, divide the mixture among six salad plates. Garnish each serving with the tortilla chips. If desired, serve with additional salsa.

Makes 6 main-dish servings.

Note: To make sure you're buying the leanest ground turkey available, check the label. Look for products made with only turkey breast meat. Many ground turkey products contain the dark meat and the fatty skin.

24-Hour Layer Salad

Here's a salad you can prepare the day before and the lettuce will stay crisp until you're ready to serve it. Calories, fat and cholesterol were reduced by:

- Replacing the bacon with turkey bacon and reducing the total amount

- Reducing the amount of cheddar cheese and using its reduced-fat alternate (less than 5 grams of fat per ounce of cheese)

- Using a reduced-fat Parmesan dressing instead of mayonnaise

- Using only the egg white portion of the hard-cooked eggs

Nutrition Scorecard
(per serving)

	Before	After
Calories	276	123
Fat (g.)	24	4
% Calories from fat	78%	29%
Cholesterol (mg.)	80	12

    4 cups torn lettuce
    1 cup sliced fresh mushrooms
    1 (10-ounce) package frozen peas
    1 cup coarsely shredded carrots
    4 hard-cooked egg whites, chopped; discard yolks
    5 slices turkey bacon, cooked, drained and crumbled
    ½ cup (2 ounces) finely shredded reduced-fat cheddar cheese
  1¼ cups Creamy Parmesan Dressing (page 245)
    2 tablespoons snipped fresh chives

Place the lettuce in a large clear-glass bowl with straight sides. In the following order, layer the mushrooms, frozen peas, carrots, egg whites and turkey bacon on top. Sprinkle with ¼ cup of the cheddar cheese. Then carefully spread the dressing over the top, sealing the dressing to the edge of the bowl. Sprinkle with the remaining ¼ cup of cheese and the chives. Cover and refrigerate for 24 hours.

To serve, toss the salad until the lettuce and vegetables are coated.

Makes 8 side-dish servings.

Creamy Parmesan Dressing

No one will ever guess that this rich, creamy dressing is virtually fat free. I like to use it on 24-Hour Layer Salad (page 244), but it's also delicious over plain lettuce or fresh tomatoes or as a dip for raw vegetables. Calories, fat and cholesterol were reduced by:

• Replacing regular sour cream with a combination of fat-free yogurt and fat-free sour cream

• Using reduced-fat Parmesan cheese (3 grams of fat per ounce of cheese)

Nutrition Scorecard
(per 2 tablespoons)

	Before	After
Calories	76	29
Fat (g.)	7	<1
% Calories from fat	83%	19%
Cholesterol (mg.)	15	0

½ cup fat-free plain yogurt
½ cup fat-free sour cream
¼ cup grated reduced-fat Parmesan cheese
2 tablespoons fresh lemon juice (see note)
1 clove garlic, minced

In a small bowl, use a wire whisk to stir together the yogurt, sour cream, Parmesan cheese, lemon juice and garlic. Cover and chill in the refrigerator for at least 30 minutes to blend the flavors.

Makes 1¼ cups; 10 servings.

Note: This is a tangy dressing. If you prefer a less sour dressing, replace some of the lemon juice with skim milk.

Creamy Shrimp Salad on Romaine

Pictured on page 230

Part of what makes this shrimp salad so easy is using purchased fat-free salad dressing as a timesaver. I prefer Thousand Island dressing, but you might like creamy cucumber, honey Dijon or bacon and tomato. I reduced calories, fat and cholesterol by:

- Reducing the amount of walnuts

- Replacing the traditional mayonnaise-and-French-dressing mixture with purchased fat-free salad dressing

- Using only the egg white portion of hard-cooked eggs instead of olives

Nutrition Scorecard
(per serving)

	Before	After
Calories	357	178
Fat (g.)	31	5
% Calories from fat	78%	25%
Cholesterol (mg.)	119	110

2 cups cooked and deveined shrimp, chilled
1¼ cups sliced celery
4 hard-cooked egg whites, coarsely chopped; discard yolks
3 tablespoons chopped walnuts
2 teaspoons finely chopped onions
½ cup fat-free Thousand Island salad dressing
4 cups shredded romaine lettuce

In a large bowl, combine the shrimp, celery, egg whites, walnuts and onions. Add the dressing and stir until the shrimp mixture is coated. Cover and chill in the refrigerator about 30 minutes to blend the flavors.

To serve, divide the lettuce among four plates. Then top with the shrimp mixture.

Makes 4 main-dish servings.

Waldorf Salad

Pictured on page 295

Some fruit salads can be surprisingly high in fat. Take Waldorf Salad—the traditional dressing is quite fatty, and the salad is loaded with nuts, which contribute their own share of fat and calories. So I reduced calories, fat and cholesterol by:

- Replacing mayonnaise in the dressing with a combination of fat-free vanilla yogurt and fresh lemon peel

Nutrition Scorecard (per serving)	Before	After
Calories	187	89
Fat (g.)	15	3
% Calories from fat	72%	30%
Cholesterol (mg.)	24	0

- Substituting a combination of reduced-calorie whipped topping and additional fat-free yogurt for whipped heavy cream

- Replacing some of the walnuts with additional celery

SALAD
- 2 cups chopped apples
- 1½ teaspoons fresh lemon juice
- ⅓ cup chopped celery
- ¼ cup raisins
- 3 tablespoons chopped walnuts

DRESSING
- ⅓ cup fat-free vanilla yogurt
- ¼ cup frozen reduced-calorie whipped topping, thawed
- ½ teaspoon grated lemon peel
- ⅛ teaspoon ground nutmeg

TO MAKE THE SALAD: Place the apples in a medium bowl. Sprinkle with the lemon juice, then toss. Add the celery, raisins and walnuts.

TO MAKE THE DRESSING: Place the yogurt in a small bowl. Add the whipped topping and gently fold in. Then gently fold in the lemon peel and nutmeg.

Add the dressing to the apple mixture. Gently fold in until the apple mixture is coated.

Makes 6 side-dish servings.

New-Fashioned Potato Salad

I changed the dressing of this picnic favorite, which drastically cut calories and fat but kept the flavor and creamy texture of an old-fashioned potato salad. Calories, fat and cholesterol were reduced by:

- Using only the egg white portion of hard-cooked eggs

- Replacing most of the mayonnaise in the dressing with a mixture of tofu and fat-free yogurt

Nutrition Scorecard
(per serving)

	Before	After
Calories	218	60
Fat (g.)	21	2
% Calories from fat	85%	36%
Cholesterol (mg.)	120	2

SALAD
3 medium potatoes (1 pound)
5 hard-cooked egg whites, coarsely chopped; discard yolks
1 stalk celery, chopped
¼ cup chopped green onions

DRESSING
3 ounces tofu
2 tablespoons reduced-calorie mayonnaise
2 tablespoons fat-free plain yogurt
1 teaspoon white vinegar
½ teaspoon dry mustard or 1 tablespoon Dijon mustard
1 clove garlic, minced
¼ teaspoon salt
⅛ teaspoon ground black pepper
Paprika

TO MAKE THE SALAD: In a medium covered saucepan, cook the potatoes in boiling water for 20 to 25 minutes or until tender. Drain, then peel and cube the potatoes. Transfer to a medium bowl and chill in the refrigerator.

Add the egg whites, celery and green onions to the potatoes.

TO MAKE THE DRESSING: In a blender or small food processor, puree the tofu on low speed until creamy. Add the mayonnaise, yogurt, vinegar, mustard, garlic, salt and pepper. Blend or process until smooth.

Add the dressing to the potato mixture. Gently toss until the potato mixture is coated. Lightly sprinkle the top with the paprika to garnish. Cover and chill in the refrigerator for at least 2 hours to blend the flavors.

Makes 6 side-dish servings.

Oil-Free Three-Bean Salad

This salad improves with age! I always plan ahead when serving this salad so the beans have plenty of time to soak up the tangy-sweet dressing. Calories and fat were reduced by:

• Replacing the salad oil with a mixture of chicken broth and grape juice

Nutrition Scorecard (per serving)		
	Before	After
Calories	161	77
Fat (g.)	9	<1
% Calories from fat	50%	4%
Cholesterol (mg.)	0	0

DRESSING
- ⅓ cup white vinegar
- 3 tablespoons chicken broth, defatted
- 2 tablespoons white grape juice
- 2 tablespoons sugar
- 1 teaspoon celery seeds
- 1 clove garlic, minced

SALAD
- 1 (8-ounce) can cut waxed beans, drained
- 1 (8-ounce) can cut green beans, drained
- 1 (8-ounce) can red kidney beans, drained
- ½ cup finely chopped onions
- ½ cup chopped green peppers

TO MAKE THE DRESSING: In a small bowl, stir together the vinegar, broth, juice, sugar, celery seeds and garlic.

TO MAKE THE SALAD: In a large bowl, combine the waxed beans, green beans, kidney beans, onions and peppers. Add the dressing. Gently stir until combined. Cover and chill in the refrigerator for 4 to 24 hours to blend the flavors, stirring often.

Makes 6 side-dish servings.

Italian Pasta Salad

My love for deli-style pasta salad inspired me to create this copycat. It's just as tasty as the purchased version but has only half the calories and less than a third of the fat. Calories, fat and cholesterol were reduced by:

- Reducing the amount of provolone cheese

- Using reduced-fat Parmesan cheese (3 grams of fat per ounce of cheese)

- Replacing the salami with additional sweet peppers

- Reducing the amount of olives

- Using a commercial fat-free Italian salad dressing instead of a homemade oil-and-vinegar dressing

Nutrition Scorecard
(per serving)

	Before	After
Calories	201	99
Fat (g.)	13	2
% Calories from fat	59%	20%
Cholesterol (mg.)	15	3

4 ounces corkscrew pasta (rotini)
½ small zucchini
1 ounce provolone cheese, cubed
½ cup broccoli florets, chopped
½ cup finely chopped sweet red peppers
½ cup finely chopped green peppers
½ small red onion, sliced
3 tablespoons reduced-fat grated Parmesan cheese
3 tablespoons snipped fresh parsley
3 tablespoons sliced pitted ripe olives
½ cup fat-free Italian salad dressing
½ teaspoon dried oregano
2 tablespoons fat-free Italian salad dressing (if necessary)

Cook the pasta according to the directions on the package. Drain well. Transfer the pasta to a large bowl.

Cut the zucchini lengthwise into quarters, then thinly slice it (you should have about ½ cup). Add the zucchini to the pasta. Then add the provolone cheese, broccoli, red and green peppers, onion, Parmesan cheese, parsley and olives.

Add the ½ cup dressing, then toss until the pasta mixture is coated. Sprinkle with the oregano. Cover and chill in the refrigerator for at least 2 hours to blend the flavors. If necessary, add the 2 tablespoons dressing to moisten the salad. Gently toss.

Makes 8 side-dish servings.

Chinese Noodle Salad

Going to a potluck picnic? Take this oriental coleslaw—it serves ten, is delicious with grilled chicken, burgers and fish and always receives rave reviews. Calories and fat were reduced by:

- Replacing the salad oil in the dressing with a mixture of chicken broth and pineapple juice

- Reducing the amount of sugar in the dressing

- Reducing the amount of sesame oil in the dressing

- Reducing the amount of almonds and enhancing their flavor by toasting them

- Using reduced-fat ramen noodles

Nutrition Scorecard
(per serving)

	Before	After
Calories	453	89
Fat (g.)	40	3
% Calories from fat	79%	32%
Cholesterol (mg.)	0	0

DRESSING
⅓ cup seasoned rice vinegar
3 tablespoons chicken broth, defatted
3 tablespoons pineapple juice
2 tablespoons sugar
1 tablespoon oriental sesame oil

SALAD
⅓ cup slivered blanched almonds
5 cups finely shredded cabbage
1 package reduced-fat ramen soup noodles, crumbled (discard the soup-seasoning packet)
½ cup loosely packed snipped fresh cilantro
3 tablespoons snipped fresh chives

TO MAKE THE DRESSING: In a small bowl, stir together the vinegar, broth, juice, sugar and oil.

TO MAKE THE SALAD: Preheat the broiler. Spread the almonds on a cookie sheet. Broil 3" to 4" from the heat for about 5 minutes or until golden brown, stirring occasionally.

In a large bowl, combine the almonds, cabbage, *uncooked* noodles, cilantro and chives. Add the dressing and toss until the cabbage mixture is coated. Cover and chill in the refrigerator for at least 1½ hours to blend the flavors.

Makes 10 side-dish servings.

Carrot and Raisin Salad

It took just one change to whip this classic salad into shape. I cut calories, fat and cholesterol by:

• Switching to fat-free vanilla yogurt instead of sour cream

Nutrition Scorecard
(per serving)

	Before	After
Calories	147	111
Fat (g.)	6	<1
% Calories from fat	37%	1%
Cholesterol (mg.)	13	1

DRESSING
1 cup fat-free vanilla yogurt
2 tablespoons powdered sugar
1 teaspoon grated orange peel

SALAD
4 cups coarsely shredded carrots (about 5 medium)
1 (8-ounce) can crushed pineapple (in its own juice), well drained
½ cup raisins

TO MAKE THE DRESSING: In a small bowl, use a wire whisk to stir together the yogurt, sugar and orange peel.

TO MAKE THE SALAD: In a large bowl, combine the carrots, pineapple and raisins. Add the dressing and fold in until the carrot mixture is coated. Cover and chill in the refrigerator about 30 minutes before serving.

Makes 8 side-dish servings.

Watch That Topping!

Toppings can make or break a salad. Many salad bar favorites—including regular dressings, bacon bits, avocado slices and sunflower seeds—contain quite a bit of fat. That doesn't mean you can never have them. It does mean you should be extra choosy about which ones you select and the amount you use.

TOPPINGS	CALORIES	FAT (g.)	% CALORIES FROM FAT
Avocado (¼)	84	8	86%
Bacon bits (2 tablespoons)	54	3	53%
Cheddar cheese, shredded (2 tablespoons)	57	5	74%
Chow mein noodles (2 tablespoons)	30	2	52%
Coconut (2 tablespoons)	35	3	85%
Croutons (2 tablespoons)	14	<1	8%
Crumbled bacon (2 tablespoons)	36	3	78%
Granola (2 tablespoons)	74	4	50%
Olives (5)	26	2	83%
Parmesan cheese, grated (2 tablespoons)	46	3	43%
Raisins (2 tablespoons)	54	<1	<1%
Sunflower seeds (2 tablespoons)	104	10	84%

DRESSINGS	CALORIES	FAT (g.)	% CALORIES FROM FAT
Blue cheese (2 tablespoons)	155	16	91%
Caesar (2 tablespoons)	102	10	91%
French (2 tablespoons)	134	18	84%
Italian (2 tablespoons)	137	18	91%
Mayonnaise-type (2 tablespoons)	115	10	77%
Olive oil (2 tablespoons)	239	27	100%
Ranch (2 tablespoons)	109	11	92%
Russian (2 tablespoons)	151	16	90%
Thousand Island (2 tablespoons)	168	11	83%

Tabbouleh

Pictured on page 296

This light version of a Middle Eastern grain salad is a great way to help you meet the Food Guide Pyramid's recommended 6 to 11 servings of grains a day. Calories and fat were reduced by:

• Replacing most of the olive oil in the dressing with a mixture of chicken broth and lemon juice

Nutrition Scorecard
(per serving)

	Before	After
Calories	127	84
Fat (g.)	7	2
% Calories from fat	50%	21%
Cholesterol (mg.)	0	0

SALAD
- ¾ cup bulgur
- ¾ cup boiling water
- 2 tomatoes, chopped
- ¾ cup snipped fresh parsley
- ¼ cup snipped fresh chives
- ¼ cup snipped fresh mint

DRESSING
- ¼ cup lemon juice
- 2 tablespoons canned chicken broth, defatted
- 1 tablespoon olive oil
- 1 clove garlic, minced

TO MAKE THE SALAD: In a large bowl, stir together the bulgur and water. Let stand about 15 minutes or until the water is absorbed. Gently stir in the tomatoes, parsley, chives and mint. Set aside.

TO MAKE THE DRESSING: In a small bowl, stir together the lemon juice, broth, oil and garlic.

Add the dressing to the bulgur mixture. Gently stir until combined. Cover and chill in the refrigerator for at least 2 hours to blend the flavors.

Makes 8 side-dish servings.

Greek Salad

Pictured on page 297

This salad is bursting with flavor, but it's low in calories and fat. I was able to slim it down by jazzing up a commercial fat-free salad dressing. Calories, fat and cholesterol were also reduced by:

• Replacing some of the feta cheese with fat-free cottage cheese

Nutrition Scorecard
(per serving)

	Before	After
Calories	195	83
Fat (g.)	19	4
% Calories from fat	87%	43%
Cholesterol (mg.)	25	3

3 cups torn romaine lettuce
3 cups torn iceberg lettuce
1 cucumber, sliced
1 green pepper, chopped
½ red onion, sliced and separated into rings
2 stalks celery, sliced
1 tomato, cut into thin wedges
½ cup sliced pitted ripe olives
4 ounces feta cheese
½ cup fat-free cottage cheese
⅔ cup fat-free Italian salad dressing
1½ teaspoons chopped fresh dill

In a large bowl, combine the romaine, iceberg lettuce, cucumbers, green peppers, onions, celery, tomatoes and olives.

In a small bowl, use a fork to crumble the feta cheese. Stir in the cottage cheese. Sprinkle the cheese mixture on top of the lettuce mixture.

Stir together the dressing and dill. Pour the mixture over the salad. Gently toss until well coated. Cover and chill for at least 1 hour to blend the flavors.

Makes 8 side-dish servings.

Tropical Avocado and Fruit Salad

Colorful and tasty fruits make up this paradise delight. I like to use papaya, pineapple and mandarin oranges, but almost any fruit combination would be delicious. Calories, fat and cholesterol were reduced by:

- Reducing the amount of avocado

- Using a homemade reduced-fat salad dressing

Nutrition Scorecard *(per serving)*		
	Before	After
Calories	175	115
Fat (g.)	11	4
% Calories from fat	57%	31%
Cholesterol (mg.)	6	0

1 papaya, seeded, peeled and cubed
2 cups fresh pineapple chunks
1 (11-ounce) can water-packed mandarin oranges, drained
1 avocado, seeded, peeled and diced
⅔ cup Creamy Lime Dressing (see below)
1 tablespoon snipped fresh mint (optional)

In a large bowl, combine the papaya, pineapple, oranges and avocados. Add the dressing and gently fold in until the fruit mixture is coated. If desired, sprinkle with the mint to garnish.

Makes 8 side-dish servings.

Creamy Lime Dressing

Pictured on page 298

This dressing is also good as a dip for fresh fruit. I cut back on calories, fat and cholesterol by:

- Using fat-free plain yogurt instead of sour cream

Nutrition Scorecard *(per 2 tablespoons)*		
	Before	After
Calories	68	37
Fat (g.)	4	<1
% Calories from fat	53%	1%
Cholesterol (mg.)	9	0

½ cup fat-free plain yogurt
2 tablespoons honey
5 teaspoons fresh lime juice

1 tablespoon powdered sugar
½ teaspoon finely shredded lime peel

In a small bowl, use a wire whisk to stir together the yogurt, honey, lime juice, powdered sugar and lime peel until combined.

Makes about ¾ cup; 6 servings.

Strawberry Cream Gelatin Salad

This fruity gelatin salad frosted with cream cheese has been a favorite of mine since my childhood. So when my clients request a healthier version of it, I'm always thrilled to give them this recipe. I reduced the calories, fat and cholesterol by:

- Using a mixture of fat-free ricotta cheese and light cream cheese instead of regular cream cheese

- Using sugar-free gelatin instead of regular gelatin

- Reducing the amount of sugar

Nutrition Scorecard
(per serving)

	Before	After
Calories	309	174
Fat (g.)	13	3
% Calories from fat	38%	13%
Cholesterol (mg.)	37	8

1½ cups boiling water
1 (8-serving) package sugar-free strawberry gelatin
2 (10-ounce) packages frozen sliced strawberries, partially thawed
1 (16-ounce) can crushed pineapple (in its own juice), drained
½ cup powdered sugar
½ cup soft-style light cream cheese (see note)
1 cup fat-free ricotta cheese

In a large bowl, stir together the water and gelatin until the gelatin is dissolved. Stir in the strawberries and pineapple. Pour half of the mixture into an 11" × 7" × 1½" baking dish. Chill in the refrigerator about 30 minutes or until semi-firm. Set the remaining gelatin mixture aside at room temperature.

Meanwhile, in a small bowl, stir together the powdered sugar and cream cheese until well combined. Fold in the ricotta. Carefully, spread the cheese mixture on top of the semi-firm gelatin. Then spoon on the remaining gelatin mixture. Chill in the refrigerator for 3 to 4 hours or until firm. Cut into pieces to serve.

Makes 8 side-dish servings.

Note: Be sure to use light cream cheese rather than the fat-free variety. Using fat-free cream cheese will result in a runny topping.

Pineapple Lime Molded Salad

This salad is particularly popular at potluck dinners. And this version is nearly fat free. Calories, fat and cholesterol were reduced by:

• Replacing cream cheese with a combination of fat-free yogurt and fat-free ricotta cheese

• Replacing chopped nuts with celery

• Using sugar-free gelatin rather than regular gelatin

Nutrition Scorecard
(per serving)

	Before	After
Calories	347	107
Fat (g.)	19	<1
% Calories from fat	49%	1%
Cholesterol (mg.)	41	2

> 1 cup boiling water
> 1 (4-serving) package sugar-free lime gelatin
> 1 (16-ounce) can crushed pineapple (in its own juice)
> ½ cup fat-free plain yogurt
> ½ cup fat-free ricotta cheese
> 1½ cups miniature marshmallows
> ½ cup chopped celery

In a large bowl, stir together the water and gelatin until the gelatin is dissolved.

Drain the pineapple, reserving the juice. Set the pineapple aside. Add enough water to the juice to make 1 cup, and stir it into the gelatin mixture. Gradually stir in the yogurt and ricotta cheese. Chill in the refrigerator about 30 minutes or until thickened but not set.

Fold the pineapple, marshmallows and celery into the gelatin mixture. Transfer to a 1-quart mold. Chill in the refrigerator about 2 hours or until firm. Unmold the gelatin onto a serving plate and serve.

Makes 6 side-dish servings.

Pineapple Ambrosia

Years ago when I first made this ambrosia, I was surprised how good it tasted with yogurt instead of sour cream. Now, this salad has become a favorite at family gatherings. Calories, fat and cholesterol were reduced by:

- Using fruit canned in juice instead of syrup

- Using plain or tropical-flavored fat-free yogurt instead of sour cream

- Reducing the amount of coconut

Nutrition Scorecard
(per serving)

	Before	After
Calories	223	133
Fat (g.)	10	1
% Calories from fat	40%	7%
Cholesterol (mg.)	10	0

3 cups miniature marshmallows
1 (20-ounce) can crushed pineapple (in its own juice), drained
1 (20-ounce) can pineapple chunks or tidbits (in their own juice), drained
1 (11-ounce) can water-packed mandarin oranges, drained
1 cup fat-free plain or tropical-flavored yogurt
½ cup flaked coconut

In a large bowl, gently combine the marshmallows, crushed pineapple, pineapple chunks or tidbits, oranges, yogurt and coconut. Cover and chill in the refrigerator for at least 1 hour.

Makes 10 side-dish servings.

Note: Leftover ambrosia keeps well in the refrigerator for up to two days. If you like, you can also serve this as a light dessert.

SIMPLY SIDE DISHES

While a "side dish" may sound unimportant in the scheme of a meal, it can easily contain as many calories or as much fat as the main course. Take the case of traditional bread stuffing. It often has a lot of butter—not to mention cream, egg yolks, sausage or another fatty meat. It certainly has more fat than the turkey it accompanies.

Even healthy-sounding vegetable dishes can have their nutritional integrity clouded when fatty ingredients are part of the recipe. It's not unusual for super-nutritious steamed carrots, broccoli and such to be coated with butter or sprinkled with bacon before they arrive on the table. There are smarter ways to treat these vegetables.

In this chapter, I'll give you some of my favorite methods for reducing the fat in traditional side dishes. When a recipe calls for bacon, for instance, I use the leaner turkey version and enhance the flavor with a small amount of liquid smoke. When butter really is vital to maintain the richness of a dish, I use only enough to satisfy the taste buds. All of which underscores my philosophy that you don't need to banish certain foods from your diet—just cut the fat where you won't miss it.

Healthy Ways with Vegetables

The best thing you can do with most vegetables is cook them quickly and serve them simply. Microwaving and steaming are ideal reduced-fat cooking methods. Both preserve the vegetables' bright colors and fresh flavors. As an added bonus, they leave valuable vitamins intact.

You can serve the cooked vegetables plain or you can dress them up with a spritz of lemon juice, a sprinkling of herbs or a luscious—but reduced-fat—sauce like the one on the next page.

To microwave or steam vegetables to perfection, follow the general directions given here and use the estimated cooking times on the chart. Keep in mind that microwaving time varies according to the ripeness of your vegetables, the size of the pieces and the wattage of your particular microwave oven.

- STEAMING. Use a large saucepan with a tight-fitting lid. Bring about 1" of water to a boil. Then place the vegetable in a steamer basket. Set the basket in the saucepan, making sure the basket sits above the water. Cover the saucepan and steam for the time on the chart or until the vegetable is crisp-tender.

- MICROWAVING. Use the amount listed on the chart. Place the vegetable in a casserole or baking dish and add 2 tablespoons of water. Cover with a lid or vented plastic wrap and cook on high power (100%) for the time listed or until the vegetable is crisp-tender; rearrange or stir the vegetables halfway through the cooking time.

| | | TIME (MINUTES) | |
VEGETABLE	QUANTITY	MICROWAVING	STEAMING
Artichokes, whole	1 (10 ounces)	9-10	30-40
Asparagus, whole spears	1 pound	5-8	10-15
Beans, green or waxed whole	1 pound	12-14	10-15
Broccoli florets	1 pound	5-7	10-15
Brussels sprouts, whole	1 pound	6-8	10-15
Carrots, sliced ¼" thick	1 pound	9-10	10-15
Cauliflower florets	1 pound	7-8	10-15
Corn kernels	2 cups	5-6	5
Peas, shelled	2 cups	7-8	10-15
Winter squash, cut into 1" cubes	1 pound	5-7	10-15

Lite Cheddar Cheese Sauce

This creamy reduced-fat cheese sauce is great on all types of steamed or microwaved vegetables, especially cauliflower, broccoli and asparagus. I also like to serve it over baked potatoes. I reduced calories, fat and cholesterol by:

- Eliminating the butter

- Using evaporated skim milk instead of whole milk

- Using a combination of fat-free and reduced-fat (less than 5 grams of fat per ounce) cheddar cheeses

Nutrition Scorecard
(per 2 tablespoons)

	Before	After
Calories	73	47
Fat (g.)	6	1
% Calories from fat	70%	27%
Cholesterol (mg.)	18	6

½ cup (2 ounces) finely shredded reduced-fat sharp cheddar cheese
¼ cup (1 ounce) finely shredded fat-free cheddar cheese
3 teaspoons cornstarch
¾ cup evaporated skim milk

In a small bowl combine the reduced-fat and fat-free cheeses. Sprinkle with 1 teaspoon of the cornstarch and toss until coated. Set the cheese mixture aside.

In a small saucepan, use a wire whisk to stir together 2 tablespoons of the milk and the remaining 2 teaspoons of cornstarch until smooth. Then stir in the remaining milk.

Cook and stir the milk mixture over medium heat until slightly thickened and bubbly. Cook and stir for 1 minute more. Reduce the heat to low. Then slowly stir in the cheese mixture. Cook and stir just until melted.

Makes 1 cup; 8 servings.

Glazed Carrots

Don't be alarmed by seeing butter instead of margarine in this recipe. I used only a tiny amount to give these carrots a rich, buttery taste. It makes a big difference! I reduced calories, fat and cholesterol by:

• Replacing some of the butter with apple juice

Nutrition Scorecard (per serving)		
	Before	After
Calories	113	74
Fat (g.)	6	1
% Calories from fat	62%	1%
Cholesterol (mg.)	16	3

1 pound carrots
4 teaspoons apple juice
1 tablespoon brown sugar
1 teaspoon butter
¼ teaspoon ground nutmeg (optional)

Cut the carrots into 2"-long pieces. Then cut each piece lengthwise into quarters.

In a large saucepan with a tight-fitting lid, bring about 1" of water to a boil. Place the carrots in a steamer basket and set the basket in the saucepan, making sure the basket sits above the water. Cover the saucepan and steam for 8 to 10 minutes or until crisp-tender.

Meanwhile, in a 1-cup microwave-safe measuring cup or custard cup, stir together the apple juice, brown sugar and butter. Cook in a microwave oven on high power (100%) about 25 seconds or just until the brown sugar and butter are melted.

To serve, transfer the carrots to a serving bowl. Drizzle with the apple juice mixture and toss until coated. If desired, sprinkle with the nutmeg and toss again.

Makes 4 servings.

Note: Since sodium is a concern for many people, I reduced the amount in this recipe by omitting the salt that's usually sprinkled on cooked vegetables. You can do that with virtually any vegetable, and you'll never notice the difference.

Easy Cheesy Cauliflower

Here's a dish that's quick and easy—and it's a winner with my six-year-old. Whenever I prepare this creamy dish, my daughter asks for seconds. Calories, fat and cholesterol were reduced by:

- Replacing a traditional white sauce (butter, flour and milk) with a mixture of reduced-fat cream of mushroom soup and evaporated skim milk

- Using a combination of fat-free and reduced-fat (less than 5 grams of fat per ounce) cheddar cheeses

Nutrition Scorecard
(per serving)

	Before	After
Calories	189	117
Fat (g.)	12	3
% Calories from fat	54%	27%
Cholesterol (mg.)	38	11

4 cups small cauliflower florets
1 (10¾-ounce) can 99%-fat-free condensed cream of mushroom soup with ⅓ less salt
¼ cup evaporated skim milk
½ cup (2 ounces) finely grated or shredded fat-free cheddar cheese (see note)
½ cup (2 ounces) finely shredded reduced-fat sharp cheddar cheese (see note)

In a large saucepan with a tight-fitting lid, bring about 1" of water to a boil. Place the cauliflower in a steamer basket and set the basket in the saucepan, making sure the basket sits above the water. Cover the saucepan and steam for 6 to 8 minutes or until crisp-tender.

Meanwhile, in a medium saucepan stir together the condensed soup and milk. Cook and stir until bubbly. Add the fat-free cheese; cook and stir until melted. Then stir in the reduced-fat cheese. Add the cauliflower. Gently toss until coated and heated through.

Makes 4 servings.

Note: Be sure to *finely* grate or shred the fat-free cheddar cheese so that it melts easier. Also, use a *sharp-flavored* reduced-fat cheddar cheese in the sauce for a better cheddar flavor.

Spicy Vegetable Stir-Fry

Pictured on page 299

Stir-frying can be a quick and healthy way to prepare vegetables. This fast, waterless method locks in nutrients, preventing vitamins and minerals from leaching out. Calories and fat were reduced by:

- Using no-stick spray instead of oil to stir-fry the vegetables

Nutrition Scorecard
(per serving)

	Before	After
Calories	77	34
Fat (g.)	5	1
% Calories from fat	58%	6%
Cholesterol (mg.)	0	0

¼ cup chicken broth, defatted
1 tablespoon orange juice
1 tablespoon reduced-sodium soy sauce
1½ teaspoons cornstarch
1½ teaspoons grated ginger root
1½ teaspoons minced garlic (about 3 cloves)
⅛ teaspoon crushed red pepper
1½ cups small cauliflower florets
1 cup carrots cut into julienne pieces
8 ounces zucchini, halved and thinly sliced

In a small bowl, stir together the broth, orange juice, soy sauce and corn starch. Set the broth mixture aside.

Lightly spray an unheated wok or large skillet with no-stick spray. Heat the wok or skillet over medium-high heat. Add the ginger, garlic and red pepper. Stir-fry about 30 seconds or until fragrant.

Add the cauliflower and stir-fry for 2 minutes. Then add the carrots and stir-fry for 2 minutes. Finally, add the zucchini and stir-fry for 2 minutes more.

Stir in the broth mixture. Bring to a simmer. Cover and simmer about 1 minute or until the vegetables are crisp-tender and the sauce turns glossy and thickens. Serve immediately.

Makes 4 servings.

Creamy Green Bean and Onion Bake

If you have company for dinner or need a vegetable dish for a potluck party, make this reduced-fat version of the ever-so-popular green bean casserole with french-fried onions. Calories, fat and cholesterol were reduced by:

- Using a homemade reduced-fat onion topping instead of canned french-fried onions

- Replacing bacon with turkey bacon, reducing the amount used and enhancing the flavor with liquid smoke

- Using reduced-fat cream of mushroom soup

- Using fat-free yogurt instead of sour cream

Nutrition Scorecard
(per serving)

	Before	After
Calories	227	103
Fat (g.)	15	2
% Calories from fat	60%	19%
Cholesterol (mg.)	29	7

⅓ cup chopped onions
⅓ cup fine dry plain bread crumbs
4 slices turkey bacon
1 (10¾-ounce) can 99%-fat-free condensed cream of mushroom soup with ⅓ less salt
½ cup fat-free plain yogurt
½ teaspoon liquid smoke
3 (9-ounce) packages frozen French-style green beans, thawed

Preheat the oven to 350°. Lightly spray a cookie sheet with no-stick spray.

In a small bowl, stir together the onions and bread crumbs. Evenly spread the mixture on the cookie sheet. Bake about 12 minutes or until golden brown. Remove the onion mixture from the oven and set aside.

Meanwhile, in a medium skillet, cook the bacon according to the directions on the package. Chop the bacon and set aside.

In a large bowl, stir together the condensed soup, yogurt and liquid smoke. Then stir in the beans and bacon.

Lightly spray an 11" × 7" × 1½" baking dish with no-stick spray. Transfer the bean mixture to the baking dish. Top with the onion mixture. Bake for 25 to 30 minutes or until bubbly.

Makes 6 servings.

Crockpot Baked Beans

Pictured on page 300

Here's a hearty side dish that's always a favorite at picnics. Calories, fat and cholesterol were reduced by:

- Reducing the amount of ground beef (you could omit it entirely to save even more calories, fat and cholesterol)

- Replacing bacon with turkey bacon, reducing the amount used and enhancing the flavor with liquid smoke

- Replacing the ketchup with tomato sauce

- Adding maple flavoring to enhance the perception of sweetness ordinarily contributed by ketchup

Nutrition Scorecard
(per serving)

	Before	After
Calories	332	206
Fat (g.)	14	3
% Calories from fat	36%	14%
Cholesterol (mg.)	40	15

½ medium onion, chopped
5 slices turkey bacon, chopped
4 ounces ground beef (80% lean)
1 (16-ounce) can vegetarian beans in tomato sauce
1 (16-ounce) can vegetarian baked beans
1 (16-ounce) can red kidney beans, rinsed and drained
½ cup tomato sauce
2 tablespoons brown sugar
1–2 teaspoons liquid smoke
½ teaspoon maple flavoring

Lightly spray an unheated medium skillet with no-stick spray. Add the onions and bacon. Cook and stir over medium-high heat until the onions are tender. Add the ground beef and cook until browned, stirring occasionally.

Transfer the onion mixture to a 4- to 6-quart crockpot. Stir in the beans in tomato sauce, baked beans, kidney beans, tomato sauce, brown sugar, liquid smoke and maple flavoring. Cover and cook on the medium-high heat setting for 4 to 6 hours (if necessary, adjust the heat setting so the beans slowly simmer during cooking). Stir before serving.

Makes 10 servings.

Eggplant Parmigiana

Here's a great-tasting side dish that can also double as a vegetarian main dish. (In that case, I serve heartier portions.) Calories, fat and cholesterol were reduced by:

- Baking the eggplant slices instead of frying them

- Using egg whites instead of a whole egg

- Using reduced-fat mozzarella cheese (less than 5 grams of fat per ounce of cheese)

Nutrition Scorecard
(per serving)

	Before	After
Calories	298	186
Fat (g.)	17	5
% Calories from fat	51%	25%
Cholesterol (mg.)	81	12

1 eggplant (about 12 ounces)
⅓ cup fine dry plain bread crumbs
1 tablespoon grated Parmesan cheese
1 teaspoon dried oregano
2 tablespoons all-purpose flour
2 egg whites, lightly beaten
1 cup marinara sauce
½ cup (2 ounces) finely shredded reduced-fat mozzarella cheese

Preheat the oven to 350°. Spray an 8" × 8" × 2" baking pan with no-stick spray; set aside.

Trim the ends from the eggplant. If desired, remove the skin. Then slice the eggplant crosswise into ½"-thick slices. Set aside.

In a pie plate, stir together the bread crumbs, Parmesan cheese and oregano. Dip the eggplant slices into the flour. Then dip them into the egg whites and coat them with the bread crumbs.

Arrange the eggplant in the prepared pan. Bake for 20 to 25 minutes or until light brown. Remove from the oven. Spoon the marinara sauce over the eggplant. Sprinkle with the mozzarella cheese. Bake about 10 minutes or until the cheese is melted.

Makes 4 servings.

Herbed Mushroom Sauté

<table>
<tr><td rowspan="2">With their hint of sherry, garlic and rosemary, these mushrooms make a wonderful complement to grilled chicken breasts or poached fish. Calories, fat and cholesterol were reduced by:

• Using chicken broth instead of butter for sautéing the mushrooms and onion rings</td><td colspan="3">*Nutrition Scorecard*
(per serving)</td></tr>
</table>

		Before	After
Calories		95	46
Fat (g.)		6	<1
% Calories from fat		59%	11%
Cholesterol (mg.)		16	0

> 1 pound fresh large mushrooms
> 2 tablespoons dry sherry, dry white wine or nonalcoholic white wine
> 2 tablespoons chicken broth, defatted
> ½ small onion, thinly sliced and separated into rings
> 2 cloves garlic, minced
> 2 teaspoons snipped fresh rosemary or oregano
> Freshly ground black pepper

Cut the mushrooms into quarters. Lightly spray an unheated large skillet with no-stick spray. Add the sherry or wine and chicken broth. Then add the mushrooms, onions and garlic. Cook over medium-high heat, stirring occasionally, about 5 minutes or until the mushrooms are tender. Stir in the rosemary or oregano and season to taste with the pepper.

Makes 4 servings.

Ratatouille in Roasted Peppers

Pictured on page 301

Traditionally, this mixture of eggplant, sweet peppers, tomatoes and zucchini is simmered in olive oil. But by using olive oil no-stick spray when cooking the vegetables, I was able to dramatically lower the fat and calories and still maintain the dish's character-istic flavor. Calories, fat and cholesterol were also reduced by:

- Using olive oil no-stick spray instead of olive oil for roasting the sweet peppers

- Reducing the amount of mozzarella cheese and using its reduced-fat alternate (less than 5 grams of fat per ounce of cheese)

Nutrition Scorecard (per serving)

	Before	After
Calories	185	44
Fat (g.)	16	1
% Calories from fat	77%	15%
Cholesterol (mg.)	6	2

PEPPER SHELLS
> 4 *sweet red, green or yellow peppers*

RATATOUILLE
> 2 *cups diced eggplant*
> 1 *medium zucchini, sliced ¼" thick*
> 1 *cup sliced fresh mushrooms*
> 1 *(8-ounce) can diced stewed tomatoes (with juices)*
> ½ *cup chopped onions*
> ¼ *cup loosely packed chopped fresh basil*
> 2 *tablespoons dry white wine*
> 2 *cloves garlic, minced*
> ¼ *cup (1 ounce) finely shredded reduced-fat mozzarella cheese*

TO MAKE THE PEPPER SHELLS: Preheat the oven to 450°. Lightly spray a cookie sheet with the olive oil no-stick spray. Cut the peppers in half length-wise, then remove the stems, seeds and membranes. Arrange the pepper halves, cut side down, on the cookie sheet. Spray the skins of the peppers with the no-stick spray. Bake for 25 to 35 minutes or until the skins just begin to blister. Remove the peppers from the oven and slightly cool.

When the peppers are cool enough to handle, remove and discard the skins. Return the peppers, cut side up, to the cookie sheet; set aside.

TO MAKE THE RATATOUILLE: Preheat the broiler. Lightly spray an unheated large skillet with the no-stick spray. Add the eggplant, zucchini, mushrooms, tomatoes (with juices), onions, basil, wine and garlic. Bring to a boil. Reduce the heat, cover and simmer about 20 minutes or until the vegetables are ten-der. Then uncover and simmer for 5 to 10 minutes more, stirring occasionally, until the mixture slightly thickens.

Spoon the ratatouille mixture into the pepper shells. Sprinkle with the cheese. Broil 3" to 4" from the heat about 1 minute or until the cheese melts.

Makes 8 servings.

Savory Creamed Spinach

Here's a dish with only one-quarter the fat of its original version. Yet all the richness and creaminess of traditional creamed spinach remain. I cut calories, fat and cholesterol by:

- Using olive oil no-stick spray instead of margarine to sauté the onions

- Reducing the amount of cheese and using its reduced-fat alternate (less than 5 grams of fat per ounce of cheese)

Nutrition Scorecard
(per serving)

	Before	After
Calories	216	129
Fat (g.)	16	4
% Calories from fat	64%	27%
Cholesterol (mg.)	31	17

    1 (10-ounce) package frozen chopped spinach
    ¾ cup evaporated skim milk
    2 teaspoons cornstarch
    ½ cup finely chopped onions
    ¼ teaspoon dried basil
    ¼ teaspoon dried oregano
       Dash of nutmeg
    ¾ cup (3 ounces) finely shredded reduced-fat Monterey Jack cheese

Cook the spinach according to the directions on the package. Drain the spinach well and set it aside.

In a small bowl, stir together the milk and cornstarch. Set the mixture aside.

Lightly spray an unheated medium skillet with olive oil no-stick spray. Add the onions, basil, oregano and nutmeg. Cook and stir over medium heat until tender.

Stir in the milk mixture. Cook and stir until thickened and bubbly. Add the cheese, then cook and stir until melted. Stir in the spinach and heat through.

Makes 4 servings.

Classy Potatoes

Serve this delicious cheese-and-potato casserole when company's coming for dinner. It's ideal because you can assemble it before your guests arrive. This leaves you more time to spend with them instead of being in the kitchen doing last-minute preparation. Calories, fat and cholesterol were reduced by:

• Using reduced-fat sharp cheddar cheese (less than 5 grams of fat per ounce of cheese)

• Using reduced-fat cream of chicken soup

• Replacing sour cream with fat-free yogurt

• Using evaporated skim milk instead of butter

Nutrition Scorecard (per serving)		
	Before	After
Calories	521	334
Fat (g.)	38	8
% Calories from fat	65%	21%
Cholesterol (mg.)	58	35

> 2 cups (8 ounces) finely shredded reduced-fat sharp cheddar cheese
> 1 (10¾-ounce) can 99%-fat-free condensed cream of chicken soup with ⅓ less salt
> 1 cup fat-free plain yogurt
> ¾ cup evaporated skim milk
> ½ cup very finely chopped onions
> 2 cups cornflakes
> 6 medium potatoes (2 pounds), peeled

Preheat the oven to 350°. In a large bowl, stir together the cheese, condensed soup, yogurt, milk and onions. Set the soup mixture aside.

In a blender or food processor, blend or process the cornflakes into coarse crumbs (you should have about 1 cup). Set the cornflakes aside.

Coarsely shred the potatoes. Immediately stir the potatoes into the soup mixture to prevent browning. Spray a 10" × 9" × 2" or 11" × 7" × 1½" baking dish with no-stick spray. Transfer the potato mixture to the baking dish. Top with the cornflakes. Bake about 1 hour or until the potatoes are tender.

Makes 8 servings.

Sweet Potato Puff

Just a tiny amount of butter (yes, butter!) makes a big flavor difference. The trick is to eliminate the butter from the potato mixture and use only a small amount in the topping. Calories, fat and cholesterol were also reduced by:

• Using egg whites instead of whole eggs

• Reducing the amount of sugar (*sweet* potatoes are naturally sweet on their own)

• Reducing the amount of pecans

Nutrition Scorecard
(per serving)

	Before	After
Calories	737	335
Fat (g.)	36	11
% Calories from fat	42%	28%
Cholesterol (mg.)	126	10

POTATO PUFF
- 2 (18-ounce) cans vacuum-packed sweet potatoes or 3 cups cooked and cubed sweet potatoes
- 4 egg whites
- ¼ cup sugar
- 1 teaspoon vanilla
- 2 tablespoons all-purpose flour

PECAN TOPPING
- ½ cup packed brown sugar
- 3 tablespoons all-purpose flour
- 2 tablespoons butter
- ½ cup chopped pecans

TO MAKE THE POTATO PUFF: Preheat the oven to 350°. Spray a 1¼-quart casserole with no-stick spray. Set the casserole aside.

Using a food processor or electric mixer, process or mix the sweet potatoes, egg whites, sugar, vanilla and flour until smooth. Transfer the mixture to the prepared casserole. Set aside while preparing the topping.

TO MAKE THE PECAN TOPPING: In a small bowl, use your fingers to rub together the brown sugar, flour and butter until crumbly. Stir in the pecans. Sprinkle the mixture on top of the potato puff.

Bake about 30 minutes or until golden brown.

Makes 6 servings.

Twice-Baked Potatoes

Pictured on page 302

I love making a large batch of these stuffed potatoes for "planned leftovers." They're great for a quick lunch or snack, and they're even good for breakfast. Calories, fat and cholesterol were reduced by:

- Replacing sour cream with a combination of fat-free yogurt and fat-free cottage cheese (this substitution also supplies more calcium and protein than fat-free sour cream)

- Eliminating the butter in the pulp mixture

- Using reduced-fat sharp cheddar cheese (less than 5 grams of fat per ounce of cheese)

Nutrition Scorecard
(per potato half)

	Before	After
Calories	439	179
Fat (g.)	34	3
% Calories from fat	68%	13%
Cholesterol (mg.)	88	11

3 medium potatoes
1 cup fat-free cottage cheese
¼ cup fat-free plain yogurt
2 tablespoons minced fresh parsley
¾ cup (3 ounces) finely shredded reduced-fat sharp cheddar cheese
Paprika (optional)

Preheat the oven to 350°. Using a fork, prick the potatoes. Bake for 40 to 50 minutes or until tender. Cut the potatoes in half lengthwise. Scoop out the pulp, leaving thin shells. Set the pulp and shells aside.

In a food processor, process the cottage cheese, yogurt and parsley until smooth. Add the potato pulp and process again until smooth. Divide the mixture among the potato shells.

Place the filled shells on a cookie sheet. If necessary, bake about 10 minutes to heat through.

Top with the cheddar cheese and bake about 5 minutes or until the cheese melts. If desired, sprinkle with paprika.

Makes 6 potato halves; 6 servings.

Note: You may also use a blender to puree the mixture. For best results, blend the cottage cheese and yogurt until smooth. Then blend half of the cheese mixture with half of the potato pulp. Repeat blending with the remaining cheese mixture and pulp.

Duchess Potatoes

This recipe is even easier if you use leftover cooked potatoes. I cut calories, fat and cholesterol from this classic dish by:

• Replacing butter with buttermilk

• Using egg whites instead of a whole egg

Nutrition Scorecard (per serving)	Before	After
Calories	229	122
Fat (g.)	13	<1
% Calories from fat	50%	2%
Cholesterol (mg.)	84	0

3 medium potatoes (1 pound), peeled and halved
2 egg whites, lightly beaten
3 tablespoons buttermilk
¼ teaspoon salt (optional)

Place the potatoes in a medium saucepan. Add cold water to cover and bring to a boil. Reduce the heat. Cover and simmer about 30 minutes or until tender when tested with a fork.

Meanwhile, in a small bowl, combine the egg whites and buttermilk. Set the egg mixture aside. Lightly spray a cookie sheet with no-stick spray. Set the cookie sheet aside.

Drain the potatoes and transfer them to a large bowl. Using an electric mixer, beat the potatoes on low speed until fluffy. Slowly add the egg mixture and continue beating until combined.

Preheat the broiler. If desired, spoon the potato mixture into a pastry bag fitted with a large star- or round-shaped pastry tip. Pipe or spoon the potato mixture into four mounds on the prepared cookie sheet, leaving 2" between mounds. Broil about 3" from the heat for 5 to 8 minutes or until the potatoes are golden brown.

Makes 4 servings.

German Potato Pancakes

Now you can enjoy classic potato pancakes—with only a fraction of the fat and calories of the original version. And for a traditional no-fat topping, choose applesauce rather than sour cream or butter. I cut calories, fat and cholesterol by:

• Using egg whites instead of whole eggs

• Using no-stick spray instead of oil for cooking the pancakes

Nutrition Scorecard
(per potato pancake)

	Before	After
Calories	170	69
Fat (g.)	12	<1
% Calories from fat	61%	1%
Cholesterol (mg.)	106	0

  2 cups shredded potatoes
  6 egg whites, lightly beaten
1½ tablespoons all-purpose flour
  1 tablespoon grated onions
  ½ teaspoon salt (optional)
  ⅛ teaspoon ground black pepper

Squeeze the excess moisture from the potatoes. Transfer the potatoes to a large bowl. Stir in the egg whites. Then stir in the flour, onions, salt (if desired) and pepper.

Lightly spray an unheated large skillet or griddle with no-stick spray. Heat over medium heat. Meanwhile, shape the potato mixture into six ¼"-thick patties. Add the patties to the hot skillet or griddle. Cook about 5 minutes on each side or until lightly browned and crisp. Serve immediately.

Makes 6 pancakes; 6 servings.

Hoppin' John

A two-in-one dish—this side dish of black-eyed peas and rice can double as a main dish. Just serve larger portions. Calories, fat and cholesterol were reduced by:

• Replacing bacon with turkey bacon (and adding liquid smoke to enhance the flavor)

Nutrition Scorecard
(per serving)

	Before	After
Calories	324	186
Fat (g.)	14	2
% Calories from fat	40%	12%
Cholesterol (mg.)	24	8

2½ cups water
½ cup dried black-eyed peas, sorted and rinsed
3 slices turkey bacon
¼ cup chopped onions
1 clove garlic, minced
½ cup long-grain brown rice (see note)
⅓ cup chopped green pepper
1 bay leaf
¼ teaspoon ground thyme
¼ teaspoon hot-pepper sauce
¼ teaspoon liquid smoke

In a medium saucepan, bring the water to a boil. Add the peas and reduce the heat. Cover and simmer about 45 minutes or until the peas are tender but not mushy.

Meanwhile, lightly spray a medium skillet with no-stick spray. Add the bacon and cook according to the directions on the package. Then drain the bacon on paper towels, chop it and set it aside.

Add the onions and garlic to the skillet. Cook and stir just until golden.

To the peas, add the bacon, onion mixture, rice, green peppers, bay leaf, thyme, hot-pepper sauce and liquid smoke. Stir until well combined.

Cover and cook over medium-low heat about 35 minutes or until the rice is tender. Remove the lid and simmer about 15 minutes or until the liquid has evaporated. Before serving, remove and discard the bay leaf.

Makes 4 servings.

Note: For best results, be sure to use regular brown rice rather than the instant or quick-cooking variety.

Mexican Rice

	Nutrition Scorecard (per serving)		
For this spicy rice dish, I chose to use brown rice because it both enhances the nutritional value of the dish and imparts a toasty "fried" color. Calories and fat were reduced by:		Before	After
	Calories	207	147
• Using no-stick spray instead of oil for browning the rice	Fat (g.)	8	1
	% Calories from fat	33%	5%
	Cholesterol (mg.)	0	0

    1 cup long-grain brown rice (see note)
    ½ cup chopped onions
    1 clove garlic, minced
    2 cups chicken broth, defatted
    ½ cup tomato sauce
    1 (4-ounce) can diced green chili peppers, drained
    ¼ teaspoon ground cumin
    ⅛ teaspoon ground black pepper

Lightly spray an unheated large skillet with no-stick spray. Heat the skillet over medium-high heat. Add the rice, onions and garlic. Cook until the rice is browned, stirring occasionally.

Stir in the broth, tomato sauce, chili peppers, cumin and pepper. Bring to a boil, then reduce the heat. Cover and simmer about 45 minutes or until the liquid is absorbed.

Makes 6 servings.

Note: For best results, be sure to use regular brown rice rather than the instant or quick-cooking variety.

Chinese Fried Rice

Chock-full of vegetables and flavor, this tasty dish can easily be a meal in itself. Calories, fat and cholesterol were reduced by:

- Replacing most of the whole eggs with egg whites

- Using no-stick spray instead of oil for "frying"

- Replacing ham with more vegetables

Nutrition Scorecard (per serving)		
	Before	After
Calories	113	80
Fat (g.)	4	1
% Calories from fat	29%	15%
Cholesterol (mg.)	39	36

> 2 egg whites
> 1 egg
> ¾ teaspoon grated ginger root
> ¼ cup chopped fresh mushrooms
> ¼ cup finely shredded carrots
> 2 tablespoons chopped fresh chives
> 1½ cups cooked medium-grain brown rice, well-chilled
> ¾ cup chopped Chinese cabbage or green cabbage
> 1 tablespoon reduced-sodium soy sauce
> ½ teaspoon dry mustard

In a small bowl, beat together the egg whites and egg until combined. Lightly spray an unheated large skillet with no-stick spray. Heat the skillet over medium heat. Pour in the eggs. Cook, without stirring, until the eggs begin to set. Then cook and stir until the eggs are crumbly and broken into small bits. Transfer the eggs to a bowl and set aside.

Slightly cool the skillet, then spray it again with the no-stick spray. Heat over medium-high heat. Add the ginger and cook and stir for 30 seconds. Add the mushrooms, carrots and chives. Cook and stir about 3 minutes or until the vegetables are tender.

Stir in the rice, cabbage and eggs. Sprinkle with the soy sauce and mustard. Cook for 3 to 5 minute or until heated, gently tossing to coat the rice with the soy sauce.

Makes 6 servings.

Risotto

This Italian rice dish requires a lot of stirring, but believe me the creamy end result is well worth the effort. Calories, fat and cholesterol were reduced by:

- Using olive oil no-stick spray instead of butter to sauté the onions, carrots and garlic

Nutrition Scorecard (per serving)		
	Before	After
Calories	194	134
Fat (g.)	7	1
% Calories from fat	33%	1%
Cholesterol (mg.)	18	0

3 cups beef broth, defatted
½ cup finely chopped onions
1 medium carrot, peeled and chopped
1 clove garlic, minced
¼ cup dry red wine or nonalcoholic red wine
1 cup Arborio rice (see note)
3 tablespoons snipped fresh parsley

In a medium saucepan, bring the broth to a simmer. Meanwhile, lightly spray an unheated large skillet with olive oil no-stick spray. Add the onions, carrots and garlic. Cook and stir over medium heat until tender.

Add the wine to the onion mixture. Cook and stir until almost all of the liquid has evaporated. Then stir in the rice and mix until the rice is coated.

Add 1 cup of the simmering broth to the rice mixture. Cook and stir about 10 minutes or until almost all of the liquid has been absorbed. Repeat the cooking and stirring process two more times, using 1 cup of broth each time. Transfer the rice mixture to a serving dish and sprinkle it with the parsley.

Makes 6 servings.

Note: Arborio rice is a special short-grain variety that has a high starch content and is ideal for achieving the creamy texture that's characteristic of risotto. Look for it in well-stocked supermarkets and specialty food shops.

Spiced Couscous

When I'm short on time, I turn to this flavorful side dish that I can have on the table in minutes. Look for couscous in the rice or pasta section of the supermarket or at a specialty food store. Calories, fat and cholesterol were reduced by:

- Using olive oil no-stick spray instead of olive oil to toast the couscous

- Eliminating the butter

Nutrition Scorecard
(per serving)

	Before	After
Calories	323	213
Fat (g.)	14	1
% Calories from fat	39%	6%
Cholesterol (mg.)	16	0

1½ cups couscous
2 cups chicken broth, defatted
¼ teaspoon ground black pepper
¼ teaspoon ground allspice

Lightly spray an unheated large skillet with olive oil no-stick spray. Heat the skillet over medium heat. Add the couscous. Cook and stir for 2 minutes.

Stir in the broth, pepper and allspice. Cook and gently toss with two forks until the liquid is absorbed.

Makes 4 servings.

Harvest Apple Stuffing

Pictured on page 303

This fruit-and-walnut dressing is the perfect complement to roasted chicken. Calories, fat and cholesterol were reduced by:

• Using apple juice instead of butter to sauté the vegetables

Nutrition Scorecard (per serving)		
	Before	After
Calories	307	197
Fat (g.)	18	5
% Calories from fat	50%	21%
Cholesterol (mg.)	31	0

> 2 cups finely chopped apples
> 1 teaspoon lemon juice
> 1 cup coarsely shredded carrots
> 1 cup thinly sliced celery
> ½ cup chopped onions
> ½ cup apple juice
> ¼ teaspoon ground nutmeg
> 8 cups dry plain bread cubes
> ⅓ cup chopped walnuts
> ¼ cup toasted wheat germ
> 1–1½ cups chicken broth, defatted

Preheat the oven to 350°.

Place the apples in a small bowl. Sprinkle with the lemon juice, then toss until coated. Set aside.

Spray a large skillet with no-stick spray. Add the carrots, celery, onions and apple juice. Cook over medium heat until tender, stirring occasionally. Stir in the nutmeg.

Lightly spray a 3- to 4-quart casserole with no-stick spray. Add the bread cubes, apples, walnuts, wheat germ and the carrot mixture; toss to combine. Drizzle with 1 cup of the broth. If necessary, drizzle with enough of the remaining ½ cup of broth to moisten the bread; gently toss to mix well. Bake, uncovered, for 30 to 40 minutes or until heated through.

Makes 8 servings.

Old-Fashioned Cornbread Stuffing

Here's an easy, made-from-scratch bread stuffing I often recommend to my clients who want to enjoy a traditional Thanksgiving feast and still stay within healthy limits. I cut calories, fat and cholesterol by:

- Using no-stick spray instead of butter to sauté the vegetables

- Replacing melted butter in the stuffing mixture with additional chicken broth

Nutrition Scorecard
(per serving)

	Before	After
Calories	225	135
Fat (g.)	13	1
% Calories from fat	50%	8%
Cholesterol (mg.)	31	0

½ cup finely chopped celery
½ cup sliced fresh mushrooms
¼ cup chopped onions
2 tablespoons snipped fresh parsley
1½ teaspoons ground sage
2¾ cups (from 12-ounce package) unseasoned cornbread dressing cubes (see note)
1–1½ cups chicken broth, defatted

Preheat the oven to 350°.

Lightly spray a medium skillet with no-stick spray. Add the celery, mushrooms and onions. Cook and stir over medium heat until tender. Stir in the parsley and sage.

Lightly spray a 1½- to 2-quart casserole with no-stick spray. Place the cornbread in the casserole. Then add the onion mixture. Drizzle with 1 cup of the broth. Gently toss. If necessary, drizzle with enough of the remaining ½ cup of broth to moisten the bread; gently toss to mix well. Bake, uncovered, for 30 to 40 minutes or until heated through.

Makes 4 servings.

Note: If unseasoned cornbread dressing cubes are unavailable, use the stuffing crumbs from a 6-ounce package of cornbread stuffing mix; discard the vegetable/seasoning packet.

Southern Sweet Corn Pudding

	Nutrition Scorecard (per serving)	
	Before	After
Calories	367	249
Fat (g.)	22	4
% Calories from fat	53%	12%
Cholesterol (mg.)	66	1

The flavor of this corn pudding is similar to that of corn cakes. I reduced calories, fat and cholesterol by:

• Replacing margarine with a combination of applesauce and buttermilk

• Using fat-free yogurt instead of sour cream

• Using egg whites instead of whole eggs

• Replacing canned cream-style corn with a combination of pureed corn and buttermilk

> 2 (11-ounce) cans vacuum-packed whole kernel corn (no salt or sugar added) (with juices)
> ¼ cup buttermilk
> 4 egg whites, lightly beaten
> 1 cup fat-free plain yogurt
> ¼ cup unsweetened applesauce
> ½ cup sugar
> 1 (8½-ounce) package corn muffin mix

Preheat the oven to 350°. Lightly spray a 3-quart casserole with no-stick spray. Set the casserole aside.

In a blender of food processor, pulse blend or process one of the cans of corn (with juices) and the buttermilk until creamy but slightly lumpy (the mixture will resemble the texture of cottage cheese). Set the pureed corn mixture aside.

In a large bowl, stir together the egg whites, yogurt and applesauce until combined. Drain the remaining can of corn. Stir the drained corn, pureed corn mixture, and sugar into the yogurt mixture. Add the muffin mix and stir just until combined.

Transfer the mixture to the prepared casserole. Bake about 1 hour or until golden brown and set.

Makes 8 servings.

SWEET ENDINGS

My fondness for chocolate desserts was so well known during my postgraduate dietetic internship that I was given a chocolate cookbook when I graduated. Since then, my sweet tooth has prompted me to develop healthier versions of many luscious desserts. The recipes in this chapter are among my favorites.

As I've converted dessert recipes over the years, I've discovered several nontraditional techniques for replacing fat in baked products. Here are just a few of them:

- BABY-FOOD PRUNES can be used as an alternative to butter in chocolate desserts. Pureed prunes not only impart a rich chocolate color to brownies and other baked goods but also add moistness normally associated with fat.

- APPLESAUCE, like prunes, can replace butter. It too adds moistness to cakes, bars and sweet breads. It's especially suitable for light-colored products.

- MARSHMALLOW CREME adds creaminess to frostings without the fat.

Try these techniques on your own favorite recipes. With just a little practice, you too can slash excess fat and calories from desserts without sacrificing good taste. Experiment and enjoy!

Carrot Cake

Pictured on page 304

A traditional carrot cake is often perceived as healthy because of the carrots it contains. But usually it also contains at least 1½ cups of oil—not good when you're watching your fat intake. Here's my version, which contains no oil and tastes fabulous (if I do say so myself). Calories, fat and cholesterol were reduced by:

- Using egg whites instead of whole eggs

- Replacing oil with a combination of buttermilk and applesauce

- Reducing the amount of walnuts

- Replacing the traditional cream cheese frosting with one made with reduced-fat cream cheese

Nutrition Scorecard
(per serving)

	Before	After
Calories	449	243
Fat (g.)	29	5
% Calories from fat	58%	17%
Cholesterol (mg.)	44	4

---

    1 cup all-purpose flour
    1 cup whole-wheat flour
 2½ teaspoons ground cinnamon
    2 teaspoons baking soda
    ½ teaspoon ground nutmeg
    ½ teaspoon ground cloves
    6 egg whites
 1⅓ cups sugar
    1 cup unsweetened applesauce
    ½ cup buttermilk
 1½ teaspoons vanilla
    1 (8-ounce) can crushed pineapple (in its own juice), undrained
    2 cups coarsely shredded carrots
 ⅔ cup chopped walnuts
    ½ cup raisins
 1¾ cups Light Cream Cheese Frosting (page 289)

Preheat the oven to 350°. Lightly spray a 13" × 9" × 2" baking pan with no-stick spray. Set the pan aside.

In a large bowl, stir together the all-purpose flour, whole-wheat flour, cinnamon, baking soda, nutmeg and cloves; set aside.

In another large bowl, beat the egg whites with clean, dry beaters until soft peaks form. Slowly beat in the sugar. Then slowly beat in the applesauce, buttermilk and vanilla.

Using a spoon, stir in the flour mixture just until combined. Then stir in, one ingredient at a time, the crushed pineapple, carrots, walnuts and raisins.

Spread the batter in the prepared pan. Bake about 40 minutes or until a toothpick inserted near the center comes out clean. Cool completely on a wire rack. Then spread the frosting on top.

Makes 20 servings.

Lemon Lace Cake

Here's a luscious lemon cake that's not only healthier than its original version but also tastier, according to my taste testers. One trick I used was to replace the water with boiled-down pineapple juice to enhance the sweetness and create a rich texture. Calories, fat and cholesterol were reduced by:

- Replacing oil with applesauce

- Using egg whites instead of whole eggs

- Reducing the amount of powdered sugar in the topping

Nutrition Scorecard *(per serving)*

	Before	After
Calories	429	297
Fat (g.)	19	4
% Calories from fat	41%	12%
Cholesterol (mg.)	71	0

> 1 cup unsweetened pineapple juice
> 8 egg whites
> ¾ cup unsweetened applesauce
> 1 package 2-layer yellow cake mix
> 1 (4-serving) package regular lemon gelatin
> 2 teaspoons finely shredded lemon peel
> 1½ cups powdered sugar
> ½ cup fresh lemon juice

Preheat the oven to 350°. Lightly spray a 13" × 9" × 2" baking pan with no-stick spray. Set the pan aside.

In a small saucepan, bring the pineapple juice to a boil. Then reduce the heat. Simmer, uncovered, until the juice has reduced to ½ cup. Set the juice aside.

In a large bowl, beat the egg whites until foamy. Stir in the applesauce. Then stir in the cake mix, gelatin and lemon peel.

Slowly drizzle the pineapple juice into the batter. Using an electric mixer, beat the mixture on medium speed for 5 minutes. Spread the batter in the prepared pan. Bake for 30 to 40 minutes or until the cake springs back when lightly touched in the center.

Meanwhile, in a small bowl, stir together the powdered sugar and lemon juice until smooth.

Remove the cake from the oven. Use a toothpick to poke holes in the top of the cake, then pour the lemon juice mixture over the hot cake. Cool the cake before serving.

Makes 12 servings.

Pumpkin 'n' Cheese Cake Roll

This jelly-roll cake is always a big hit with my family and friends because of its moist, dense texture and rich pumpkin flavor. Best of all, it only has about a third the calories of its original counterpart. Calories, fat and cholesterol were reduced by:

- Replacing some of the egg yolks with buttermilk

- Replacing regular cream cheese with a combination of fat-free ricotta and light cream cheese

- Reducing the amount of sugar in the filling and enhancing the sweetness by using more ricotta cheese than cream cheese (ricotta is sweeter than cream cheese)

Nutrition Scorecard *(per serving)*

	Before	After
Calories	443	178
Fat (g.)	17	3
% Calories from fat	35%	16%
Cholesterol (mg.)	129	47

CAKE
- ½ cup all-purpose flour
- 2 teaspoons pumpkin pie spice
- 1 teaspoon baking powder
- 2 egg yolks
- ⅓ cup + ½ cup sugar
- ½ cup canned pumpkin
- 3 tablespoons buttermilk
- 4 egg whites
- Powdered sugar

FILLING
- ½ cup soft-style light cream cheese
- ½ cup powdered sugar
- 1 teaspoon vanilla
- 1 cup fat-free ricotta cheese

TO MAKE THE CAKE: Preheat the oven to 375°. Spray a 15" × 10" × 1" baking pan with no-stick spray. Line the bottom of the pan with wax paper, then spray the wax paper with no-stick spray. Set the pan aside.

In a small bowl, stir together the flour, pumpkin spice and baking powder; set aside.

Place the egg yolks in a large bowl. Use an electric mixer to beat the yolks on high speed about 5 minutes. Slowly add the ⅓ cup sugar, beating constantly. Then add the pumpkin and buttermilk. Beat until well combined. Add the flour mixture to the yolk mixture and beat on low speed just until combined.

In another large bowl, beat the egg whites with clean, dry beaters until soft peaks form. Then slowly beat in the ½ cup sugar. Stir one-quarter of the egg white mixture into the pumpkin mixture, then gently fold in the remaining egg white mixture.

Spread the batter evenly in the prepared pan. Bake for 12 to 15 minutes or until the cake springs back when lightly touched in the center. Meanwhile, lightly sift the powdered sugar onto a clean dish towel.

Immediately loosen the cake from the sides of the pan and invert it onto the towel. Remove the wax paper and roll up the towel and the cake together, jelly-roll fashion, starting from a short end. Transfer the cake to a wire rack, seam side down, and cool completely.

TO MAKE THE FILLING: In a small bowl, beat together the cream cheese, powdered sugar and vanilla until well mixed. Stir in the ricotta cheese until well combined. Cover and refrigerate until ready to use.

TO ASSEMBLE THE CAKE ROLL: Unroll the cake. Spread the filling on the cake to within ½" of its edges. Then roll up the cake without the towel. Transfer the cake to a serving plate. Cover it with plastic wrap and chill it in the refrigerator for at least 1 hour before serving.

Makes 10 servings.

Light Cream Cheese Frosting

Marshmallow creme replaces the butter in this super-easy frosting. To keep things neat and simplify cleanup, coat the measuring cup with no-stick spray before measuring the marshmallow creme. Calories, fat and cholesterol were also reduced by:

- Replacing regular cream cheese with light cream cheese

Nutrition Scorecard (per ¼ cup)		
	Before	After
Calories	263	214
Fat (g.)	13	5
% Calories from fat	42%	20%
Cholesterol (mg.)	36	10

1 (8 ounce) container soft-style light cream cheese
1 cup marshmallow creme
1 teaspoon fresh lemon juice
1 teaspoon vanilla
1 cup powdered sugar

In a medium bowl, stir together the cream cheese, marshmallow creme, lemon juice and vanilla until well combined. Then gradually beat in the powdered sugar.

Makes 1¾ cups; 7 servings.

Fudge Sundae Cake Roll

Here's a summertime delight: a rich chocolate cake filled with fat-free frozen yogurt. I like using frozen yogurt from my neighborhood yogurt shop rather than that from the supermarket. It's tastier and much softer to spread. Calories, fat and cholesterol were reduced by:

- Using cocoa powder instead of chocolate

- Replacing some of the egg yolks with a combination of egg whites and buttermilk

- Using fat-free frozen yogurt instead of ice cream

- Using fat-free fudge topping

- Reducing the amount of almonds

Nutrition Scorecard
(per serving)

	Before	After
Calories	281	181
Fat (g.)	10	2
% Calories from fat	31%	11%
Cholesterol (mg.)	98	43

⅓ cup all-purpose flour
¼ cup unsweetened cocoa powder
¼ teaspoon baking soda
2 egg yolks
⅓ cup + ½ cup sugar
3 tablespoons buttermilk
½ teaspoon almond extract
4 egg whites
Powdered sugar
1 pint fat-free frozen vanilla yogurt, softened if necessary
½ cup fat-free fudge ice-cream topping, softened
2 tablespoons chopped almonds

Preheat the oven to 375°. Spray a 15" × 10" × 1" baking pan with no-stick spray. Line the bottom of the pan with wax paper, then spray the wax paper with no-stick spray. Set the pan aside.

In a small bowl, stir together the flour, cocoa and baking soda; set aside.

Place the egg yolks in a large bowl. Use an electric mixer to beat the yolks on high speed about 5 minutes. Slowly add the ⅓ cup sugar, beating constantly. Then beat in the buttermilk and almond extract. Add the flour mixture to the yolk mixture and beat on low speed just until combined.

In another large bowl, beat the egg whites with clean, dry beaters until soft peaks form. Slowly beat in the ½ cup sugar. Continue beating until stiff peaks form. Then stir one-quarter of the egg white mixture into the chocolate mixture; gently fold in the remaining egg white mixture.

Spread the batter evenly in the prepared pan. Bake for 12 to 15 minutes or until the cake springs back when lightly touched in the center. Meanwhile, lightly sift the powdered sugar onto a clean dish towel.

Immediately loosen the cake from the sides of the pan and invert it onto the towel. Remove the wax paper and roll up the towel and the cake together, jelly-roll fashion, starting from a short end. Transfer the cake to a wire rack, seam side down, and cool completely.

Unroll the cake. Spread the softened yogurt to within ½" of its edges. Then roll up the cake without the towel. Transfer the cake to a freezer-safe serving plate. Cover it with plastic wrap and freeze it for at least 1 hour before serving.

Just before serving, frost the cake roll with the fudge topping and sprinkle it with the almonds.

Makes 10 servings.

To MAKE CHOCOLATE RICOTTA CAKE ROLL: Use the following filling instead of the frozen yogurt: Place ½ cup semisweet chocolate chips in a blender or small food processor. Blend or process until coarsely chopped. Add 1½ cups fat-free ricotta cheese, 1 tablespoon unsweetened cocoa powder and 1 teaspoon almond extract. Blend or process until smooth. Transfer the mixture to a small bowl and stir in ¼ cup powdered sugar. (Per serving: 185 calories, 5 g. fat, 21% calories from fat, 46 mg. cholesterol.)

Macaroon-Filled Chocolate Cupcakes

These moist, easy-to-make cup-cakes conceal a delightful surprise: coconut filling. To keep these cakes tender and fresh, freeze what you won't use within a day. Reduced-fat baked goods tend to become chewy when stored at room temperature for more than one day. Calories, fat and cholesterol were reduced by:

- Using fat-free ricotta cheese instead of regular cream cheese

- Using less coconut and adding coconut extract

- Using egg whites instead of whole eggs

- Using cocoa powder instead of chocolate

- Replacing oil with applesauce

Nutrition Scorecard (per cupcake)		
	Before	After
Calories	184	116
Fat (g.)	9	1
% Calories from fat	41%	8%
Cholesterol (mg.)	15	2

FILLING
- 1 cup fat-free ricotta cheese
- ¼ cup sugar
- 1 egg white
- ⅓ cup flaked coconut
- 1 teaspoon coconut extract

CUPCAKES
- 1¼ cups all-purpose flour
- 1 cup sugar
- ⅓ cup unsweetened cocoa powder
- ½ teaspoon baking soda
- 2 egg whites, lightly beaten
- ¾ cup buttermilk
- ⅓ cup unsweetened applesauce
- 1 teaspoon vanilla

TO MAKE THE FILLING: In a medium bowl, beat together the ricotta cheese, sugar and egg white until smooth. Stir in the coconut and coconut extract. Set the filling aside.

TO MAKE THE CUPCAKES: Preheat the oven to 350°. Lightly spray 18 cup-cake cups with no-stick spray; set aside. In a large bowl, stir together the flour, sugar, cocoa and baking soda. In a small bowl, combine the egg whites, butter-milk, applesauce and vanilla. Add the buttermilk mixture to the flour mixture and mix until smooth.

Spoon half of the batter evenly into the prepared cupcake cups. Then spoon 1 tablespoon of the filling on top and in the center of each. Spoon the remaining batter evenly on top of the coconut filling in each cupcake.

Bake for 25 to 30 minutes or until a toothpick inserted in the center comes out clean. Cool for 5 minutes. Then remove cupcakes and cool on a wire rack.

Makes 18 cupcakes; 18 servings.

To MAKE ALMONDINE-FILLED CHOCOLATE CUPCAKES: Omit the flaked coconut and replace the coconut extract with 1 teaspoon almond extract. (Per cupcake: 108 calories, 1 g. fat, 4% calories from fat, 2 mg. cholesterol.)

Good-for-You Gingerbread

Pictured on page 305

I've given traditional gingerbread a nutritional boost by substituting whole-wheat flour for a portion of the all-purpose flour. The molasses and spices mask the whole-wheat flavor so your family won't even notice the difference. Calories, fat and cholesterol were reduced by:

• Replacing shortening with applesauce

• Using egg whites instead of a whole egg

Nutrition Scorecard (per serving)		
	Before	After
Calories	246	149
Fat (g.)	12	1
% Calories from fat	44%	2%
Cholesterol (mg.)	24	0

    1 cup all-purpose flour
    ½ cup whole-wheat flour
    ¼ cup packed brown sugar
    ¾ teaspoon ground ginger
    ¾ teaspoon ground cinnamon
    ½ teaspoon baking powder
    ½ teaspoon baking soda
    2 egg whites, lightly beaten
    ½ cup buttermilk
    ½ cup unsweetened applesauce
    ½ cup light molasses

Preheat the oven 350°. Lightly spray an 8" × 8" × 2" baking pan with no-stick spray. Set the pan aside.

In a large bowl, stir together the all-purpose flour, whole-wheat flour, brown sugar, ginger, cinnamon, baking powder and baking soda.

In a small bowl, combine the egg whites, buttermilk, applesauce and molasses. Add the buttermilk mixture to the flour mixture. Beat with an electric mixer until combined.

Transfer the batter to the prepared pan. Bake for 30 to 35 minutes or until a toothpick inserted in the center comes out clean. Cool on a wire rack for 10 minutes. Then remove from the pan and serve warm.

Makes 9 servings.

Dark Chocolate Brownies

Pictured on page 306

Oh so rich . . . oh so gooey . . . and oh so good—these cocoa brownies are almost fat free (there's just a little from the walnuts). Cocoa powder has all of the great taste of chocolate but a lot less saturated fat. Calories, fat and cholesterol were also reduced by:

- Replacing the butter with baby-food prunes or applesauce

- Reducing the amount of sugar

- Using egg whites instead of whole eggs

- Reducing the amount of walnuts

Nutrition Scorecard
(per brownie)

	Before	After
Calories	135	80
Fat (g.)	8	2
% Calories from fat	51%	18%
Cholesterol (mg.)	38	0

    1¾ cup sugar
    ¾ cup unsweetened cocoa powder
    ½ cup all-purpose flour
    ½ cup whole-wheat flour
    ½ teaspoon baking powder
    7 egg whites
    2 (4-ounce) jars baby-food prunes or ⅔ cup unsweetened applesauce
    ¼ cup buttermilk
    2 teaspoons vanilla
    ⅔ cup chopped walnuts
       Powdered sugar

Preheat the oven to 350°. Lightly spray a 13" × 9" × 2" baking pan with no-stick spray. Set the pan aside.

In a large bowl, stir together the sugar, cocoa, all-purpose flour, whole-wheat flour and baking powder. Set the flour mixture aside.

In another large bowl, beat the egg whites until foamy. Slowly stir in the prunes or applesauce, buttermilk and vanilla. Add the egg mixture to the flour mixture and beat with an electric mixer until thoroughly combined. Fold in the walnuts.

Transfer the batter to the prepared pan. Bake about 30 minutes or until the brownies just begin to pull away from the sides of the pan (do not over-bake). Cool completely on a wire rack. Lightly sprinkle with the powdered sugar, then cut into bars.

Makes 36 brownies; 36 servings.

Waldorf Salad (page 247)

Tabbouleh (page 254)

Greek Salad (page 255)

Creamy Lime Dressing (page 256)

Spicy Vegetable Stir-Fry (page 265)

Crockpot Baked Beans (page 267)

Ratatouille in Roasted Peppers (page 270)

Twice-Baked Potatoes (page 274)

Harvest Apple Stuffing (page 282)

303

Carrot Cake (page 286)

Good-for-You Gingerbread (page 293)

Dark Chocolate Brownies (page 294)

Cherry Delicious Pie (page 316)

Summertime Fruit Pizza (page 320)

Chocolate Marble Cheesecake (page 322)

Georgia Peach Crisp (page 324)

Layered Raspberry Bars

All-fruit preserves are an easy and healthy replacement for the cooked fruit-and-sugar filling originally used in these bars. I prefer the flavor of raspberry with the whole-wheat crust and topping, but almost any flavor will be delicious. Calories, fat and cholesterol were also reduced by:

• Replacing butter with a combination of buttermilk and an egg white in the dough mixture

Nutrition Scorecard
(per bar)

	Before	After
Calories	145	106
Fat (g.)	5	1
% Calories from fat	30%	11%
Cholesterol (mg.)	12	0

1 cup whole-wheat flour
1 cup quick-cooking rolled oats
⅔ cup firmly packed brown sugar
½ teaspoon ground cinnamon
¼ teaspoon baking soda
¼ cup chopped walnuts
½ cup buttermilk
1 egg white
1 (10-ounce) jar all-fruit red raspberry spread

Preheat the oven to 350°. Lightly spray a 9" × 9" × 2" baking pan with no-stick spray.

In a medium bowl, stir together the flour, oats, brown sugar, cinnamon and baking soda. Stir in the walnuts.

In a small bowl, use a fork to beat together the buttermilk and egg white. Add the buttermilk mixture to the oat mixture. Using a pastry blender or fork, cut or mix in the buttermilk mixture until combined (the mixture will be sticky). Set ¾ cup of the oat mixture aside for the topping.

To assemble, press the remaining oat mixture in the bottom of the prepared pan to form the crust. Spread the preserves on top. Then drop small spoonfuls of the reserved oat mixture on top (the surface will not be entirely covered).

Bake for 25 to 30 minutes or until the top is golden brown. Cool completely on a wire rack, then cut into bars.

Makes 20 bars; 20 servings.

Cinnamon-Cocoa Bars

These chocolate-cake bars can double as a mid-afternoon snack as well as an ending to a light lunch or homey dinner. Calories, fat and cholesterol were reduced by:

- Replacing the margarine and oil with a combination of concentrated pineapple juice, applesauce and buttermilk

- Reducing the amount of sugar in the bars

- Using egg whites instead of whole eggs

- Replacing margarine with marshmallow creme in the frosting for a creamy texture

- Reducing the amount of pecans in the frosting

Nutrition Scorecard
(per bar)

	Before	After
Calories	362	161
Fat (g.)	20	3
% Calories from fat	49%	17%
Cholesterol (mg.)	19	0

BARS
- 1 cup unsweetened pineapple juice
- ¾ cup unsweetened applesauce
- ½ cup + ⅓ cup buttermilk
- 3 tablespoons unsweetened cocoa powder
- 2 cups all-purpose flour
- 1½ cups sugar
- 1 tablespoon ground cinnamon
- 4 egg whites
- 1 teaspoon baking soda

FROSTING
- ¾ cup marshmallow creme
- ¼ cup unsweetened cocoa powder
- 2 tablespoons fat-free dry milk
- 1 tablespoon light corn syrup
- 2 teaspoons vanilla
- ¾ cup chopped pecans

TO MAKE THE BARS: Preheat the oven to 350°. Lightly spray a 13" × 9" × 2" baking pan with no-stick spray. Set the pan aside.

In a medium saucepan, bring the pineapple juice to a boil. Reduce the heat and simmer, uncovered, until the juice has reduced to ½ cup.

Meanwhile, in a medium bowl, stir together the applesauce, ½ cup of the buttermilk and the cocoa; set aside. In a large bowl, stir together the flour, sugar and cinnamon; set aside.

When the pineapple juice is reduced by half, stir in the applesauce mixture. Increase the heat to medium and bring to a boil, stirring continuously. Then slowly stir the fruit mixture into the flour mixture. Cool to lukewarm.

Add the egg whites and mix well. Dissolve the baking soda in the remaining ⅓ cup buttermilk, then add the buttermilk mixture to the batter. Stir just until combined (do not overmix).

Pour the batter into the prepared pan. Bake for 35 to 45 minutes or until a toothpick inserted in the center comes out clean. Cool completely on a wire rack.

To make the frosting: In a small saucepan, combine the marshmallow creme, cocoa, dry milk and corn syrup. Heat over medium until the marshmallow creme is melted, stirring constantly. Remove from the heat, then stir in the vanilla. Stir in the pecans. Spread on top of the bars.

Makes 24 bars; 24 servings.

Note: If you're in a hurry, forget the frosting and lightly sprinkle powdered sugar over the top of these bars.

Stock Up on Reduced-Fat Staples

So that I'm always prepared for reduced-fat baking, I make sure to keep the following ingredients on hand:

- 6-ounce cans of unsweetened fruit juice (small cans cut down on leftovers)
- Baby-food prunes
- Unsweetened applesauce
- Evaporated skim milk
- Fat-free plain yogurt
- Frozen phyllo dough
- No-stick spray

Lemon Sunshine Bars

These pretty yellow bars are so rich and luscious it's no wonder they're one of my best-loved makeovers. I not only lightened the original recipe but gave it a flavor and nutrient boost by using whole-wheat flour and a small amount of hazelnuts in the crust. I reduced calories, fat and cholesterol by:

- Replacing butter in the crust with a combination of buttermilk and oil

- Replacing the eggs with fat-free egg substitute (I prefer to use egg substitute instead of egg whites in the filling to maintain a yellow color)

Nutrition Scorecard
(per bar)

	Before	After
Calories	108	88
Fat (g.)	5	2
% Calories from fat	52%	17%
Cholesterol (mg.)	34	0

CRUST
- 1 cup whole-wheat pastry flour
- ¼ cup sugar
- 3 tablespoons finely chopped hazelnuts
- 1 teaspoon finely shredded lemon peel
- ⅛ teaspoon salt (optional)
- ⅓ cup buttermilk
- 1 tablespoon oil

FILLING
- ¾ cup sugar
- 2 tablespoons all-purpose flour
- ¼ teaspoon baking powder
- ½ cup fat-free egg substitute
- 2 teaspoons finely shredded lemon peel
- 3 tablespoons fresh lemon juice
- Powdered sugar

TO MAKE THE CRUST: Preheat the oven to 350°. Lightly spray an 8" × 8" × 2" baking pan with no-stick spray and set aside.

In a medium bowl, stir together the pastry flour, sugar, hazelnuts, lemon peel and, if desired, salt.

In a small bowl, stir together the buttermilk and oil. Drizzle the buttermilk mixture over the flour mixture. Using a pastry blender or fork, cut or mix in the buttermilk mixture until combined. Press the mixture in the bottom of the prepared pan. Bake for 12 to 15 minutes or until lightly browned.

TO MAKE THE FILLING: In a small bowl, stir together the sugar, flour and baking powder. Then stir in the egg substitute, lemon peel and juice. Use an electric mixer to beat for 2 minutes on medium speed or until thoroughly combined.

Pour the filling on the hot crust, then bake about 20 minutes more or until the bars are lightly browned around the edges and the center is set. Cool on a wire rack.

Before serving, lightly sift the powdered sugar over the top. Then cut into bars.

Makes 20 bars; 20 servings.

Swedish Apple Pie

This old-time pie resembles a cobbler more than a pie. It has no crust, which eliminates a lot of fat right there. But the original was also loaded with sugar. So I tinkered with the recipe and came up with this healthier version. I cut calories, fat and cholesterol by:

• Reducing the amount of sugar

• Using egg whites instead of whole eggs

• Reducing the amount of walnuts

Nutrition Scorecard
(per serving)

	Before	After
Calories	333	238
Fat (g.)	10	5
% Calories from fat	28%	18%
Cholesterol (mg.)	53	0

2   teaspoons fresh lemon juice
2   cups coarsely chopped apples
1   cup whole-wheat pastry flour
1   cup sugar
2   teaspoons baking powder
4   egg whites, lightly beaten
½   teaspoon vanilla
½   cup chopped walnuts

Preheat the oven to 325°. Lightly spray a 9" pie plate with no-stick spray; set aside. Sprinkle the lemon juice over the apples, then gently toss until coated. Set the apples aside.

In a large bowl, stir together the flour, sugar and baking powder. Then stir in the egg whites and vanilla. Stir in the apples and walnuts (the mixture will be thick).

Transfer the apple mixture to the prepared pie plate. Bake about 35 minutes or until golden brown.

Makes 8 servings.

Cherry Delicious Pie

Pictured on page 307

When I'm looking for a less-filling dessert, I make this refrigerated cheese-cake pie. Calories, fat and cholesterol were reduced by:

• Using fat-free instead of regular cream cheese

• Replacing regular frozen whipped topping with a combination of reduced-fat ricotta cheese and frozen reduced-calorie whipped topping

• Using a reduced-calorie pie filling

• Using a reduced-fat graham cracker crust

Nutrition Scorecard
(per serving)

	Before	After
Calories	414	290
Fat (g.)	22	5
% Calories from fat	51%	16%
Cholesterol (mg.)	31	8

    1 *(8-ounce) container fat-free cream cheese*
    ⅔ *cup powdered sugar*
 1½ *teaspoons fresh lemon juice*
    1 *teaspoon vanilla*
    1 *cup reduced-fat ricotta cheese*
 1½ *cups thawed, frozen reduced-calorie whipped topping*
    1 *reduced-fat Graham Cracker Crust (opposite page)*
    1 *(20-ounce) can reduced-calorie cherry pie filling*

In a large bowl, beat together the cream cheese, powdered sugar, lemon juice and vanilla until mixed. Stir in the ricotta cheese until well combined. Then fold in the whipped topping.

Spread the mixture evenly in the crust. Then carefully spread the pie filling on top. Chill the pie in the refrigerator for at least 4 hours before serving.

Makes 8 servings.

Note: Even frozen reduced-calorie whipped topping contains a significant amount of fat, so use it judiciously.

Graham Cracker Crust

Although a traditional graham cracker crust is much lower in fat than a pastry crust, it still adds a significant amount of fat to a serving of pie. In this recipe, I made just a few changes that cut the number of calories nearly in half. Calories, fat and cholesterol were reduced by:

- Replacing margarine with a combination of reduced-calorie butter blend (60 calories per tablespoon) and apricot jam

- Reducing the amount of sugar

- Reducing the amount of graham crackers

- Replacing a portion of the graham crackers with a fat-free cereal

Nutrition Scorecard
(per serving)

	Before	After
Calories	172	110
Fat (g.)	10	3
% Calories from fat	47%	27%
Cholesterol (mg.)	21	4

2 tablespoons reduced-calorie butter blend
2 tablespoons apricot jam
¾ cup fine graham cracker crumbs
⅓ cup Grape-Nuts cereal
2 tablespoons sugar

Preheat the oven to 375°. Spray a 9" pie plate with no-stick spray. Set aside.

In a small saucepan, heat the butter blend and jam just until melted.

In a medium bowl, stir together the cracker crumbs, cereal and sugar. Drizzle in the butter-blend mixture. Using a fork, stir until well mixed.

Transfer the crumb mixture to the prepared pie plate. Using the back of a large spoon, press the crumb mixture firmly in the bottom and up the sides of the pie plate. Bake for 5 to 7 minutes or until the edges are lightly browned. Cool on a wire rack before filling.

Makes 1 pie crust; 8 servings.

Apple 'n' Raisin Strudel

You won't believe that this ultra-flaky strudel is so low in fat. This transformation was accomplished by using phyllo pastry dough and no-stick spray instead of the traditional strudel dough and butter. Then I also cut calories, fat and cholesterol by:

• Reducing the amount of sugar

• Reducing the amount of walnuts

Nutrition Scorecard
(per serving)

	Before	After
Calories	409	225
Fat (g.)	15	3
% Calories from fat	32%	10%
Cholesterol (mg.)	53	0

FILLING
    4 cups peeled and finely chopped apples
    1 tablespoon fresh lemon juice
  1–2 slices whole-wheat bread, toasted
    ¾ cup sugar
    ¼ cup finely chopped walnuts
    1 teaspoon finely shredded lemon peel
    ½ cup raisins

PASTRY
    2 tablespoons sugar
    ¼ teaspoon ground nutmeg
    6 sheets phyllo dough
      Powdered sugar

TO MAKE THE FILLING: Place the apples in a large bowl. Sprinkle with the lemon juice and toss until coated. Set the apples aside.

In a blender or food processor, blend or process the bread until it forms fine crumbs. In a small bowl, stir together 6 tablespoons of the crumbs, the sugar, walnuts and lemon peel. Set the walnut mixture aside.

TO MAKE THE PASTRY: Preheat the oven to 350°. In a custard cup, stir together the sugar and nutmeg.

Stack the phyllo sheets and cover them with a damp cloth to prevent drying out. Place one sheet on a large piece of wax paper. (Keep the remaining sheets covered.) Lightly spray the sheet with the no-stick spray. Sprinkle with about 1 teaspoon of the nutmeg mixture. Repeat layering, spraying and sprinkling the remaining sheets with the nutmeg mixture.

TO ASSEMBLE THE STRUDEL: Evenly spread the apples on top of the phyllo. Sprinkle with the walnut mixture, then sprinkle with the raisins. Spray a large cookie sheet with no-stick spray. With the help of the wax paper, carefully lift and roll up the phyllo and apples jelly-roll fashion. Then carefully transfer the strudel to the prepared cookie sheet. Fold under the ends so that the strudel does not leak out during baking.

Bake about 30 minutes or until golden brown. Cool slightly or completely on a wire rack before serving. To serve, cut the strudel diagonally into eight slices. Then lightly sift the powdered sugar over the tops of the slices and serve.

Makes 8 servings.

Pumpkin Pie

On Thanksgiving, start a new tradition. Instead of using a classic pastry crust, use the reduced-fat Graham Cracker Crust on page 317 for a pie with almost no fat. I further reduced calories, fat and cholesterol by:

- Using egg whites instead of whole eggs

- Replacing evaporated whole milk with evaporated skim milk

Nutrition Scorecard (per serving)		
	Before	After
Calories	280	244
Fat (g.)	12	2
% Calories from fat	39%	13%
Cholesterol (mg.)	66	2

4 *egg whites, lightly beaten*
1 *(16-ounce) can pumpkin*
¾ *cup sugar*
1 *teaspoon ground cinnamon*
½ *teaspoon ground ginger*
¼ *teaspoon ground cloves*
1 *(12-ounce) can evaporated skim milk*
1 *unbaked Graham Cracker Crust (page 317)*

Preheat the oven to 425°. In a large bowl, combine the egg whites and pumpkin. Stir in the sugar, cinnamon, ginger and cloves. Then stir in the milk.

Pour the mixture into the crust. Bake for 15 minutes. Then reduce the oven temperature to 350° and bake for 40 to 50 minutes more or until a knife inserted in the center comes out clean. Cool completely on a wire rack before serving.

Makes 8 servings.

Summertime Fruit Pizza

Pictured on page 308

Here's a dessert pizza that's as pretty as a picture, healthful and one of my daughter's favorites! This version uses a combination of kiwi, strawberries and nectarines, but you may want to select a different mix of fruit. Calories, fat and cholesterol were reduced by:

- Replacing the sugar-cookie crust with a reduced-fat, high-fiber crust

- Replacing regular cream cheese in the topping with a combination of fat-free ricotta cheese and light cream cheese

- Reducing the amount of glaze

Nutrition Scorecard
(per serving)

	Before	After
Calories	559	283
Fat (g.)	26	9
% Calories from fat	42%	26%
Cholesterol (mg.)	82	13

CRUST
- 1 cup whole-wheat pastry flour
- 3 tablespoons sugar
- 2 tablespoons finely chopped hazelnuts
- 1 teaspoon finely shredded lemon peel
- ¼ cup buttermilk
- 2 tablespoons oil

TOPPING
- ½ cup soft-style light cream cheese
- ½ cup powdered sugar
- 1 teaspoon vanilla
- ¼ cup fat-free ricotta cheese
- 3 kiwi fruit, peeled and sliced
- 1 cup strawberries, sliced
- 1 nectarine, sliced

GLAZE
- ⅓ cup sugar
- 1 tablespoon cornstarch
- ¼ cup fresh orange juice

TO MAKE THE CRUST: In a mixing bowl, stir together the flour, sugar, hazelnuts and lemon peel. Add the buttermilk and oil. Use a fork to stir the mixture until it begins to form a ball. Then use your hands to press the mixture into a smooth ball; flatten to 4" in diameter. Wrap in plastic wrap and refrigerate at least 30 minutes before rolling out.

Preheat the oven to 375°. Spray a pizza pan or cookie sheet with no-stick spray; set aside.

Unwrap the dough and place it between two 12"-square pieces of wax paper. Gently roll out the dough to about ⅛" thickness. Remove the top piece of wax paper. Then invert the dough onto the pizza pan or cookie sheet. Remove the remaining piece of wax paper. Bake about 12 minutes or until the edges begin to lightly brown. Remove the crust from the oven and cool.

To make the topping: In a small bowl, beat together the cream cheese, powdered sugar and vanilla. Then beat in the ricotta cheese. Spread the cheese mixture on the cooled crust. Arrange the kiwi, strawberries and nectarines on top, slightly overlapping if necessary (see photo). Chill in the refrigerator while preparing the glaze.

To make the glaze: In a small saucepan, stir together the sugar and cornstarch. Stir in the orange juice. Cook and stir over medium heat until the mixture slightly thickens and begins to gently boil. Cook and stir for 2 minutes more. Remove from the heat and cool for 5 minutes. Using a clean pastry brush, brush the glaze over the fruit. Chill for 1 hour before serving.

Makes 8 servings.

Easy Low-Sugar Fruit Glaze

For a quick fruit glaze, heat low-sugar or all-fruit preserves—such as apricot or orange marmalade—just until melted. Spread the melted preserves over fruit tarts or between cake layers. Or drizzle it over scoops of frozen fat-free yogurt.

Chocolate Marble Cheesecake

Pictured on page 309

This cheesecake is always a hit dessert. Unfortunately, though, one serving of its original version could have wiped out your fat budget for an entire day. But here's its healthy counterpart with only a fraction of the fat and half the calories. Calories, fat and cholesterol were reduced by:

- Using a reduced-fat chocolate crumb crust

- Replacing regular cream cheese with a combination of light cream cheese, fat-free yogurt cheese and fat-free cottage cheese

- Using egg whites instead of whole eggs

Nutrition Scorecard (per serving)	Before	After
Calories	427	222
Fat (g.)	30	6
% Calories from fat	62%	23%
Cholesterol (mg.)	103	11

CHOCOLATE CRUMB CRUST
1½ cups fine chocolate wafer or chocolate graham cracker crumbs (see note)
2 tablespoons apricot jam, melted

FILLING
1 cup fat-free cottage cheese
4 egg whites
1 cup Yogurt Cheese (page 83)
1 (8-ounce) package light cream cheese
¾ cup + 2 tablespoons sugar
1 tablespoon all-purpose flour
1 teaspoon vanilla
¼ cup unsweetened cocoa powder
1 teaspoon almond extract

TO MAKE THE CHOCOLATE CRUMB CRUST: Preheat the oven to 350°. Spray a 9" springform pan with no-stick spray; set aside.

In a medium bowl, stir together the crumbs and melted jam until well combined.

Using your fingers, lightly press the crumbs in the bottom and about 2" up the sides of the pan. Bake at 350° for 8 minutes. Set the crust aside. Increase the oven temperature to 375°.

TO MAKE THE FILLING: In a clean, dry blender or food processor, blend or process the cottage cheese until creamy and almost smooth. Add the egg whites, then blend or process just until smooth.

Add the yogurt cheese, cream cheese, ¾ cup sugar, flour and vanilla. Blend or process until smooth. Transfer half of the filling to a bowl; stir in the cocoa, remaining 2 tablespoons sugar and almond extract until well combined.

Pour half of each batter mixture into the crust. Then repeat pouring the remaining half of each batter into the crust. Using a small metal spatula, gently swirl the two batters.

Bake at 375° for 35 to 40 minutes or until a knife inserted in the center comes out clean. Cool on a wire rack for 15 minutes. Loosen the crust from the sides of the pan. Then cool for 30 minutes more. Remove the sides from the pan. Cool the cheesecake completely. Chill it at least 4 hours before serving. If desired, garnish it with additional fine chocolate wafer crumbs.

Makes 12 servings.

Note: To make fine chocolate crumbs, place a few wafer cookies or graham crackers in a blender or food processor. Pulse blend or process until finely ground. Repeat with more cookies or crackers until you have the amount you need.

Cream Cheese Substitutes

The following items are perfect reduced-fat alternatives to regular cream cheese. Use them when converting your own dessert recipes into slimmer versions.

- FAT-FREE OR LIGHT CREAM CHEESE. These two leaner alternatives are the most obvious substitutes. The flavor and baking characteristics vary considerably according to the manufacturer. Try several brands until you find one that you like and that works well for you.

- FAT-FREE OR REDUCED-FAT YOGURT CHEESE. Yogurt cheese is one of the tastiest substitutes for regular cream cheese. As an added benefit, it's also richer in calcium than fat-free or light cream cheese. To make yogurt cheese, see page 83.

- LIGHT CREAM CHEESE BLENDED WITH FAT-FREE RICOTTA CHEESE. This is another flavorful alternative. Use it in desserts when smoothness is not critical, such as the Chocolate Ricotta Cake Roll on page 291.

- PUREED FAT-FREE COTTAGE CHEESE BLENDED WITH FAT-FREE YOGURT CHEESE AND LIGHT CREAM CHEESE. This combination provides the delicious flavor of yogurt cheese and the creaminess of pureed cottage cheese. The light cream cheese gives the mixture a thicker consistency and imparts the characteristic flavor of regular cream cheese. I used this technique for the Chocolate Marble Cheesecake on page 322.

Georgia Peach Crisp

Pictured on page 310

Here's a wonderful homey dessert I lightened up by making only a few changes to the topping. Calories, fat and cholesterol were reduced by:

• Replacing some of the walnuts with Grape-Nuts cereal

• Using buttermilk instead of butter in the crumb topping

Nutrition Scorecard
(per serving)

	Before	After
Calories	443	364
Fat (g.)	11	2
% Calories from fat	22%	6%
Cholesterol (mg.)	21	0

FILLING
5 cups fresh or frozen unsweetened peach slices
3 tablespoons sugar
1 tablespoon all-purpose flour

TOPPING
½ cup rolled oats
½ cup firmly packed brown sugar
¼ cup whole-wheat flour
2 tablespoons chopped walnuts
2 tablespoons Grape-Nuts cereal
¼ teaspoon ground nutmeg
¼ cup buttermilk
Milk (optional)

TO MAKE THE FILLING: Preheat the oven to 350°. Thaw the peaches, if frozen. Drain and discard any juice from the peaches and place the peaches in a round 8" × 1½" baking dish.

In a custard cup or small bowl, stir together the sugar and all-purpose flour. Sprinkle the mixture over the peaches. Toss until the peaches are coated.

TO MAKE THE TOPPING: In a small bowl, combine the oats, brown sugar, whole-wheat flour, walnuts, cereal and nutmeg. Drizzle the buttermilk over the oat mixture, then use a fork to combine the mixture until it resembles coarse crumbs. Sprinkle the mixture on top of the filling.

Bake for 30 to 35 minutes or until the topping is golden brown. If desired, serve with milk.

Makes 6 servings.

Chocolate Soufflé for Two

Feel free to indulge in this healthy dessert! For a special touch, sometimes I sift a little powdered sugar over the top and serve the soufflé with fresh raspberries. Calories, fat and cholesterol were reduced by:

- Using egg whites instead of a whole egg

- Using skim milk instead of whole milk

- Using cocoa powder instead of chocolate chips

- Eliminating the butter

Nutrition Scorecard
(per soufflé)

	Before	After
Calories	448	216
Fat (g.)	26	2
% Calories from fat	52%	6%
Cholesterol (mg.)	252	0

½ teaspoon sugar
3 tablespoons unsweetened cocoa powder
2 tablespoons + ¼ cup sugar
1 tablespoon cornstarch
½ teaspoon instant coffee granules
½ cup skim milk
2 egg whites
¼ teaspoon cream of tartar
½ teaspoon vanilla

Preheat the oven to 350°. Lightly spray two 12-ounce soufflé dishes with no-stick spray. Sprinkle the sides and bottom of the dishes with the ½ teaspoon of sugar. Set the dishes aside.

In a small saucepan, stir together the cocoa, 2 tablespoons sugar, cornstarch and coffee granules. Then stir in the milk. Cook and stir over medium heat until the mixture comes to a boil (the mixture will be very thick). Then cook and stir for 1 minute more. Remove the saucepan from the heat and let stand until the mixture cools to room temperature.

Meanwhile, in a large bowl, beat the egg whites with clean, dry beaters until foamy. Add the cream of tartar. Then slowly add the ¼ cup sugar, beating until the peaks are stiff but not dry.

Stir the vanilla into the chocolate mixture, then stir in one-quarter of the egg whites. Using a rubber spatula, fold the chocolate mixture into the remaining beaten egg whites. Transfer the mixture to the prepared dishes. Use the spatula to smooth the tops.

Place the dishes in a large, deep baking pan. Pour in enough hot water so the water comes one-third up the sides of the dishes. Bake about 25 minutes or until the soufflés are puffed and the tops feel firm when lightly touched. Serve immediately.

Makes 2 soufflés; 2 servings.

Whole-Wheat Bread Pudding

Classic bread pudding has just gotten better—this new version is substantially lower in fat and cholesterol. It also supplies more fiber because I've used whole-wheat bread instead of white. (For a pudding with a smooth texture, use regular whole-wheat bread rather than a type that contains cracked wheat, wheat berries or bran.) Calories, fat and cholesterol were reduced by:

• Using egg whites instead of whole eggs

• Using skim instead of whole evaporated milk

Nutrition Scorecard
(per serving)

	Before	After
Calories	211	176
Fat (g.)	7	1
% Calories from fat	28%	4%
Cholesterol (mg.)	153	2

---

  3 cups dry whole-wheat bread cubes (4–6 slices) (see note)
  ⅓ cup raisins
  1 (12-ounce) can evaporated skim milk
  7 egg whites
  ⅓ cup sugar
  ½ teaspoon ground cinnamon
  1 teaspoon rum extract or vanilla

Preheat the oven to 325°. Lightly spray a 1½-quart soufflé dish or casserole with no-stick spray. Place the bread cubes in the dish or casserole. Sprinkle the raisins on top.

In a medium bowl, beat together the milk, egg whites, sugar, cinnamon and rum extract or vanilla until well combined. Pour the mixture over the bread. Bake for 50 to 55 minutes or until a knife inserted in the center comes out clean. Cool slightly. Serve warm.

Makes 6 servings.

Note: To make dry bread cubes, toast the bread slices, then cut them into 1" cubes. Or cut the bread into cubes, spread the pieces on a cookie sheet and bake at 300° about 15 minutes or until dry.

Easy Brown Rice Pudding

By using convenience products, you can have this old-fashioned dessert in minutes. I prefer to use brown rice instead of white because it has more fiber. If you don't have any already cooked, use the instant variety to save time. I reduced calories, fat and cholesterol by:

• Using skim milk instead of whole milk

Nutrition Scorecard
(per serving)

	Before	After
Calories	192	174
Fat (g.)	3	1
% Calories from fat	15%	4%
Cholesterol (mg.)	12	2

1 (6-serving) package vanilla pudding mix (not instant)
3 cups skim milk
¼ teaspoon ground nutmeg
¼ teaspoon ground cinnamon
3 cups cooked brown rice

In a large saucepan, stir together the pudding mix and milk. Cook according to the directions on the pudding package.

Remove the pudding from the heat and stir in the nutmeg and cinnamon. Then stir in the rice. Spoon the pudding into dessert dishes. Serve warm or chilled.

Makes 8 servings.

Fudge Surprises

The surprise in this candy is the baby-food prunes that substitute for fat and give the fudge a melt-in-your-mouth, smooth texture. Calories, fat and cholesterol were reduced by:

- Using skim instead of whole evaporated milk

- Replacing most of the butter with baby-food prunes

- Reducing the amount of sugar

- Reducing the amount of walnuts

Nutrition Scorecard
(per piece)

	Before	After
Calories	143	105
Fat (g.)	7	4
% Calories from fat	46%	32%
Cholesterol (mg.)	9	2

2 tablespoons butter
2½ cups sugar
⅔ cup evaporated skim milk
1 (12-ounce) package semisweet chocolate chips
1 (2½-ounce) jar baby-food prunes
1 (7-ounce) jar marshmallow creme
½ cup chopped walnuts
1 teaspoon vanilla

Line a 13" × 9" × 2" baking pan with wax paper, extending the paper over the edges of the pan. Set the pan aside.

In a large saucepan, melt the butter. Stir in the sugar and milk. Bring the mixture to a boil over medium heat, stirring constantly. Boil for 5 minutes, stirring constantly.

Remove the saucepan from the heat and slowly stir in the chocolate chips. Stir until the chocolate melts. Then stir in the prunes, marshmallow creme, walnuts and vanilla until well combined.

Spread the mixture in the prepared pan. Chill in the refrigerator until firm.

To serve, use the wax paper to lift the fudge from the pan. Then cut the fudge into pieces.

Makes 48 pieces; 48 servings.

Butterscotch Chip Oatmeal Cookies

Homemade cookies are a favorite with everyone. Yet they don't have to be laden with fat and calories to taste good. This oatmeal cookie has lots of butterscotch chips but is still healthful. Calories, fat and cholesterol were reduced by:

- Using extra-light corn-oil spread (25 calories per tablespoon of spread) instead of shortening

- Reducing the amount of brown and granulated sugar by 25 percent

- Using egg whites instead of a whole egg

- Reducing the amount of butterscotch chips (and enhancing the flavor by replacing water with molasses and using maple flavoring instead of vanilla)

Nutrition Scorecard
(per cookie)

	Before	After
Calories	122	75
Fat (g.)	6	2
% Calories from fat	42%	25%
Cholesterol (mg.)	4	0

¾ cup extra-light corn-oil spread, softened
¾ cup firmly packed brown sugar
¼ cup sugar
¼ cup light molasses
2 egg whites
1 teaspoon maple extract
1 cup all-purpose flour
1 teaspoon ground cinnamon
½ teaspoon baking soda
3 cups quick-cooking rolled oats
1 (6-ounce) package butterscotch chips (1 cup)

Preheat the oven to 350°. Spray 2 large cookie sheets with no-stick spray. Set the cookie sheets aside.

In a large bowl, mix together the corn-oil spread, brown sugar, sugar, molasses, egg whites and maple extract until well combined.

In a small bowl, stir together the flour, cinnamon and baking soda. Gradually mix the flour mixture into the sugar mixture. Stir in the oats and butterscotch chips.

Drop rounded teaspoonfuls of the dough 1" apart on the prepared cookie sheets. Bake for 12 to 15 minutes or until almost no imprint remains when you lightly touch a cookie in the center. Immediately remove the cookies from the cookie sheets and transfer them to a wire rack to cool. Store the cookies in a tightly covered container.

Makes 48 cookies; 48 servings.

INDEX

Note: <u>Underscored</u> page references indicate boxed text. **Boldface** references indicate illustrations and photos. *Italic* references indicate tables.

Almonds
Almondine-Filled Chocolate Cupcakes, 292–93
Ambrosia
Pineapple Ambrosia, 259
Angel hair pasta
Angel Hair Pasta with Fresh Tomato and Basil Sauce, 182
Angel Hair Pasta with Italian Spinach, 183
Reduced-Fat Pesto Pasta, 192
Three-Pepper Pesto Pasta, 191
Antioxidant, vitamin E as, <u>39</u>
Appetizers
Celery Stuffed with Blue Cheese, 83
Cheddar Cheese Straws, 77
Chinese Vegetable Egg Rolls, 89
Cocktail Party Meatballs, **67**, 90
Cream Cheese Fondue Dip for Fresh Fruit, 79
Easy Green Chili Bean Dip, 73
Fresh Tomato-Topped Mini-Pizzas, 87
Goat Cheese Rolled in Grape Leaves, 81
Greek Spinach Triangles, 88
Homemade Tortilla Chips, **64**, 75
Hot Artichoke Parmesan Spread, 52
Hot Beer Cheese Dip, 51
Hummus, 71, **227**
Marinated Tricolored Sweet Peppers, **66**, 86
Mushrooms Stuffed with Turkey, 82
Oven-Fried Potato Skins, 85
Parmesan Wonton Crisps, 76
Peanut Butter Fruit Dip, 78
Red Potatoes Stuffed with Cheese, **65**, 84
Savory Three-Cheese Ball, 50
Seven-Layer Tex-Mex Dip, **64**, 74
Spicy Chicken Wings, 91

Spinach and Chestnut Dip, 54, **63**
Split Pea Guacamole, 72
Tortilla Pinwheels with Smoked Turkey, 80
Vegetable Dill Dip, 53
Yogurt Cheese, 83
Apples
Apple 'n' Raisin Strudel, 318–19
Apple Stuffed Tenderloin with Cinnamon Raisin Sauce, 112–13, **138**
Harvest Apple Coffee Cake, 37, **58**
Harvest Apple Stuffing, 282, **303**
Swedish Apple Pie, 315
Waldorf Salad, 247, **295**
Applesauce, as fat alternative, 15
Apricots
Apricot Oat Bran Muffins, 27, **56**
Arborio rice
Risotto, 280
Artichokes
Cheesy Chicken and Artichoke Bake, 116–17, **140**
Hot Artichoke Parmesan Spread, 52
Asparagus
Cream of Asparagus Soup, **145**, 156–57
Avocados
Split Pea Guacamole, 72
Tropical Avocado and Fruit Salad, 256

Baking, reduced-fat staples for, <u>313</u>
Bananas
Cinnamon Spiced Banana Nut Bread, 34
Bar cookies. *See* Cookies
Basil
Angel Hair Pasta with Fresh Tomato and Basil Sauce, 182
Creamy Pesto Dressing, 240
Reduced-Fat Pesto Pasta, 192
Three-Pepper Pesto Pasta, 191
Beans
calories in, *8*
Crockpot Baked Beans, 267, **300**

Butterscotch
    Butterscotch Chip Muffins with Pecans,
       30
    Butterscotch Chip Oatmeal Cookies, 329

Cabbage
    Chinese Noodle Salad, 251
Cake rolls
    Chocolate Ricotta Cake Roll, 290–91
    Fudge Sundae Cake Roll, 290–91
    Pumpkin 'n' Cheese Cake Roll, 288–89
Cakes. See also Cake rolls; Cupcakes
    Carrot Cake, 286–87, **304**
    Chocolate Marble Cheesecake, **309**,
       322–23
    Cinnamon Streusel Coffee Cake, 38–39
    Good-for-You Gingerbread, 293, **305**
    Harvest Apple Coffee Cake, 37, **58**
    Lemon Lace Cake, 287
Carrots
    beta-carotene in, <u>121</u>
    Carrot and Raisin Salad, 252
    Carrot Cake, 286–87, **304**
    Glazed Carrots, 263
    Spicy Vegetable Stir-Fry, 265, **299**
Casseroles. See also One-dish meals
    Easy Cheesy Chili Relleno Casserole,
       134
    Homestyle Tuna Casserole, **144**, 151
    troubleshooting recipe makeovers of,
       24
Cauliflower
    Easy Cheesy Cauliflower, 264
    Spicy Vegetable Stir-Fry, 265, **299**
Celery
    Celery Stuffed with Blue Cheese, 83
    Creamy Celery Soup, 157
Cheddar cheese
    Cheddar Cheese Straws, 77
    Easy Cheesy Cauliflower, 264
    Lite Cheddar Cheese Sauce, 262
Cheese. See also specific cheeses
    Cheese Ravioli with Rosemary and
      Lemon, 194, **220**
    Cheesy Chicken and Artichoke Bake,
      116–17, **140**
    Cheesy Potato Soup, 161
    Easy Cheesy Cauliflower, 264
    Easy Cheesy Chili Relleno Casserole,
      134
    Easy Cheesy Lasagna, 186–87
    Fiesta Cheese Strata, 153
    Green and White Lasagna Bundles,
      184–85, **217**
    Hot Beer Cheese Dip, 51

    Meatless Cheese Burgers, 113
    Old-Fashioned Macaroni and Cheese,
      189
    Pumpkin 'n' Cheese Cake Roll, 288–89
    Red Potatoes Stuffed with Cheese, **65**, 84
    Savory Three-Cheese Ball, 50
    Sole Stuffed with Broccoli and Cheese,
      106–7
    Tomato Mac 'n' Cheese, 185, **218**
    Yogurt Cheese, 83
Cheesecake
    Chocolate Marble Cheesecake, **309**,
      322–23
Cherries
    Cherry Delicious Pie, **307**, 316
Chicken
    Cheesy Chicken and Artichoke Bake,
      116–17, **140**
    Chicken à la King, 98–99
    Chicken à la Marengo, **69**, 97
    Chicken and Biscuits, 124–25
    Chicken Cacciatore, 196, **221**
    Chicken Chow Mein, 206
    Chicken Cordon Bleu, 93
    Chicken Enchiladas, 207
    Chicken Fajitas, 203
    Chicken in a Packet, 115, **139**
    Chicken Marsala, 95
    Chicken Paprikash, 200–201
    Chicken Parmigiana, 199
    Chicken Sloppy Joes, 102
    Chicken Tostadas, 197, **222**
    Chinese Chicken Salad, **228**, 236
    Country Chicken Gumbo, 171
    Crispy Oven-Fried Chicken, **70**, 99
    Curried Chicken Divan, 117
    Deep-Dish Chicken Pot Pie, 122–23
    Hawaiian Chicken, **68**, 96
    Layered Mexican Chicken Pie, 208
    lean cuts of, *123*
    Lemon Dijon Breasts of Chicken, 94
    Mu Shu Chicken, 204–5, **223**
    Southwest Chicken Lasagna, 120–21,
      141
    Spicy Chicken Wings, 91
    Szechuan Chicken, 198
    Teriyaki Breasts of Chicken, 202
    Weekday Chicken and Dumplings,
      118–19
Chick-peas
    Falafel, **227**, 233
    Hummus, 71, **227**
Chili
    Easy Chili, 125, **142**
    Macaroni Chili, 133, **143**

Frostings
  Light Cream Cheese Frosting, 289
Fruit group, in Food Guide Pyramid, 5
Fruit juice
  as marinade, 16
  as salad dressing, 16
Fruits. *See also specific fruits*
  recommended daily servings of, 7
  Tropical Avocado and Fruit Salad, 256
  Waldorf Salad, 247, **295**
Fudge. *See also* Chocolate
  Fudge Sundae Cake Roll, 290–91
  Fudge Surprises, 328

Garlic
  Garlic Scampi, 213, **225**
  Parmesan Garlic Bread, 48, **62**
Gelatin
  Pineapple Lime Molded Salad, 258
  Strawberry Cream Gelatin Salad, 257
German-style dishes
  German Potato Pancakes, 276
Ginger
  All-Purpose Oriental Ginger Sauce, 205
  Ginger Sesame Dressing, 237
Gingerbread
  Good-for-You Gingerbread, 293, **305**
Glazes, fruit, from preserves, 321
Goat cheese
  Goat Cheese Rolled in Grape Leaves, 81
Graham crackers
  Graham Cracker Crust, 317
Grains
  Apricot Oat Bran Muffins, 27, **56**
  Buttermilk Whole-Wheat Pancakes, 46, **61**
  Butterscotch Chip Oatmeal Cookies, 329
  Chinese Fried Rice, 279
  Easy Brown Rice Pudding, 327
  Hoppin' John, 277
  Italian Eggplant and Rice Bake, 127
  Mexican Rice, 278
  Peppers Stuffed with Spanish Rice, 103
  recommended daily servings of, 6
  Risotto, 280
  Spiced Couscous, 281
  Tabbouleh, 254, **296**
  Turkey and Rice Bake, 126
  Whole-Wheat Bread Pudding, 326
  Whole-Wheat Soda Bread, 45
  Whole-Wheat Zucchini Bread, 36
  Wild Rice and Sausage Bake, 132–33
Grape leaves
  Goat Cheese Rolled in Grape Leaves, 81
Gravies, reduced-fat, 101

Greek-style dishes
  Goat Cheese Rolled in Grape Leaves, 81
  Greek Penne, 193, **219**
  Greek Salad, 255, **297**
  Greek Spinach Pie, 234
  Greek Spinach Triangles, 88
  Moussaka, 210–11
Green beans
  Creamy Green Bean and Onion Bake, 266
Guacamole
  Split Pea Guacamole, 72
Gumbo
  Country Chicken Gumbo, 171

Herbs
  Herbed Mushroom Sauté, 269
Honey
  Honey Bran Muffins, 29
Hummus, 71, **227**
Hungarian-style dishes
  Chicken Paprikash, 200–201

Italian-style dishes. *See also* Pasta; Pizza
  Angel Hair Pasta with Italian Spinach, 183
  Chicken Cacciatore, 196, **221**
  Chicken Marsala, 95
  Chicken Parmigiana, 199
  Easy Cheesy Lasagna, 186–87
  Eggplant Parmigiana, 268
  Garden Frittata, 152
  Garlic Scampi, 213, **225**
  Green and White Lasagna Bundles, 184–85, **247**
  Italian Bean and Pasta Soup, 165
  Italian Eggplant and Rice Bake, 127
  Italian Meat Loaf, 104
  Italian Pasta Salad, 250
  Ratatouille in Roasted Peppers, 270–71, **301**
  Spaghetti with Spicy Italian Meat Sauce, 176–77, **215**

Juice, fruit
  as marinade, 16
  as salad dressing, 16

Kidney beans
  Taco Salad, 242–43
Kiwi fruit
  Summertime Fruit Pizza, **308**, 320–21

Labels, food, nutrition information on, 119